About the author

Renée Goossens was born in the United States and came to Australia with her family at the age of six. Educated at school in Sydney, and at university in Paris and Oxford, she trained as a teacher of children with learning difficulties.

Never able to remain long away from Sydney, she returned in 1967 initially to teach disabled children and subsequently became Lecturer in French at the NSW State Conservatorium of Music. In 1973 she worked as language coach for the Australian Opera with company members and visiting artists on French operatic repertoire. When SBS-TV began operations in Sydney in May 1980, she worked as an administrator, editor and subtitler for twelve years.

More recently Renée spent nine years living in France and England, visiting friends and relatives, and wrote for newspapers and magazines on the challenges of travelling with a wheelchair. An Australian citizen for many decades, she returned to Sydney in 2001, where she now lives permanently, as does her son Philip.

to dear Tony, Christine
and Annabel
with love and
happy memories – music
will always unite us.
Love [signature]

2003

BELONGING

a memoir

BELONGING

a memoir

renée goossens

ABC
Books

Dedication

For my beloved father, whose gift of music continues to fill my life with happiness. He enriched my knowledge and understanding of his special world of creativity and excellence. His positive influence on the cultural life of the people of Australia should never be forgotten.

And

For Betsy Brown my mentor who, after the death of my parents, became my adopted mother, and grandmother to my son Philip. She taught me the meaning of unconditional love, guided my learning and enlightened my teaching. Her instinctive ability to accept me as I was, and above all, to help me bring up my son, gave us both strength and security. She remained a constant factor in our lives and brought a sense of belonging in years troubled by conflict and confusion.

With Betsy, I always knew where I was, and who I was.

Published by ABC Books for the
AUSTRALIAN BROADCASTING CORPORATION
GPO Box 9994 Sydney NSW 2001

Copyright © Renée Goossens 2003

First published April 2003

National Library of Australia
Cataloguing-in-Publication entry
Goossens, Renée.
  Belonging.

  Includes index.
  ISBN 0 7333 1244 6.

  1. Goossens, Renée. 2. Goossens, Eugene, Sir, 1893-1962.
  3. Conductors (Music) – Australia – Family relationships.
  I. Australian Broadcasting Corporation. II. Title.

920.72

Designed by Jane Cameron/Fisheye Design
Edited by Suzanne Falkiner
Set in 11/15 pt Adobe Garamond by
Midland Typesetters, Maryborough, Victoria
Colour reproduction by Colorwize, Adelaide
Printed and bound in Australia by
Griffin Press, Adelaide

5 4 3 2 1

CONTENTS

AUTHOR'S NOTE

My life has seen a varied procession of colourful people, all of whom have lent it meaning. Those who brought challenges taught me lessons I needed to learn, those who gave me love comforted me, those who attempted to understand me were welcome.

I would like to thank them all for being there. Most did the best they knew how to do, and we can never hope for more than that.

At my discretion and out of respect for families, I have altered the names of some of the people who would prefer not to be identified.

Carole Rosen's *The Goossens, A Musical Century*, published by André Deutsch in 1993, contributed valuable information concerning my family. Without it I would never have known, for example, that my father had been a twin. Carole was an expert author who presented her information openly and fairly and shared my loyalty and admiration for my father. Her work was essential to the preparation of this book.

Several outstanding people moulded my life and helped me towards a greater comprehension of what mattered and what was less important.

My English nanny Dorothy Cubitt gave me my first example of love and affection, discipline, humour and reliability. My sister Donie nourished me with her love and example for many years. I hope one day we may come together and renew that special understanding and closeness we once shared.

Dr David Champion came into my life in the 1980s as a physician and specialist in pain management. His compassion, expertise and belief in my ability to overcome some of my physical challenges enabled me to keep writing this and other works. In Europe 'Ak' Akhurst cared for me through a time of great physical disability, supporting me with love and understanding. Lizzie Pickering with her knowledge of literature, suffering and personal endurance, read and commented on my work, offering me the encouragement that helped me to complete this story.

Jill Hickson was the first professional agent who had faith and trust in my book and helped it towards publication. Though she is no longer a literary agent, her loving friendship continues. Joan Carden, my operatic colleague and friend, championed my work and introduced me to Margaret Gee who, as my present agent, has helped me through the practical matters of developing the book from its manuscript to this final stage of publication.

Jacqueline Kent my editor at ABC Books has reassured me at moments of self doubt, and has ensured a more polished product.

The love of an 'adopted' sister, Erica Booker Thomas, who accepted me into her family in the 1960s when we were at the Con together, gave me that sense of belonging I had been seeking all my life. Her solidarity through life's many storms proved her to be the unique friend I needed.

Betsy Brown was my mentor from the age of eight, and later

became an 'adopted' mother and also a real grandmother to my son Philip. Although her physical presence has gone, her influence, unconditional love and acceptance remain with me always.

My son Philip has been and always will be the most important person in my life. His strength and example, his humour and his achievement have gladdened my heart.

To all these people I offer my sincere thanks.

Renée Goossens
January 2003

BEGINNING

Some children recollect in perfect detail their earliest years. I do not. Where did I live? I am told I was born in Biddeford, Maine, in 1940, when the family was on holiday on the north east coast of the United States. My father was based in Cincinnati, and then in New York, which is where my first memories begin. Street sounds, old men in rags shuffling along the pavement with brown paper bags under their arms, smelling of beer. Beautiful tree-lined streets with grand hotels and uniformed doormen greeting well-dressed patrons, receiving tips as they hailed taxis for them, smiling pleasantly.

Most of all I remember things which felt good, like scrambling up onto my father's lap, usually with difficulty, when I was five, especially as he wore a thick teddy bear coat which took up so much room. I loved that coat. It smelt woolly, as one imagines a baby lamb might, a sweet scent that offered both comfort and welcome. My father used to take me out for afternoon tea sometimes, to big hotels with waiters in black, almost like players in an orchestra.

He didn't talk much, when I'd prattle and ask questions, but offered me pastries and cakes, as he took out a pen and jotted notes on napkins. If these were paper napkins, nothing was said. But on one occasion, his black notes and staves blackened a huge white starched linen napkin. He was completely absorbed in what he was doing, drawing staves, and putting notes all over them, humming and telling me they were melodies he didn't want to forget. An angry man came over and seized the napkin from him. Father was furious, saying it was part of a string quartet. The man made him pay several dollar notes for 'damaging my equipment'. Daddy protested that he was doing the hotel a favour. But we did leave rather hurriedly, so maybe it *had* been the wrong thing to do.

Music was always ringing in my ears. Often it was from our gramophone, a beautiful instrument which looked just like the covers of His Master's Voice recordings, without the dog. No music sounded strange to me. Daddy might say it was something French which friends of his had written and he was going to introduce to orchestras wherever he went. Sitting straight in a large armchair, he would tap rhythmically on the wooden table beside him muttering, "I'll do this section in two," or again "Perhaps it would be better in four." It was many years before I understood what this meant, but it seemed exactly the right thing to say then. He didn't mind if I sat at his feet and played fiddle-sticks as long as I didn't make a noise. Sometimes he would interrupt my game and ask me to listen to a particular part, and then lift the arm off the record and play that section again and again. I would hum it back to him and he would say "There's my girl," and I would feel really grown up and proud.

My father, Eugene Goossens, was born in London on 26 May 1893, and received his early musical training in Bruges, Belgium. The son and grandson of two gifted Belgian conductors, he followed the family tradition in being a musician of exceptional talent and ability. His brother Léon was one of the world's most accomplished oboists. Adolphe, who was killed in battle in World

War I, was a promising French horn player, while sisters Marie and Sidonie both became renowned harpists gracing the orchestras of England for five decades.

My father studied at the Liverpool College of Music and in 1907 won a scholarship to the Royal College of Music, London. He rapidly developed his technique as a conductor, and attracted the attention of Sir Thomas Beecham. His accomplishment as a violinist and violist enabled him to have a special rapport with the orchestra when he turned to conducting orchestral music and opera.

He travelled to America with Somerset Maugham, Noel Coward and Basil Dean in 1925, and their friendship endured throughout their careers. In Rochester, New York, he became chief conductor of the Rochester Philharmonic Orchestra, then conducted orchestras in Minneapolis and St Louis. From 1931 to 1946 he was the driving force behind the Cincinnati Symphony Orchestra, which he developed into one of the finest in the world. However, by the time of my fifth birthday we had moved to New York.

Many memories of later years came from stories people told me, but what I recall best are the instances of physical closeness, something I treasured above all else with my father.

We moved to places long hours away, with names which meant nothing to me, over long days of distance. America to me represented vast expanses, travelling by rail, through stations at which we never stopped. At other times the steam rose excitingly as people crammed on to platforms to meet their loved ones, or cried as they made farewells. We went from New York to San Francisco, over many days. I found the changes confusing and unsettling.

We finally came to Australia in 1947, where everything fell into place and Sydney became my home. Then, suddenly, there were operas and concerts—watching, participating, learning, forgetting, rehearsing, practising. And there was tennis, surf, sun, warmth; an expression of disapproval from Daddy, a smile, and sometimes even those precious yet spare words of praise. That was my new life.

My father had married an artist, Dorothy Millar, known as Boonie, in 1919. They had three daughters, Anne, then twins Julia and Jane. I never met Boonie, and it was decades before I met two of my half-sisters. Anne had been sent to America from Europe to my father and mother to be looked after, but returned to Europe prior to my birth, or when I was a very small baby. I never met Julia.

This first marriage had ended in divorce, and father married my mother Janet Lewis, or Jansi as he called her. My sister Donie was born in 1932, and I came eight years later in 1940. This second marriage did not last either.

My father was Conductor of the Cincinatti Symphony Orchestra for fifteen years but by the time of my sixth birthday we had moved to New York.

My father's prestige had meant that in Rochester, Cincinnati and New York he and Jansi were celebrated and greeted as high society, almost royalty. His skill as a conductor and composer was unquestioned. His introduction of new music, particularly the French composers with whom he was friendly from his European career, was both acclaimed and criticised. He found time to compose new works, as well as to refine work in progress: quartets, a symphony, and of course *Don Juan de Manara*, his opera. His correspondence with his parents and his brother Léon and sisters Marie and Sidonie in England kept him in touch not only with his supportive family, but also with wartime conditions. Frequently in his letters he pleaded with them to join him in the USA. This did not happen, due both to the dangers of the journey and his father's patriotic feelings for England, and of course to the constant program of musical engagements the family continued to fulfil.

Our lives changed when Father married Marjorie Foulkrod, a divorcée who was wealthy, glamorous and talented, a piano graduate of the Juilliard Music School, whom he had met while she was working for a record company. I was five years old when Daddy brought his new wife to live with us at the New York apartment.

This meant that my father, mother, stepmother, my sister Donie and my beloved English nanny Dorothy Cubitt, all lived together under the same roof. I can't recall the sleeping arrangements because that's not the sort of thing one notices as a child. Parents lived in their quarters, children in theirs. Arrangements that may have seemed strange to others I accepted unquestioningly. There were simply two mothers, and from my limited perspective it seemed perfectly normal for us all to live together. As I was unaware of my other relatives in England, this was my family.

Donie studied the harp with the famous teacher Carlos Salzedo and I attended a local Catholic infants' school. My only practical participation in music was attending ballet classes, and I loved dressing up in a tutu and following the others in beautiful sequences I didn't quite manage to get right.

One day my sister, who was just under six foot tall, came to collect me from my class while Nanny was at the dentist. The ballet teacher, on learning she was my sister, said, "There is no point your little sister having lessons, for if she grows as tall as you, there will be no role for her in any corps de ballet and certainly none as a soloist."

I was disappointed to give up ballet, with its marvellous exercises for posture which I adored and was to remember throughout my life. Unlike my sister, I grew to be only five foot four inches; but then, as my life turned out, it is just as well I was not a dancer—but that is advancing my life too rapidly.

My stepmother was tall and beautiful, and she bought me presents. My mother had always gone out to work, and continued to do so. Although father had hoped she would find literary work, she eventually found a job as a publicist for artists' releases at Columbia Concerts Corporation.

I adored my English nanny and it was her unquestioning love

and attention I sought and received. Stepmother seemed like an artificial doll and my mother seemed sad, as if she wasn't in the same play with us any more. Daddy was often away, conducting, and I didn't see much of him at all. They said he had gone to Australia, to see about a permanent job. Nanny showed me on the map where Australia was, but looking at the large piece of paper I understood nothing of what it meant or of the dramatic distance it would put between me and all that I had known before.

Before Daddy had gone away there was music in the house; he would play the piano, sitting on an old tapestry stool, his pencil in his mouth, humming a tune before writing it down on large sheets of paper on the music stand. I would sneak in and watch, fascinated, but was always told by Stepmother to be very quiet and not to disturb him. After his departure, there seemed to be no more music, just the occasional sounds of a radio not quite tuned in to orchestral concerts, sounds which came from my mother's sitting room. If she was alone, which she often was, I would knock on the door, climb up onto her lap, and she would hug me but say very little. I had no idea how badly she must have suffered then, and afterwards. Perhaps she had no choice but to stay. Maybe the flat was in her name. These were details never entrusted to me.

There was a stray cat which, with a degree of persuasion, followed me home to our apartment in 93rd Street. It was to be the first of my constant, if by force of circumstances, various feline companions. The kidnapped cat retained all the cunning of its street origins. We called him Orlando, like the marmalade cat in the book Nanny was reading to me. When he suspected imminent exile he knew to hide, and so spent most of his time asleep beneath my bed. After school, he tolerated my awkward lugging as I demonstrated my love by folding him in two under my arm, unaware of his discomfort. At night he slept unashamedly on the pillow beside my head, purring his robust engine of rhythmic sound.

For another companion I had a little boy aged five, a rascal by the name of Peter. We played in Central Park, just a few minutes' walk from our house. One snowy, ice-cold December morning we decided to go tobogganing down the slopes, but had no sled. On our dining room sideboard was proudly displayed a beautiful shiny silver tray with an inscription upon it. It had been a farewell gift from the Cincinnati Orchestra to honour Daddy for his years of service.

"Peter," I said. "Will you climb up and get it? It would make a perfect sled."

Peter climbed up onto a chair to procure the tray and put it beneath his coat. We ran out the front door and headed across the road to the park. The gleaming silver trophy sped down the snowy hill with lightning ease and us both on board.

Nanny was appalled as she watched us coming back across the road, returning from the park covered in snow. She could not believe her eyes when we handed her the silver tray, badly bent and deeply scratched.

"You naughty, wicked children," she said, smacking me on the bottom. She shook her fist at Peter. "And you, you wretched scoundrel, be home with you!" Later the tray was returned to its place in the dining room, sparkling and polished, magically teased back into shape, and nothing was said. I hugged Nanny, who shrugged her shoulders, her eyes raised upwards just like our priest at Mass.

A few evenings later I was told we were going to Australia. Daddy had been offered a permanent position there. It was decided that Donie, Marjorie and I would all travel by ship, but Daddy, who wrote to say how thrilled he was with his new position, was going to stay there conducting until our arrival.

"Is Nanny coming too?" I asked Stepmother, seeking reassurance.

"Of course, dear, Nanny will come," she said.

"And Mummy too?" as only a child would ask a stepmother.

"No. Janet will stay in New York, where she has work to do."

Bewildered, I went to ask my mother, "That's the way it is," she explained. Her voice was low and uncertain as she told me I'd be happy in Australia. She said we'd have a better life, and that we'd be able to go swimming every day if we wanted to, just as we had when we went to Maine on holiday.

The sacrifice she made was immense, yet I had no comprehension then that it would be many years before I would hear from her, or see her again. My mother bravely hugged us and waved goodbye, as if we were embarking on nothing more than a day trip to Coney Island.

It must have been in 1947 that we travelled across America by train to join our ship near San Francisco, on the West Coast. I liked the friendly hooting of the train as it raced along, the comforting regular beat of the wheels, the delicious food, the changing scene of fields, plains and finally, the ocean. I had then no eye for the beauties of the landscape, preferring the comfort of pestering Nanny with endless questions, and playing Snap with my long-suffering sister Donie.

Travelling to strange places at the age of six has no taste of the fear of the unknown experienced by adults. To me it was just the beginning of a marvellous adventure.

On board ship we were befriended by one of the officers, a Swede. We'll call him Sven, and he was very good at reading stories to me, particularly *Winnie the Pooh*. He played quoits with me on deck and made me feel special. He was a cuddly man who seemed comfortable with children. He told me how to say 'I love you' in Swedish; '*ya elska day*', it was pronounced.

The best time was when the ship crossed the Equator and we had the ceremony of Crossing the Line. I had no idea what that meant.

"Sven, how can a line be put across the water? Does it go right around the world?"

"You are a funny little thing. No, it's just an expression. Come and see the map and I'll show you." I climbed up onto his lap and he unfolded a great, crinkly Map of the World.

Our ship, a cargo liner, was not very large. There were about twenty passengers only, none of them children. I loved the smell of the salt air and the sound of the foam frothing on top of the waves.

The smell of diesel oil from the engine room was horrid, however, and made me feel quite sick. Some days the wind was blowing in such a way that you could smell the oil wherever you went.

It was difficult to imagine where we were because everywhere we looked we saw only vast expanses of ocean. I was grateful when Nanny took out the atlas that she always kept with her to show me what she thought our position was. As a special treat I was allowed on the bridge to visit the Captain to inspect his charts and marvellous maps. Everything looked immense and very far away and I couldn't imagine how we could ever run out of Pacific Ocean and reach Sydney. Sven told me Sydney was on the coast, so we would probably always see the ocean there as well.

There was a peculiar little canvas swimming pool on the deck. It was cooling to dip into when the tropical heat of the Equator made us feel as hot as bread when it first comes out of the oven.

The Captain invited me to enter his fancy dress competition, held during a big party one evening. Donie and Nanny made me a marvellously clever costume from handkerchiefs and scarves. They used pipe cleaners twisted into shapes for a funny head dress. They labelled me 'Marcia from Mars', and I won first prize. People were very kind to me. Nanny said I was becoming thoroughly spoilt.

Nobody suffered from sea sickness as the blue skies and calm seas gave us a smooth voyage most of the time. Stepmother offered Sven the position of valet to Daddy so we could keep seeing him when the voyage came to an end. She went down to see 'Sparks' (he didn't seem to have a proper name) in the radio room and asked him to send a cable to Daddy explaining Sven was to become part of our household. Sven was happy to accept as his officer's contract was to end shortly.

Our first sight of land, the coast of eastern Australia, was extremely welcome. We were going to land almost in the same place as Captain Cook had landed one hundred and seventy years before. Donie read me stories about convicts and Botany Bay so

that we would know something of our new city. I was terribly
excited. I hoped there would be kangaroos.

Sven was able to explain and identify the various boats that
met us once we entered Sydney Heads.

Before us was an amazingly beautiful sight: a vast expanse of
jewel-blue water, the leafy green trees coming right down to the
water's edge, and small sandy beaches dotted around the harbour
like shortbread biscuits on a blue plate. Tiny, energetic ferries
scuttled about. A large lumbering tug came to guide us safely into
port, followed by a faster, neater cruiser with 'Pilot' written on the
side. As it came alongside, a rope ladder was thrown down over
our ship's railings and men in smart uniforms climbed up on deck.

To our amazement and delight, Daddy climbed up too. He
could not climb as briskly as the uniformed officials. We had
been at sea for five weeks and had not seen him for ages. It was
lovely to see him again. He rushed to hug us all and shook Sven
by the hand, saying he was glad to welcome him to join the
family. When we landed, Daddy went first, then me, then Donie,
followed by Stepmother with Nanny and Sven, as we all walked
down the gangplank together. It was funny to see Daddy wearing
his teddy bear coat, for the day seemed much too hot for
lambskin. On his head was his usual dark hat with its turned-up
brim, but because of the wind he had to keep holding it down
with his right hand. This meant he had to let go of hugging me,
which was a great shame.

There was much luggage to wait for. Seven porters were
standing by to help the disembarking passengers. Stepmother had
so many cases and trunks filled with beautiful dresses that we
needed three porters just for ourselves. There were ten huge
trunks and seventeen cases, four hatboxes and lots of brown paper
carrier bags filled with last minute treasures we seemed to have
collected since leaving America. Nanny said our things just
seemed to grow in the cabin.

Life in post-war Sydney was comfortable, exciting, different,
and warmer. The colours were brighter, the people spoke with a

twang unlike my own, so that I was teased at school for having 'a foreign accent'. The nuns who accepted me into their school were kind, although it was not easy to settle at first. Stepmother could not decide on the best location for us in Sydney, which meant we kept moving from house to house and from school to school. By the time I was fourteen I would have attended over a dozen schools on three different continents.

"Your father is an important man here," Stepmother instructed, as I asked why for the millionth time as we once again packed up our belongings. "We have to live somewhere people appreciate his position. People value a good address. One day you will understand."

We therefore experimented with various addresses in the first year, all rented houses. We began in the eastern suburbs, around Bellevue Hill and Edgecliff, with beautiful harbour views. I watched for hours as ferries bustled and colourful spinnakers dazzled me with their fluttering, while occasional liners and flying boats looked fascinating as I brought them magically closer with Daddy's binoculars. Our houses were large and visitors commented that they were impressive, but I found them unfriendly.

"Where's Nanny?" I asked, surprised to see Stepmother at the school gate one day not long after our arrival.

"She has gone back to England. Her sister needed her."

"Where is England?" I asked, having no idea, but hoping it was very close.

"Many thousands of miles away. About four weeks on a ship."

My heart sank.

"But I didn't even have a chance to say goodbye," I said, tears streaming down my face all the way home.

"Don't be such a silly child. You'll soon forget her. After today, you are to find your own way home from school. Now that you're seven, you don't need to be collected any more. Bring yourself home like a big girl."

But Nanny had always been with me, and being a dependent child, I had hated it even when it was her day off, missing her, hanging around the door and waiting anxiously to hear her cheery voice saying, "Here I am."

I could not believe that Nanny would leave me. She was the most important person in my life, the only one who had always been there, who loved me, held me, told me I was her special girl. I could not imagine living without her. Surely she would return and explain? She was bound to come back. I just couldn't believe she would go away and leave me without any explanation.

I was very cross with my stepmother. She had promised that Nanny would stay with us until I was grown up. I wished I could follow my Nanny to wherever it was she had gone, even if it did take four weeks on a ship. In my late teens I sought her out in Cobham, Surrey, but either she had died, or moved on, for nobody could help me find her.

One day after school I became lost and could not find my way home. I went into a fruit shop to ask directions from the shop-keeper. I could only remember the address of our previous house, and when I got to the front door, I realised it was the wrong place and we didn't live there any more. It was a strange and frightening feeling. Seeing the familiar door, I decided to see if somebody there could help me. Perhaps they would be friends of my parents. I knocked on the door, but when the new owner heard what I had to say, she did not know what to do with me. But she told me every-thing was going to be all right and I was not to worry, then she rang the police to report me as a missing child. Two uniformed men collected me and drove me to the police station in a shiny car.

The man in charge had a sunny face and he picked me up to sit on his big fat lap. "Now, young sheila," he said, "where's your mother?"

"In New York," I replied.

He rubbed his chin, strummed his fingers on the desk, then said, "How about your father?"

"He is at a place where they learn to do music. I think it's called the . . . Con . . . something," I replied, hesitatingly, hoping I had got it right.

"No worries, pet, we'll give them a ring. That'll be the Conservatorium of Music. Look it up in the book then, lad," he said to his assistant, a man whom I did not expect to be called a lad, in his smart uniform.

"What does he do there, pet?" asked the policeman.

"I don't know. But I think it may be something very important."

He picked up the phone, dialled a number, put his hand over the receiver. "How do you spell your name, darlin'?" he asked me kindly.

I spelt it out. There was a pause.

"My goodness, darlin', and I'll be blessed!" There was the crackling sound of another voice on the phone. "It's the Director himself."

This seemed to impress him, for he lifted me down from his lap and asked somebody to bring me a cup of tea *and* a biscuit.

Stepmother came to collect me. "What a hopeless child you are!" she said, and stuck a label with my name and address and phone number onto my school case. I never got lost again.

Daddy took me with him in the hire car one day, to the Conservatorium. He wanted to enrol me in the school there and asked for one of the teachers to come to his office. The wonderful Miss Betsy Brown, acting headmistress at the time, came along to meet me. She was spindly and thin, like a bird, with sparkling eyes of fun. When my father told her he wanted me enrolled she had to explain, politely, that it was a high school, and I couldn't attend until I was at least eleven years old. He seemed surprised, saying he had attended musical institutions in Bruges in Belgium when his parents had wanted him to go there. Miss Brown explained that things were different in Australia. He muttered something to indicate disappointment, then asked if she could look after me for the rest of the day till it was time for me to accompany him home.

It was a great privilege to spend the day with Miss Brown and

I had an instinctive feeling that I would always know her, rather as I had known Nanny. Watching her working with the children, interviewing parents, teaching lessons, I sat beside her desk and just knew she would be a great friend, even if I had to wait a few years before attending the Con.

While awaiting enrolment at the Conservatorium I was sent to a local piano teacher, and told I would later be going to Miss de Mestre at the Con, and also that I was to learn the violin. My teacher did not inspire me, and I went to my lessons just to please Father, although I wasn't making much progress. Some time after we moved to the North Shore I was sent to one of the nuns at Prouille convent in Water Street, Wahroonga, a little school only ten minutes' walk from home. Although I received a lot of bangs on the hand with a wooden ruler when I played wrong notes, I soon began to play passably well.

Wherever we lived, and we moved several times, I knew Daddy was somewhat aloof, although not in an unkind way. He seemed lost in his own world of which I was no part. He would talk pleasantly, give me a hug, even play Scrabble with me if I was very good. But he would seem suddenly to leave the present and his mind would move away to something more important. Perhaps he was composing in his head, or thinking about an opera, or a performance. It was clear he was not present with me, but in another place, quite alone, doing his thinking.

In 1950, when we moved up to Wahroonga, life suddenly changed wonderfully for the better. Wahroonga was half an hour's drive from the Harbour Bridge on the northern side of the city.

In New York I had often watched Nanny transplanting seedlings from one pot to another; sometimes they did well and sometimes they looked as if they weren't going to make it. I had felt like one of her unhappy seedlings until we found the house in Burns Road.

It had an immense garden surrounded by low stone walls. A spectacular carpet of purple flowers lay beneath a tall, wide-branched tree, there were higgledy-piggledy rambling bushes and unfamiliar flowers in brilliant blues. My favourite flower had little white petals that went brown when you touched them but smelt like the scent bottle on Stepmother's dressing table which I wasn't really meant to touch. We had many of these gardenia bushes.

The lawn was painted with daisies, and to the right of the house lay a vast tennis court, while at the back the soil was recently dug for vegetables.

I loved it all from the moment we saw it and I jumped up and down, and to my own surprise even kissed Stepmother on both cheeks when she said to the sales agent, "I shall buy this one." It was strange to hear her saying that she would pay in cash, but it would take a few days to arrange. A house would require a great many banknotes, I imagined.

Buying had an air of permanence to it. Perhaps we might stay this time, like when you bought something at a shop and it was yours to take home. It was a wonderful house, such as I had seen only in storybooks, painted white but with creepers climbing energetically up one front wall.

The house seemed immediately to welcome us to live comfortably and happily, as people did in fairytales. There was a large room for me, one for Donie, a wing for Daddy, with its own bathroom and little kitchenette—although I didn't know what he needed that for as I didn't think he was very good in kitchens. There were three extra bedrooms. Stepmother's room, opposite father's wing, was the prettiest and most beautifully decorated, as ever, with the best materials and feminine articles of which little girls dream. Silver hairbrushes and trinkets stood on a polished glass table beside gleaming mirrors with brightly coloured beads hanging from them: costume jewellery, for effect, not the things Stepmother usually wore when going out. Beside the tennis court was a covered veranda for sitting in the afternoon shade. I was totally contented with the house.

To make it even more perfect, on our first afternoon, a meowing by the garden shed led me to a thin, bedraggled, mangy, scruffy bundle of matted fur. It was honestly not a very special sort of cat, and it definitely did not wish to be picked up, scratching me at the first opportunity and spitting and hissing.

Father approved of it, at a distance. "We'll call it George," he pronounced the moment he saw it.

George, a tortoiseshell, gradually became more friendly and obliging, if defying its name by producing, quite soon after our arrival, five hefty kittens. They all lived in my room. The night they were born Daddy was listening to a recording of some beautiful French music. When I asked him what it was, he said it was an opera by Debussy, *Pelléas and Mélisande*. He told me it had been written for a soprano called Mary Garden and that he had first conducted it at its American première in 1931 in Chicago. Much later I learned that the audience had not approved of its first performance at all, so Daddy had turned to them and shaken his head violently to show his disapproval, but they never got the point. He explained that people took a long time to grow accustomed to new combinations of sounds. I didn't want to be like that. I hoped to learn to love everything he introduced.

The title of the work appealed to me so much that I christened the first two black and white kittens Pelly and Melly. My father said it was funny to shorten names but supposed, reluctantly, that it would be easier to say, specially when calling them to meals. He seemed a little bored by my insistent explanations about such matters.

At my Catholic girls' school, Prouille, it was good to hear the familiar Latin of the Mass I recognised from New York. It meant that something stayed the same, even though nobody I knew understood the words. I liked watching people using the same customs, dipping a hand in the holy water and making the sign of the cross.

There was also a collection plate, just like the one in New York where I had once pulled the button off my coat so it would make a noise like a coin because I had left my money at home and knew I had to put in something for the priest's dinner. A sense of belonging was gradually developing.

At last, it seemed, it was worth remembering the names of the nuns and the other girls, for I was certain that we were going to stay here this time. I had never been able to remember names, never having had time to learn them before it was time to move on again. This was my fifth school, and I was only nine.

"Babies come from Paris," announced Jacintha.

"No they don't! The stork brings them," insisted Penny.

"They're found under the lids of grand pianos," I said, just for something to say, then blushed and put my hand to my face as I shook my head, adding, "sometimes".

We were playing under the passionfruit vine, its name having provoked a mischievous discussion about passion and babies despite our having only the remotest of notions that passion could possibly be connected with birth.

In 1949, most nine-year-old girls in Sydney were very innocent.

I wanted Penny to be my best friend. Jacintha came from Uruguay. There was also Mary, whose father worked on the Snowy River Scheme and was seldom at home. The three girls were allowed to play at my house after school, provided I did my piano practice first. We could even use the tennis court if we always wore our soft sandshoes.

"What was it like where you lived before?" Penny asked.

"You mean before we crossed the bridge?"

"No, stupid. You know. Before you came to Sydney. My mum said you came from America. She said that's why you talk so funny."

"I can't help the way I talk," I protested. "New York was nothing like here. We lived in an apartment and we had no garden. When you opened the front door you stepped straight out onto the sidewalk."

Penny stopped me. "What's a sidewalk?"

"You know, the thing that you walk along beside the road to keep you safe from the traffic."

"You mean a pavement. See, that's what I meant about you talking funny."

There were other words she would correct me on, so I had to remember to stop saying elevator and call it a lift. Penny thought it was terribly funny, having different words for things, but after the first weeks of teasing, she made me feel it was cute rather than different.

I had been playing a noisy game of tennis with Penny when Stepmother came out. "Hello, aren't you going to introduce me to your friend? " she asked.

"This is Yady," I said to Penny, for I thought the word 'Step-mother' sounded unfriendly.

'Yady' was what I had called her when she had first been presented to me. "This is the lady who is going to marry your father," said Nanny. Unable to pronounce 'Marjorie' I gave her the nickname 'Yady', as I could not pronounce the letter 'l'. She seemed pleased that I had a special name for her.

Yady announced, "Tomorrow I'm going to drive up to Whale Beach for an early swim. Penny, why don't you ask your mother if you can come with us? If you'd like to."

"Yippee, Mrs Goossens, I'd love that. We don't go to the beach often, 'cos my Dad's car isn't big enough for us all. You know, with my five brothers. I'm sure Mum will say yes."

Penny threw her arms around me, but did not quite know what to do with Yady, so shook her awkwardly by the hand and ran away at full speed to her house just two streets away. In about fifteen minutes she was back, red in the face from excitement.

"Ma says I can come, and she'll do us a picnic. Something really Australian, just to say thank you. She's going to make some lamingtons and give us bottles of home-made lemonade. And she wants to know if you're wanting meat for a barbecue. She says to ring her if you need anything else." Totally out of breath now, she added, with her best manners, "And Ma says to say thanks a lot."

Yady was somewhat taken back by Penny's enthusiasm, but I

was proud of Stepmother for being polite and ringing Mrs Dwyer, thanking her and asking about barbecues.

Mrs Dwyer was very well informed and did her best to be friendly. "You're allowed to light fires now, as there's no fire ban, and there are grates near the parking area, on the grass. You can either take your own wood or use the kindling you'll find all over the ground after last night's storm. And thanks a million for including Penny in your plans. She misses a lot of outings because our Dad takes the boys to the footie."

Yady put her hand over the mouthpiece of the phone and asked me, "Where or what is the 'footie'?"

"It's Australian for football. They like to shorten lots of words," I explained, brimming with knowledge.

Mrs Dwyer would have gone on forever, but Yady brought an end to the conversation, saying we would collect Penny at eight o'clock in the car, so that nobody had to carry anything over to our house.

When we arrived to collect Penny, Mrs Dwyer came to greet us. "I hope you don't mind, but our Dad's taken four of the boys off to play footie, and left Bruce at home. Can he come with you too?"

To his sister's disgust, Bruce came. Penny had told me that Bruce was a pain in the neck, but to me he looked like a perfectly normal, cute little boy of four. I loved the way he called the purple tree on our front lawn a 'Jack and Rhonda'. Nobody had told me it was a jacaranda, so I used Bruce's name for it and made everybody laugh.

"Is it true your dad works in a greenhouse?" he asked, as we piled into the car.

"Sorry about him," said Penny apologetically, "I told him your Dad was at the Conservatorium. I suppose he thought I meant he worked in a conservatory."

I ruffled Bruce's hair and asked him, "What's your Dad do, then?"

"He's a Count Ant."

"Well, then, your Dad and my Dad should get on just fine."

Penny raised her eyes heavenwards. "He's far too stupid to think that's funny. Shut up, Bruce." The little boy promptly went to sleep.

I had never been to Whale Beach before. The journey was spectacular; we passed gum trees in more shades of green that I had ever seen, and hundreds of majestic fan-like ferns.

Bruce woke up and shouted with delight when glimpses of the ocean appeared. We drove for about an hour, passing little traffic, in our funny little Fiat station wagon with its wood-finished back and loads of room for our bathing things and the picnic.

The surf was crashing in, the waves breaking high with the spray shooting upwards like fireworks and making a heavy thumping sound as the breakers bolted in against the golden sandy beach. It was so exciting I was dying to go into the water.

Penny grabbed my hand and we threw ourselves into the waves, shouting with delight. Bruce followed, but played near the edge, as his mother had insisted. "He's not really too bad," I remarked to Penny.

"As long as you don't see him often, he's okay," she said none too fondly.

Yady lay on the sand with a book, on a large bath towel, and she had brought extra rugs, towels and Nivea cream to help us 'to get nice and brown'. We were allowed to stay in the water until lunch time.

"Bet you didn't have beaches like this in New York," boasted Penny.

"No, we didn't," I replied, wanting to tell her all about it. "New York was full of crowded streets, taxicabs, police sirens, and it smelt of petrol. In winter it was dreadfully cold and in summer there never seemed to be any breeze to blow away the heat."

Penny was sifting sand through her fingers onto her toes and squirming as it trickled down. "Go on," she said.

"Maybe there were beaches, but we never went to them except in the summer holidays. Our beach trips were to Maine, the place where I was born. It seemed a long way from New York. Not like this. Nothing in the world is like this."

"Do you like it here, then?" asked Penny.

"This is the most wonderful place in the whole wide world. I adore it. But I am finding it hard to live with Yady. I don't really like her," I confided, glad to have a friend to tell.

"She's okay. Not nearly as bad as my five brothers," Penny insisted. Then, looking quite wise, she said, "You know in fairy tales and Cinderella stories? How there are difficult stepmothers in books? Perhaps it's the way they think they have to be. Maybe she'll turn out okay in the end, when you get used to her." Then she looked at me inquisitively. "What happened to your real mum?"

"My mum never even writes to me. I don't know why. I write to her, even though I'm not sure what to say. Maybe she never writes back because I've upset her by letting her know how much I love it here."

"Things will work out for you," said Penny, dragging me over to the strange cold-water shower on the promenade, instructing me and Bruce: "Better shower off the sand before we get back to Mrs G. Can I call her that, d'you suppose? I couldn't call her that 'Yady' name."

The barbecue was an immense success. We had never had one before, so Penny showed us how to light the fire, turn the sausages and take them off with two sticks so that we did not burn our fingers. When I tried, I dropped one in the sand. We gave it to Bruce.

"Don't you ever cook things, Mrs G?" Penny asked with some amazement.

"I don't suppose I do. No, people have always done the cooking for us. It's not really my sort of thing."

"Lamingtons," Penny explained, proudly showing off her mother's offerings, "are a special Australian cake. It's a sponge dipped in chocolate then rolled in dejected coconut."

Bruce shoved four of them into his chocolate-smeared mouth,

and just as he was about to gobble yet another, Penny smacked his hand. "You rude little boy. Mum says you just graze at your food like a cow. Now, go and play and make sandcastles. You're not to go into the water while your tummy is so full, or you'll drown." As he left, she added behind her hand, "If only I could be so lucky!"

Yady returned to her sunbathing and her book, thanking Penny for her help and reminding us to bathe between the flags.

"What are the flags for?" I asked.

"You really don't know anything, do you!" said Penny. She pointed to the Surf Life Saving Club, and the men with cotton hats tied around their chins—"so you can see them better," she explained.

"My brother Steve is fifteen. He's learning to do resuss-something which he says is a great excuse for kissing girls, 'cos he puts his mouth over theirs and breathes heavily, saying it will save their lives. Trust him!"

As I had never been taught, I didn't know how to swim properly. When we went to Maine we had a swimming pool, blue and warm. Nanny used to put an inflated tyre around my middle so I could float around. She used to watch from the side in her starched white uniform. Donie swam superbly and would come in with me sometimes. I could put my arms around her neck while she did backstroke, allowing me to cling on, safely, even without my tyre.

Penny was learning to swim but stayed in the shallow water with me, jumping the waves. After we had been bouncing around in the waves for a while, Yady called us, "We have to go now. Remember, it's your father's first concert of the subscription series."

I hadn't learned about a composer with that name, but Yady had told me Daddy was going to introduce many new works to Sydney audiences. Maybe this was a special new person.

We washed the sand off our feet under the tap near the gravel area where the cars were parked, put our towels around our middles and climbed into the car.

"Would all the children like to come to the concert with us

tonight?" asked Yady as she deposited Penny and Bruce, thanked Mrs Dwyer for the picnic, and was unloading the car.

"They can't come tonight. They got really sunburnt at the footie. I'm not sure they'd know how to behave at a concert, I'm ashamed to say. Thanks anyway. And thank you for giving these two a lovely day." She waved as we went down the drive and I missed Penny already.

I could not quite believe the contrast to our life in New York. The beach, a concert, and all in one day. I was excited at being able to enjoy everything almost at once. Donie, very grown up for eighteen, was already at the Town Hall for a rehearsal. Daddy had been there all day, and they were going to change into their concert clothes in Daddy's studio at the Conservatorium, then come with us to the Town Hall where the orchestra was to play beneath the gigantic organ pipes.

Yady wore a pink chiffon straight-skirted long dress with an exquisitely delicate beaded scarf at her neck. She looked like a movie star. I was plain and awkward, even though the dressmaker had made me quite a pretty dress. It was in white organdie with dainty spots, a full skirt just to the knees with a lace collar and long sleeves that came down the back of my hands in rather impractical points. It wasn't really me and my hair, in childish sticky-out braids, was all wrong. My nose and forehead were terribly red from our day at the beach, but Yady was already bronzed with a beautiful tan.

"There, you look really cute," said Yady, smoothing my dress and taking me by the hand as we got into the black hire car with a chauffeur that collected us from Wahroonga. It felt very grand. I had never been to a concert before, only to rehearsals. In New York, they had always refused to let me go to concerts, saying I was too little to stay up so late.

During the journey it was already becoming dark, much earlier than it used to in New York. Crossing Sydney Harbour Bridge was particularly beautiful at night. We counted the illuminated ferries and an ocean liner festooned with strings of lights that made it look like an enormous, strangely shaped Christmas tree. With the water sparkling with reflections, it was much more beautiful than anything I had ever seen before.

Parking at the Conservatorium, we went straight to Daddy's rooms. The Director's Studio, as it was called, was one huge room with a lustrous grand piano, a dark brown leather sofa and several comfortable velvet armchairs. There were French doors opening onto a terrace leading to a tropical garden which overlooked the Botanic Gardens and, in the distance, dancing water.

"Is this really your room, Daddy?" I asked, running into his outstretched arms and enjoying a hug.

"Yes, my little one. This is where I work. Piano students come here for auditions. I rehearse with the chamber music groups, rest before concerts, and talk to members of the staff and the orchestra. The sofa is comfy enough for an afternoon nap. It's a quiet place for composing, too. I rather like it."

"Time to go, Gene dear." Yady was keeping an eye on her watch. Daddy liked to be at the Town Hall at least half an hour prior to a concert. Donie had walked down ahead of us, to tune her harp.

Sydney Town Hall was dark, tall, wide and seemed to me to be a very old building. But once you walked up the stairs—we usually went in by a side entrance—and across the foyer, it was like being in a film. Glass chandeliers hung from ceilings edged with gold. It seemed enormous. We went straight to the green room, which was large with brown walls, lots of dark wood, rather dreary and—and to my surprise—with no green anywhere at all.

"Why is it called a green room, Daddy?" I asked.

"It always is, little one. Don't ask silly questions." His reply made me wonder if he really knew either.

To the side of the green room was a small room with 'Private' marked on the door. Daddy put on his bow tie and dress coat in there. Then he came out, looking so very handsome, tall and important that I was proud of him.

A man in a dinner jacket collected us and showed us to our seats in the eastern gallery. I loved settling down early, listening to the chattering audience and to the exciting sounds of the tuning of the orchestra. All those different hesitant noises, some perfect, some peculiar, some scratchy as tunes were played, all at different times.

I could see my sister sitting calmly, her feet on the pedals of her harp as she finished her tuning, patting her arms against the strings, to feel the balance of the instrument, but I couldn't quite hear the sounds she was making against the volume of the other instruments.

A hush fell over the hall, voices cut off abruptly as they do on the radio before the announcer's voice is heard. There was a boisterous, friendly-sounding clapping of hands as Daddy walked to the little stand in the centre of the stage, climbed up on it, bowed to the audience, then turned his back to us as he paid attention to his orchestra. The music began.

The first item was the Overture to Wagner's *The Mastersingers*. It overwhelmed me. Sometimes a piece of music would flood into me and I would have to hear it over and over again, playing it all day, given the opportunity. I never grew out of that habit. Nothing else in the programme made any impression. A pianist played beautifully, but the vitality of the opening piece was so important that I wished to hear no further sounds. It came back into my head, playing with a constancy that drowned all else. I was mesmerised.

At interval, we went to see Daddy, who was splashing himself from a bottle labelled 'bay rum' to freshen himself up, rubbing himself down and looking red in the face but very happy.

"Daddy, I adored that first piece. Can I hear it again? Do we have a record at home? Will you teach me all about it, and the story? I read my programme notes but they don't tell me enough."

"I'm glad you liked it, little one. Yes, I will tell you more later. But now go back to your seats or we will be late with the second half."

I read in the *ABC Weekly* that there was a concert at eight a.m.

the very next day, with the Sydney Symphony Orchestra and Daddy conducting. It seemed peculiar that nobody had mentioned it, for I had never heard of him having to be at work so early. It also seemed unfair that he had to work on a Sunday.

I knew he liked to be in the green room half an hour before the concert began. The car journey took about an hour. So I decided I had better wake him at just before six a.m. He always had breakfast alone in his room.

I had watched Sven preparing breakfast so I knew just what to do. It had to be Indian tea in a heated pot. One hard-boiled egg, just three and a half minutes, with two slices of toast and butter, with 'dialectic marmalade' as Daddy insisted it was called, because he was not allowed sugar. Of course, I must not forget the five prunes.

Pleased with myself, but also a little apprehensive, I knocked on the door at five past six. The room was very dark, as there were double curtains on the windows and the walls were a sombre green. Heavy, wooden furniture made the place seem even darker, so it was difficult to find my way across to open the curtains. Music was strewn all over the lid of the black piano, and I nearly tripped on the thick pads of scores on the floor.

"It's me, Daddy. Good morning. Here is your breakfast. I thought I'd better get you ready for your concert this morning."

He was flabbergasted, and not at all pleased.

"What concert?" he asked, and I felt very important at being the only person who knew.

"I read about it in the *ABC Weekly*. It's terribly unfair for you on a Sunday morning, so I've given you extra marmalade. I suppose the hire car will be here in a moment."

"Listen, you silly child. Haven't you ever heard of records?"

I was too wounded to reply, and walked towards the door, feeling disgraced, wondering why the orchestra and Daddy would be on a record when people could come and see them instead.

"I thought recordings were only of dead people," I said, mortified, as I reached the door.

"You'll be dead too, if you do this again," he said, then called me back when he saw the tears streaming down my face. He hugged me, kissing me on both cheeks against his stubbly face.

"Now run along. We'll talk later about the music you enjoyed last night. But first of all what I need is some more sleep."

Just before lunch, Daddy called for me by ringing a large bell. It was our special signal, and just hearing it excited me. I knew the importance of the bell, and it certainly was loud, even in our big house. I had been sitting outside by the tennis court and was still able to hear it, right from the other side of the house, sounding in his composing room.

The bell was one of a set of six cow bells Daddy had brought back from Italy in his hand luggage. He adored their sounds and wanted to use them in a composition. He had not minded in the least that they weighed eight pounds each, even when the man at the airline desk made him pay what he considered a fortune in excess weight. I used to love hearing about it. When he told the story he exaggerated wildly, making it funnier with each telling. But as he only rang the bells when he wanted to see me, I was afraid he might still be angry about my silly mistake.

"There's a surprise for you on the floor. I found it for you last night. It's the piano reduction of *Die Meistersinger von Nürnberg*. You seemed so excited about the overture. If you are a good girl, I'll play some of it for you after lunch. I've got some work to do until then. Run along again now."

We had lunch outside, on the veranda by the tennis court. Our new Dutch cook Nell had prepared roast lamb with all the trimmings, such as Daddy liked best, and a heavy Dutch style pudding, the closest she could get to an English steamed pudding. Everybody was in a good mood.

"May we, Daddy?" I asked, with nothing but *The Mastersingers* on my mind.

The moment pudding was finished, he took me by the hand to his precious shiny black piano. It had been shipped out from England and had belonged to his father, who had also been a well-known conductor. The instrument had been damaged in transit and the music stand did not stay up properly. He propped it up with two pairs of scissors, which made it look rather odd, but served the purpose and he did not want anybody 'fiddling about to fix it'.

He began to play the first melody on the piano. "This is how it goes, as you will remember from last night. Wagner introduces his themes as if they were people, so that when you hear that tune, you can expect the person, or something about that person, to appear in the story."

Spellbound, I listened as he explained the significance of *leit-motifs* (leading motifs) together with the plot and the stories of the lives of the people taking part in the song contest, after which the winner would be given the hand of Eva, Pogner's daughter.

"What if Eva doesn't like the winner?" I asked with utmost concern.

"That's the secret you'll discover when you see the opera," Daddy replied.

"May I, Daddy, may I? When? Where? How?"

"Sit down, child, you're getting far too excited," he said, flustered by my enthusiasm. "Rehearsals begin very soon at the Con, and once the singers have tidied themselves up a bit musically, you may come and sit in. It's a treat, though. You cannot come to every opera, or you'll be up every night. I think this one will be your special introduction."

Nothing else seemed to matter to me, my cats, the tennis court, visits to the beach, playing with my friends. I awaited the rehearsals of *The Mastersingers* as if my very life depended upon it. I even asked if I could have a better piano teacher, as I wasn't getting on with mine. I would need to improve if I wanted to play some of the tunes for myself. I found a record and wore out the tracks of 'The Prize Song', driving Nell to distraction by singing the theme endlessly.

"Other children, they sing the pop songs, the jolly sounds which I hear on the radio," she would complain.

Nell lived in her own rooms at the back of the house with her husband and their baby daughter Helen. They had arrived to help us just before that first Town Hall concert. She wasn't the same as Nanny, and she didn't look in the least like her. Nanny was twenty-eight. She had always been twenty-eight at every birthday.

"How old are you, Nell?" I asked, surprised by her startled expression.

"My age, he is my secret. Little girls, they do not ask the grown-up peoples how old they are. It is not a good manner." She said it quite sternly, making me feel ashamed.

"Sorry, Nell. I didn't mean to be rude, but I wondered if you were like Nanny, that's all."

"Tell me about your nanny," she said in a soft, friendly voice.

I loved talking about Nanny and had not been encouraged to do so since her unexpected departure. "Nanny used to collect me from school. But I'm much older now so I don't get lost any more. She used to take me to church but didn't stay with me because she was Presbyterian and I'm not. I couldn't even press those buttons at road crossings because of it."

"What do you mean?" asked Nell.

"You know it has words on the lights where you have to cross, but I wasn't a good speller in New York."

"You mean 'stop' and 'go'?" interrupted Nell, surprised.

"No, long words. I think it could have been Presbyterian."

"You are a stupid girl! Even I have been learning that word. It is pedestrian!"

"Well, nearly the same," I protested. We looked at each other and both burst out laughing.

"You must miss your Nanny very much. I miss my mother and father," she told me. A tear rolled down her cheek, so I ran over and put my arm around her commodious tummy, for she seemed very tall.

"Don't cry, dear Nell. Missing is an awful feeling, but some days it is not so bad."

She kissed me on the forehead and gave me the sort of teddy bear squeeze Nanny used to give. "You will be all right, you funny little girl. And I am too big to be missing my parents. How about something to eat?"

She made me delicious snacks of little fat pancakes and fed me nuts and raisins because, "You are too, how do you say, skinly."

"Skinny, Nell," I corrected.

"Well, nearly the same," she laughed.

She also saved left-overs for my cats and cleaned up the messes the kittens made.

"These kittens, they do bad things with the bed clothings," she observed, as my operatic kittens Pelly and Melly constantly clawed everything from my bed onto the floor to make comfy nests. My school friends would chide me about their names, saying Pelléas and Mélisande were funny words, even if they came from an opera. They certainly didn't understand about opera either.

After a concert one night I sat with Daddy in the back seat of the hire car, enjoying the special treat of discussing the following week's programmes.

He was going to introduce Stravinsky's *The Rite of Spring*, and a work by Scriabin, *Poème d'Extase*. He hummed a few melodies from the second piece, then stopped suddenly. "Look at those lights behind us. I could swear we must have someone following us. Take another route and see what happens," Daddy instructed the driver. His voice sounded amused rather than afraid.

The driver turned down a side street, tracked back through a few parallel roads, and we emerged in Wahroonga more quickly than usual. No car had followed.

"I'm very tired, so I'll go straight to bed. See you in the morning," he said to me.

Ten minutes later two more cars pulled up outside. One held Yady and Donie, the other was a new hire car with important guests. Meanwhile Daddy had changed into his checked dressing gown, couldn't find his slippers and was walking barefoot through the living room, calling out, "I can't find any Milo. Where *is* the kitchen?"

Embarrassed to see people he did not know, then some whom he did, he retreated into my bedroom where I was feeding the cats.

"Don't you really know where our kitchen is, Daddy?" I asked, amazed. "We've lived here for almost a year now."

"Kitchens are of no interest to me," he said defensively. "Although I do enjoy making my own hot Milo in my kitchenette. But the tin was empty."

I wanted to save Daddy the embarrassment of being seen in his shabby bedclothes. I told him that we had important guests, from the theatre. Yady had invited them, telling their hire car driver to follow ours, but apparently they got a bit lost when we changed directions. I thought it was very funny, but was sad to see Daddy perplexed.

Daddy was not at all amused. He insisted on his cup of Milo, and braved out the evening in his dressing gown, for some of the visitors were old friends and he quickly forgot what he was wearing.

Two of England's greatest actors were among the guests. Dame Sybil Thorndike, in Australia on a theatre tour, was beautiful, although to me she seemed very old. She was especially kind to me, even asking me about myself.

"What do you enjoy doing? Are you going to be a musician?"

"Daddy has promised to take me to the rehearsals for *The Mastersingers*. I absolutely adore opera but I haven't been to one yet," I replied enthusiastically.

"You must come to one of our plays. Now, come and meet my husband." Her equally famous husband, Sir Lewis Casson, asked me why I liked *The Mastersingers*.

"Would you like to hear some of it?" I asked, hurrying them

into the study beside the music room, taking out a record and playing the overture. They listened attentively, describing a performance they had recently attended in Germany.

"The Bayreuth Festival is quite an event. You must ask your father to take you one day. Or you could listen to the broadcasts on the radio, even if it will be at some unholy hour here, as it is broadcast live."

Daddy rescued them from my record playing, promising we would all attend the premiere of *The Mastersingers* the following week, if it fitted in with their schedule, which it did.

So, my first visit to the opera, accompanied by my new friends, was all the more exciting. Dame Sybil looked radiant, and agreed with me that the tenor was quite the most handsome man on earth. Allan Ferris was his name, and he became the object of my adoration. I pinned his picture to my bedroom wall and kissed it goodnight before I went to sleep every single night. A pretty soprano played Eva and I would have loved to be grown up and to have been the character she played. It was such a romantic story.

The stage set represented Germany several hundred years ago, and the singers wore gorgeous period costumes. James Wilson sang the important role of the blacksmith Hans Sachs. He had broken his arm and so wore it in a sling, even though the libretto had no explanation for it.

I knew every melody well, each ensemble, and now that it was all combined with acting and costumes, it was absolutely fantastic. When the opera ended and all the wonderful tunes I had learned had been played, I felt terribly sad that the event I had waited for so eagerly was over. I wanted it to go on forever.

"May I come to another performance, Daddy?" I asked.

"We'll see," he said, appropriately.

BOUILLABAISSE

"We're going to France," said Yady conversationally, as if it were just around the corner.

"But what about my exams at Prouille, my piano lessons and Pelly and Melly?" I pleaded. Now I was having lessons with a better teacher, even if she was a strict nun, and I was beginning to make progress at last, to prepare me for going to the Conservatorium.

"We are only going for six months, and I am sure you will be able to catch up at school when we get back. Nell will look after the cats, and it will do you good to learn some French. You can go to school there. You might even lose your peculiar accent. Now that you speak half American and half Australian, you sound as if you have had no education at all."

I was mortified, and anxious about leaving Wahroonga. I hoped they would bring me back.

"Can Nell come too?" I asked, unable to forget Nanny whose absence still distressed me.

"Nell will be here when we come back. Stop worrying, child."

Daddy had conducting engagements in Italy and was to fly out later, but Yady preferred us to take a house in the south of France for most of the time. Daddy could join us when he was free, and we could live as a family in comfortable circumstances, in a warm climate. It was the Australian autumn, which meant, I learned, that it would be spring in France.

We went by ship, through the Suez Canal. It was a long journey, six weeks. Crossing the Great Australian Bight we all became very seasick. The diesel fumes from the engine room penetrated everything and when I was not being sick, I felt as if I was about to be. All I could eat was dry Sao biscuits, a cracker with no taste, or fresh oranges which made the cabin smell. Orange peel was an improvement on diesel fumes.

The ship landed at Tilbury, then we took a boat train across the English Channel and on to Paris. We did not stay there, but travelled in a *couchette*, a sleeping carriage much more comfortable than the one we had slept in when we went from New York to San Francisco. Stepmother had paid for us to go first class. It was just the three of us, my sister and me following in line as Stepmother strode elegantly ahead of her impeccable suitcases and trunks, two or three porters in tow, making rather a quaint sight.

It was never the same without my darling Nanny, and I particularly missed her on voyages. After the train there were taxis, then we arrived in Nice, going straight to the villa where Daddy would join us later.

Our rented house was called Villa Namouna. It was close to the village of St Jean Cap Ferrat, a small unspoiled fishing port nestling beneath the Alpes Maritimes. Daddy had learned of the house from his friend the writer Somerset Maugham, who lived in a house opposite and had written to say that it was vacant. Our villa had its own private beach but, compared to Bondi and Whale Beach, it did not impress me at all with its pebbles and dirty, shallow sand.

The weather was not as warm as in Sydney and the house was on three levels, all a bit of a muddle. I knew nobody and almost no French. The differences between 'pavement' and 'sidewalk' were nothing compared to an entire new language. Now it was '*le trottoir*' with something called an article in front of it, sometimes masculine, sometimes feminine, and very difficult to remember. I was afraid and shy. I didn't really want to be there, missing my darling Pelly and Melly, Nell, Sven, Wahroonga, Penny and even my more interesting piano lessons. Stepmother said I was most ungrateful.

It must have been difficult for Stepmother to cope with me, having had no experience of children, and not understanding my attachment to the security of Sydney, my home at Wahroonga and the presence of cats, friends and a regular school routine. She felt I should have jumped at the chance of being abroad, but I was probably too confused by the travelling we had already done, and too immature, to appreciate the experience.

"Will we go to the opera?" I asked, brightening at the prospect when Yady mentioned performances in Nice.

"We'll see," she said, and promptly made several bookings for us. Donie was eighteen and had enrolled at Nice University to study French. I was very proud of her. She seemed to fit in wherever we went, bravely going out on her own, finding her way everywhere by public transport. She had a poise and dignity I hoped one day to acquire, much more natural and sincere than the poses I perceived my stepmother assuming. Donie was a natural lady.

Now I was nine, I was to attend the village school, which was not even a proper Catholic one. Daddy had always been very particular about the importance of my attending 'a proper Catholic school' when I had been in Sydney, having insisted on my attending first Rose Bay Convent and later Prouille, at Wahroonga, all schools with dedicated teaching nuns who kept strict discipline and who honoured the rituals of the Mass. So, now that I was to go to a school which had no church connections, I hoped that he would not be cross.

However, it was the only school in the tiny village. "It doesn't matter for such a short time," Yady assured me soothingly. As it turned out, it was a friendly little school. My greatest fear, as it always had been when I was small, was getting lost on the way there. However, St Jean Cap Ferrat was then but a tiny fishing village. There were not many wrong streets to take.

In 1994 I had the opportunity to visit it again, in a journey of nostalgia, as one does, trying to find places to which one belonged. Nowadays it has been taken over by millionaires and pop stars and is so crowded that it is almost unrecognisable. I couldn't locate the tiny village school, which could either be a factor of my ability to still get lost or because it has closed due to there being so few children in the neighbourhood.

When we went to the opera in Nice, it was quite a funny event. The singers had come from all over the world for a special festival. The opera was Puccini's *La Bohème*, and I enjoyed its wonderful melodies. A rotund Romanian lady sang the role of Mimi. When I read in my programme that she was weak and dying of consumption, I expected her to be as thin as a stick. She sang in her own language very loudly all the time, even when she was supposed to be dying. Because the music was so beautifully moving, however, we couldn't help crying at the end, unconvincing though her performance had been.

The tenor, Rodolfo, was obviously English although he did his best to sing in Italian. In Sydney the only operas I had attended had been sung in English. Of course I knew it was different at this performance, because I recognised the words from records. The other performers sang in French, German and Russian, and when there was a quartet they all faced in different directions, looking not at each other but at the conductor, who was not looking at them anyway, but was so alarmingly engrossed in the score that we wondered if he had ever seen it before. The sounds emanating from the orchestra suggested he had not. Stepmother was quite surprised when the orchestra all ended together. We had our best laugh over supper later, agreeing it was one of the most dreadful performances anybody could be expected to endure.

Daddy came to Villa Namouna occasionally and brought friends with him, usually other conductors. His engagements in Italy were part of a contract with the British Council. He worked in Naples with the composer William Walton. There was one visitor whom I particularly liked. Years later I learned that this was Charles Groves, subsequently knighted for his services to music. I was too young to be impressed by names. What I liked about him was his kindness and sense of humour. He was a large bear of a man, stylishly dressed, always in a three-piece suit with shiny black leather shoes. He was not at all old. At his suggestion, I called him Uncle Charlie.

"Can you play billiards, Renée, my sweet?" he asked the first time he met me.

"I never have, but I'd love to try," I assured him as he took me downstairs to *le rez-de-chaussée*. 'Ground floor' seemed a very dull term in comparison. The French phrase sounded to me like a beautiful song. Loving beautiful expressions, I found it was fun to master a few attractive words.

On the *rez-de-chaussée* was a huge table covered in green felt with little nets around the edges. On the wall, gripped by pegs, were long wooden cues. Charles Groves taught me the rules, helped me to hold the cue, to chalk it before hitting the balls across the table, and all the time he was laughing his head off. He never asked me to play the piano or to read to him in French as other adults seemed compelled to do. Instead he would take me on long walks down to the fishermen's nets on the little port quay.

We watched a curious man in red flannel trousers with a checked woollen shirt and a blue cap on his head. Everything about him was interesting and colourful. He had a thick needle in his left hand and was struggling to capture pieces of net stuck in the wooden planks of the wharf. When he beckoned to me to step forward, I held on tightly to Uncle Charlie.

"You'll be all right, go on over, I'll wait here. The man looks as if he has something to show you." And when I walked towards him, the man took a little silver fish out of the net. The poor creature was still wriggling. The fisherman beckoned to me again and put it into my hand.

I shuddered, but he said *"N'ayez pas peur,"* which I knew meant I was not to be afraid. The fish was slimy and I dropped it onto the ground. He threw it back into the water, then gave me a piece of the net, indicating I was to hold it for him while he made some repairs with his needle and thread.

"Eh bien, ma petite. Merci." And he took a packet of toffees out of his pocket and gave me one to eat. It was extremely sticky and covered in little pieces of fluff that got under my tongue and made me cough. He laughed. *"C'est délicieux,"* he said reassuringly. Stretching his arms high, he threw the mended net back into the water with a mighty splash.

Uncle Charlie took my hand and led me over to the street market. The stalls were piled high with colourful vegetables. The vendors were yelling enthusiastically, shouting their prices, arguing, shaking their fists at each other, then laughing happily when customers stepped up and bought anything.

We chose some vivid red tomatoes, shiny green peppers and the most beautiful purple aubergine I had ever seen. There was a stall with polished apples, yellow pears, green bananas and spiky pineapples. Uncle Charlie bought himself a little blue French beret and put it on his head, then made little bows to me, muttering and pretending to be an eccentric Frenchman, gesticulating wildly and, instead of saying real words, making distinctly French noises at which we both hooted with laughter. I liked him very much, he was such fun to be with, not like an adult at all.

Next he pretended to tap on an imaginary rostrum, conducting the people in the market place. They looked at him with interest, and pointed to him, cheering, as a young woman with her hair piled on top of her head appeared and, crooking her right arm in his, joined in the dance, kicking her legs in the air. It was very jolly.

One of the fishmongers opened up a large accordion and played a melody everybody knew. They all sang words to it, as loudly as possible, clapping their hands rhythmically like a strange dance routine. Then there was quite a commotion when two dogs got into a fight in front of the meat display, and Uncle Charlie said it was time for us to go home to dinner.

An old woman from the village called Marie came to look after me. She was quite short and chubby, her face cheerfully rosy and smiling. She always wore a red-and-white apron, even out on the street, and spent more time laughing than talking. In preparation for our visit to France Yady had given me books to study on the ship, but my pronunciation was not very good. As a result, Marie would smile whenever I uttered a phrase, but then say it the right way and make me practise it several times. I began to gain confidence, as at least Marie understood my efforts. She reminded me of Nell rather than Nanny.

Uncle Charlie suggested, "Why don't we go out again and do some shopping? You can ask for things in French. You know so many more words than I do."

"I really don't, honestly. Please don't make me. I feel such a fool. I get everything wrong."

"You can do it. I know you can. So here is a challenge. Go down on your own to the newsagent's and ask for four sheets of brown wrapping paper."

Marie helped me to work it out, using my little dictionary because I wasn't good at getting the words in the right order: "*Quatre grandes feuilles de papier brun*". I said it five times to Uncle Charlie, set off alone to the shop, got lost on the way, began to cry, and ran home saying the shop was closed.

"You're a naughty little girl," he proclaimed, "because I know it isn't closed. And you mustn't tell fibs. Don't worry, I won't tell anybody. What we will do is go there together." He gave me a hug, wiped away my tears and took me down to the shop. He also bought me a bar of chocolate.

After dinner he and Daddy played billiards, and they promised to take me with them next day on an excursion to

St Paul de Vence, a small village about fifty kilometres away in the hills. Yady had gone by train to Paris and would be away for several days, so it was just the three of us. Donie didn't want to miss her classes.

Marie packed us a picnic of camembert, brie, tomatoes, olives, two baguettes and a bottle of Daddy's favourite red wine, three glasses, and a corkscrew. She put in a lemon drink for me. We took the local bus up into the hills and I looked down at the fierce blue of a wintry-looking Mediterranean as we zigzagged around steep hairpin bends. The men spoke of music, Ravel and Debussy. Daddy told anecdotes about Stravinsky and Diaghilev. I was entranced, listening as if to history. I couldn't wait to return to Sydney and to the Conservatorium, to school and my studies, so as to become part of their world and the magic of music.

Marie was married to a fisherman who gave us an unbelievable variety of *fruits de mer*. Daddy adored *bouillabaisse*, which she made using what seemed like every single fish of the sea. She put in huge lumps of garlic and herbs so rich and pungent that the entire house smelt of *bouillabaisse* for weeks.

"*Veux-tu un petit chaton?*" Marie asked me one day, bringing a purring, fuzzy bundle out of her red and white apron pocket.

I clutched the kitten to my face, "*Merci, c'est magnifique!*" I told her, rushing to show Yady as she walked in the door after her trip to Paris.

"Not you and your cats again!" she said, but with a smile which suggested she did not mind. "But you can't bring it back to Sydney with us next month," she continued.

"*Ça ne fait rien. Je le garderai,*" Marie assured her.

Now that I had been given the precious kitten, especially as it was on loan for only one month, I was not going to let it out of my sight.

"We'll call it George," said Daddy.

"Please may we call it something else?" I blurted with new-found confidence, remembering my tiny triumph over naming Pelly and Melly.

"But cats are always called George," he said.

"May I call her Eva, after the heroine in *Mastersingers*?"

"Only because she is a temporary acquisition," he allowed, "and provided we can have her without the tunes."

They were all immensely tired of my rendition of the 'Prize Song' and I had to admit I could not blame them. My friend Penny had told me at school that the only way to get a tune out of your head was to sing another one.

"Try *Well sung, Matilda*," she said, although she had to explain to me that I had misheard the words and that was not what it was called at all. The singing trick always worked for her, she said, but it didn't work for me.

Eva was going to be an educated kitten if I had anything to do with the matter, so she sat in the pocket of my navy school coat and came to the *école maternelle* with me. The other children were much younger, and the teachers had accepted me only because I knew so little French that I could not possibly go to primary school. I loved playing with the younger children, who enjoyed teaching me songs and games and how to read simple words. The teacher was not amused by Eva, as she obviously did not like kittens: "*Jamais on ne prend les chats dans notre classe. Retournez-la vite à la maison!*"

I did not want to take Eva home, specially without Marie to show me the way, for she always came to collect me. But I managed to reach the villa without getting lost, crying all the way like a baby, kitten pressed to my face.

"Do I have to go back to school?" I pleaded with Yady.

"Yes you do," she said. "Marie," she ordered, speaking French which I understood by the gesticulations, "take her back, and do the shopping while you wait to collect her for lunch. Hopeless child; knowing her, she will probably get lost otherwise. It must have been sheer fluke that she made it home alone just now. She really is such a nuisance."

We weren't staying in France much longer, just four more weeks and then we would go back to Sydney. So I made a calendar and struck off the days. Everybody else was having a really good time. I felt guilty that I wanted to go home. Eva was a sweet kitten and I would miss her, but Marie would be kind to her, I was certain. Pelly and Melly were at Wahroonga waiting for me, and there might even be new kittens by now, although Daddy said he hoped not.

THE CONSERVATORIUM

The journey back was by ship again. I hated ships. This was my third long journey. Once from San Francisco to Sydney, six weeks which had not been too bad. Then Sydney to Tilbury, six weeks again, when everybody was extremely seasick due to storms so fierce that most of the dining-room crockery had been flung from the tables and broken into thousands of pieces. The worst times were crossing the Great Australian Bight and the Bay of Biscay. They said it was gale force nine, which sounded most impressive and it was obvious what it meant. We were to join our ship at Tilbury again, Sydney bound, then we would be home at last. Hopefully, I would not be seasick.

There was an old rattler of a piano in the hold. Hours of solid practice produced four Mozart sonatas to a standard almost accept-able for the Con. I also read some 'classics' from the ship's library which were too hard for me to understand. The works of Dickens and Jane Austen were long and their descriptions full of atmos-phere. Some of the women characters had strong personalities and

I hoped one day to be able to speak my mind as clearly and as eloquently as they did. I struggled avidly though them, savouring the imagery and the unhappiness of the characters portrayed. Oliver Twist particularly appealed to me. There were also difficult and complex myths and legends. I wished later I had understood them for, of course, they feature in many of the operas I later learned to love. In the library I found a 1922 edition of Kobbé's book of opera. It made up for everything. I read it from cover to cover, learning the plots of dozens of operas, finding the stories ridiculous but making me eager to see them on stage nonetheless. I could scarcely wait to attend an operatic performance again.

Back in Sydney, my friends all said they were jealous because I had such a perfect older sister: Donie was so kind to me and let me join in things she was doing. She took me with her to the movies, on picnics and on ferry rides and never made me feel a nuisance. Sometimes I must have been an absolute pest.

She knew I had fallen in love with the music of *The Mastersingers*, so when she told me she was playing for a new opera company, I was ecstatic. She promised I could come with her sometimes. Her harp had to be in a special box at the side of the Tivoli Theatre stage because the pit was too small for it. If I sat back and kept as still as a statue, I was allowed to watch performances. I felt like a princess. The magical sound of the orchestral instruments tuning up before the beginning of overtures was the moment I loved best.

My first treat was Puccini's *La Bohème* again. It was a thousand times better than it had been in Nice. All the singers looked at each other, sang in English, and gave the impression that they knew what they were singing about. One of Donie's friends played Musetta, and she looked even prettier on stage than off, although I was shocked to see her being such a flirt. When I asked her if she was really in love with Marcello, she said no, only on stage, and she still loved her boyfriend. I gave a sigh of relief.

I wanted to be one of the children who ran after Papignol's balloons, but Yady told me I was not old enough. Opera, I thought, was the best thing on earth.

Donie also took me to the Town Hall with her. At nineteen, she was the youngest member of the Sydney Symphony Orchestra and she worked with them most of the time. It was most exciting when Daddy was conducting and introducing new works.

Sydney audiences had never heard Stravinsky until Father came, so the night he introduced *The Rite of Spring*, people were shocked by the different sounds. He first introduced it in 1946, and conducted it again in 1953. There is a pause in the middle of the piece when the orchestra stops playing, quite abruptly. Daddy had always told us how, on once occasion, he found it difficult to prevent himself from laughing out aloud when a woman in the organ gallery continued her conversation in a very loud voice, "I fry mine in butter, how about you?"

Many of Donie's friends were musicians too, so she used to bring them home for chamber music rehearsals in our music room. Being nine years younger than Donie, I was too shy to call her friends by their first names, so Maureen Jones and Brenton Langbein, amongst the most frequent visitors, had to be Miss Jones and Mr Langbein. As they disliked my addressing them in this old-fashioned way, I ended up calling them nothing, which sounded rather rude. Donie was always patient with me, answering my endless questions about music, school, homework, what was fair, what was not. She was a true friend to me and I admired her immensely.

Daddy wanted me to attend the Sydney Conservatorium High School, even though I was still only nine. He still did not understand about age restrictions or my being too young for high school. Miss Brown had explained some time previously, when he took me to see her, that I would have to be eleven, but this seemed to have slipped his mind. I was certainly not advanced for my age, nor had anybody led me to believe I was particularly talented. Despite my enthusiastic efforts, I scarcely coped with fourth grade piano exams, and the prospect of learning a second instrument appalled me. Nonetheless, with the audition for the Conservatorium school entrance in mind, piano practice continued and the violin was to be introduced.

Thankfully, tennis occupied my only free time after school in the afternoon. Daddy became too involved in his own schedule to remember that I had not started the obligatory second instrument, and Yady was developing into an important personality on the Sydney social scene, spending little time observing me. She held fabulous suppers after concerts, bringing international artists and musicians to our home, something she said was very important for Daddy's career.

Sometimes the visitors brought their children and I really liked playing with them, or looking after babies.

Elsie Morison, the Australian soprano, was married to the Czech conductor Rafael Kubelik and they were touring for the Australian Broadcasting Commission. Their son, who was four or five years old, sat at the sitting-room fireplace, and earnestly dismantled the brick surround piece by piece until a terrible avalanche was created and everything came tumbling down— including the treasures on the mantelpiece.

Everybody was very cross, particularly Stepmother.

"You are a wretched child," they admonished me in almost one voice. "You were supposed to be looking after the little chap."

I was sent to my room without cats, a subtle but effective punishment.

The very next day, Daddy rang the clanging cow bell to let me know he wanted to see me. Usually I was joyous when I heard our special signal but this time I feared he would be cross about the fireplace.

"Come here, little one. I want to teach you something. And I could do with your help." He took a beautiful stopwatch out of his breast pocket, undid the chain from his waistcoat button, and gave it to me.

"We have some timing to do. Next week's concert is to be

broadcast. I'm making an alteration to the planned programme and I need to see which of the pieces I have chosen will fit into the first half. With radio they make such a fuss about their precious time slot."

He flipped through some music on the top of his piano, taking out the orchestral parts for the *Mother Goose Suite* by Ravel and Debussy's *La Mer*. He explained how the timing was done, starting the metronome and using his stopwatch; I was to read the music in time to the metronome.

"You do know how to follow a score, don't you?" he asked as I considered nervously the task ahead of me.

"Not really, Daddy. I can read the music, of course, and I can follow the time signatures. But I'm not used to looking at this long page with all the instrumental parts. What if I make a mistake?"

"I'll help you with the first piece. Then you'll manage the second on your own."

He made me feel so important. I had never experienced such satisfaction. He tapped the rhythm for the first few pages, then went back to the start, set the metronome, then the stopwatch, and sat down at his desk to go through some further programmes.

"Just tell me when you've finished and I'll check to see how you've done."

It was terribly exciting. He found I was only twenty seconds out, which was, he said, "Very good for your first time. The announcer can always mumble something until the next item comes on!"

Yady's striking good looks and elegant European clothes, combined with her graceful posture, had brought her to the fashion pages of the *Sydney Morning Herald* and the *Australian Woman's Weekly*. I was proud of the fact that people knew and admired her.

I wished I could have loved her as I had loved Nanny, but the feeling was not there and I couldn't help that. She was kind to me, saw that I received a good education and showed me the importance of good manners by her own example. She also stressed the value of clear diction and good deportment. More importantly, she said that my friends were always welcome. She had never had children of her own, and I could imagine it was difficult for her to know what to do with me.

Before her first marriage, as Marjorie Fetter, she had been a gifted piano student at the prestigious Juilliard School in New York. She would occasionally perform in chamber music sessions with Donie's friends. They played Ravel, Brahms, Mozart, and Beethoven. Donie played Ravel's *Introduction and Allegro for Strings* so hauntingly that whenever I hear this music, I always think of my sister.

When Yady created a design for a fabulous music room at Wahroonga, she went to an antique shop to buy a desk she had admired in its window. Inside, she became enamoured of a little black and tan dachshund which was visiting the store, its breeder-owner showing it off to the shopkeeper. Yady was so entranced with the puppy that she bought it and came straight home, completely forgetting the desk.

At the rear of the same antique shop she found the most beautiful piano I have ever seen in my life. It was a Bechstein grand with very pale green relief paintings all over its lid and across its side, decorated in the Chinese style. First we had the dachshund, then two weeks later the piano.

The dachshund was named Trilby and spent a great deal of her time digging holes in the tennis court, escaping, and being looked for. She could drive us mad with worry until we found her, although she never strayed outside the front gates and was unable to climb over the stone wall. Once found, we scolded, petted and cuddled her. The little rascal would sit and observe us refilling her holes and trampling them down. She seemed to find our antics most amusing. Fortunately, she was totally uninterested in the cats.

The new piano encouraged my lessons, for simply being allowed to play on it was a privilege. The music room was totally redesigned to complement it. The floor was sanded and varnished, revealing a rich reddish wood, curtains were hung in the exact pink of the flowers and Chinese women's clothing on the piano, with a striking dark fringe sewn along the base. An elegant settee was chosen for its pale green silk covering and gilded wooden back, and before it was placed a luxuriously thick Chinese rug with pale pink and green flowers. The fringe, originally white, was dyed a deep green which looked far more impressive and original.

The walls were painted in a much darker green than the background colour of the piano, creating a contrast which made the whole room appear like a Renaissance painting. I had seen pictures of rooms in Versailles palace that looked just like it.

The Bechstein offered a warm, almost luscious tone so that anything played on its keys sounded better and more professional than any beginner deserved. It was unrecognisable from my teacher's ugly but stoic brown upright, very scratched and lacking a fashionable pedigree.

I squirm to admit I cannot recall my piano teacher's name. Lessons were tedious, probably even more so for her than for me. Bespectacled, her hair in a bun, she had a very straight back, as upright as her piano. She looked rather like it; tall, thin, unfriendly, brittle as toffee and usually inanimate. She looked old, but then I wasn't good with ages, she might have been only forty.

Clementi's obligatory piano studies were purgatory, scales an endless litany of complaint and arpeggios bore no resemblance to the glorious sounds my sister produced on her elegant harp. I did not think my playing would qualify me for that special paradise reserved for harpists.

My dog-eared music book bore testimony to the frequency with which pages were flicked in an attempt to correct my incessant errors of notation and fingering.

"How's the piano going, my little one?" Daddy asked from time to time. He always managed to sound both encouraging and absent-minded.

"I'm not very good yet, Daddy," I would reply truthfully, after eighteen months of lessons.

"All you need is practice, my dear. And plenty of it."

I was grateful he didn't ask me to play for him, not for some time, anyway.

I never did become competent at the piano. More proficient, or less disastrous, that was how it should be described. After I passed fourth grade, Donie took me to the Conservatorium where an appointment was made for me to be considered by Miss de Mestre. Other children had mispronounced her name, so I was expecting a man when I asked to see 'Mr. Mestre'.

The receptionist at the front desk glared at me in an intimidating manner. "So, *you* are the Director's youngest daughter, then?"

I smiled, and because she was a kind person, she wiped away her scowl and smiled back. She stepped out of her glassed-in cabin and showed me up the stairs and along a dusty corridor to find my new teacher.

Going into the Conservatorium gave me a thrill every time. To start with, it was an amusingly shaped building with funny little turrets almost like a castle. It had a pretty slate roof which was very shiny after rain. When first built over a hundred years before, it had been the horse stables to Government House. The long corridors must have been where horses were once tethered because there were cast-iron rings on the walls.

The best thing about the building was the variety of sounds coming from the practice rooms. You could hear the raucous bellowing of a trumpet lesson, then the ma-ma-ma-ma-ing arpeggios of a would-be singer, next a cello with mellow tones competing with the bird-like squeaks of a beginner on the cor anglais. I adored being there.

I hoped the dreadfulness of my playing might be masked by the quality of my new teacher's magnificent black grand piano. But I was permitted to use it only once, for the audition.

Miss de Mestre took me on, she made it clear, merely because my father was the Director and she must not let him down. Unable to disguise the disgust on her face after hearing me play, her disappointment caused her to say, "As you are such an un-talented beginner, I think you might sound better on the small upright."

I felt sorry for her, and disappointed to have started off so badly.

"Miss de Mestre is the very best technical teacher on my staff," Daddy insisted. "You have all the music within you that will ever be needed, dear child. Technique is what you need, then you will play quite well. Don't worry, things will settle down."

However, my progress did not ever meet my teacher's expectations.

"Surely you *must* not have practised this week," she would moan crossly as I displayed my best effort at a Mozart sonata after having prepared it for endless hours. "Mozart wrote that piece when he was little more than your age himself. Show some respect for him, if not for me, by playing it correctly."

And up would go her *Sydney Morning Herald*, behind which she would hide for half an hour, finishing whatever story caught her interest or even doing a crossword while I pounded away. Even as my fingers battled, my ears would delight in the oboe lesson the other side of the wall, a Bach concerto, then a piece by Vivaldi.

After a while she would inevitably declare, "That's *much* better. See what practice can do?" Her voice was smug, her face unfriendly as she made ready for her next victim. I shuddered to imagine what she would tell Daddy.

I began studying piano at the Con while I finished primary school. Schooldays at Prouille continued to be happy and enjoyable. We were a mischievous bunch. The worst thing we did was to borrow a fishing line from Penny's brother Bruce, sit on the wall by the chapel, and try to snatch the nuns' bloomers off the washing line, but we were caught. The nuns made us say fifteen Hail Marys as a penance, even before we went to Confession.

The Dominican nuns seemed to have found the right balance between allowing us to express ourselves and have fun, while being mindful of manners, discipline and punctuality. They spoke in kind, Irish-tinted voices, their long habits of black and white became them and gave them a dignity and grace that set them apart.

Daddy remained kindly but, if not really distant, not as close as I wanted him to be. He often seemed lost in a world of his own, but I was accustomed to that. One day his demeanour changed dramatically towards me and he announced enthusiastically, "Don't catch the train from Wynyard after your piano lesson today. You're staying in town, having dinner with me, then I'll tell you a secret."

I was astonished. Such a treat had never happened before. I adored my father and the idea of having special time with him was just magical. After school, we walked across Macquarie Street to a little coffee shop where they served soup, a hot meal and a pudding. Daddy went to pay for the meal before we sat down, then discovered he had no money.

"That's all right, sir. I'll put it on tick, like I usually do. Your secretary can come over and pay me at the end of the month."

We settled down to an unpleasant-tasting brownish soup.

"Do tell me the secret, please, Daddy."

"No. Not yet. Eat your soup. Tell me, what is your very favourite thing?" He spooned some of the brown liquid into his mouth, shook his head, added salt and pepper, then smiled with apparent satisfaction.

"Cats," I said in a flash.

"Old George, I suppose, and his endless scrawny kittens! I thought there was something else as well?" He gave his voice an expectant note.

"Oh, yes, Daddy, yes, really. It's opera. You know I adore anything to do with opera. I keep reading the Kobbé book

I found on the ship and I listen to your recordings of *Die Meistersinger*, even in German. I can follow the score and the dialogue. I love opera more than cats."

"Just as well," he said, tucking into his roast beef and lump of something purporting to be Yorkshire pudding smeared with oily gravy.

Hunger had not overtaken me to the point where I could eat this concoction, but I piled it towards centre plate to make it easier to hide beneath a doorstop of thick spongy bread. It was never difficult to distract his attention, which I did by enquiring about his students. He did not seem to notice that I had left my food.

Pudding was a congealed cake with a gelatinous glaze of syrup on top. Hunger had now set in sufficiently for me to gobble it up and politely say thank you for the meal. The idea of the surprise was becoming more exciting by the minute.

Daddy put on his teddy bear coat even though it was a warm evening. He still wore it all the time, and everybody was used to him in it. It made him look friendly and cuddly. "It keeps the cold out and also protects me from the heat," he used to say if anybody suggested he might not need it.

Under my chair was my new violin which did not fit in my locker, and so I bent down and picked it up. Stepmother had told me it was not insured and I was to keep it with me, which was a nuisance. It gave me pleasure to imagine that strangers might think I was a member of the orchestra when I carried it, for I would have loved to have been really clever and talented. We ambled back to the Con, straying through the gates of the Botanic Gardens just as the sun was setting bright red around us.

"You'd better come along to my studio," Father said. I followed him. There was a flurry of sound from what sounded like a full orchestra rehearsing in the hall. I could not recognise the music at first. Then I remembered Father had played me excerpts from Debussy's opera *Pelléas and Mélisande* at the time I had named my kittens. We had listened to the whole opera at home many times since, and I had read the story and followed the libretto.

As I sat quietly in Daddy's studio, waiting for him to dress in what he called his 'penguin suit' which made him look so handsome and important, I could not wait for the performance to begin.

With the sounds of the orchestra in the background, I asked him if he thought Pelléas had really loved Mélisande. He looked at me seriously and said, "Tell me what you think afterwards."

There was a knock at his door, "Your ten-minute call, sir," said the man I knew to be a producer.

It was time to go, so he couldn't tell me any more about the opera until I had seen it for myself.

"You had better go into the auditorium or you will miss the beginning," he said.

I went towards the hall alone, and he strode confidently backstage. The house lights had already been lowered, so I had difficulty finding the seat with the 'Reserved' card on it specially for me. It was in the best position, in the centre row, where the important people sat. I was tremendously happy.

The orchestra were putting the finishing touches to their tuning. My heart nearly stopped as I heard the oboe giving the orchestra an A. The hall was silent as people waited. A loud burst of clapping acknowledged and welcomed Daddy as he entered the pit. The orchestra played 'God Save the King', which broke the spell. We stood, as always, for the anthem, which steadied my excitement.

The atmosphere created on stage was of dark, forest gloom. King Arkel's rooms were dimly lit as well, so that the luxuriant ankle-length hair of Mélisande was the only brightness on stage. Her vivid blue dress had pieces of glass on it which sparkled and captured the light. She looked unreal, as if she had stepped out of the pages of a fairytale. When I saw her leaning down from a wall, she made me think of Rapunzel.

Although the orchestral music was beautiful, there were no

real tunes to remember. The production created a spellbinding mood. A French mood, Daddy had said, but I did not think all French people would be so sad and sombre. Mélisande's words told us she had a sense of foreboding, was afraid of her husband and was terribly unhappy.

When she dropped her ring down the well, it was thrilling to hear the *glissando* of a harp as it descended deep into the water. I guessed my sister was playing that harp in the pit.

I imagined being in the forest with them and was dying to know if Pelléas would kiss Mélisande. He obviously wanted to, but never quite touched her. The harp music represented their passion, I remembered reading, so it was dramatic when it stopped abruptly, almost as a warning, as Golaud appeared. The next scenes showed signs of menace as Golaud told Pelléas he must never see Mélisande again.

My heart nearly stopped during the scene when the jealous husband held up his son Yniold to spy on the couple. It was a tense scene and I pitied the child but felt sorry for the husband. It was a relief when Mélisande and Pelléas finally embraced. Inevitably, tragedy struck as Golaud killed Pelléas. It was merciless of Golaud, still crazed with jealousy, to continue questioning his wife even as she lay dying. It was heartrending to see Arkel bring the baby she had just borne for Mélisande to hold, and all the more poignant when he performed the last rites. Tears streamed down my face in sympathy for them all.

Applause and curtain calls interrupted such emotions. I wanted a happy ending for everyone, and as they came forward to take their bows, I wished they could change the story and start afresh.

Various important people in my row asked me how I had liked the performance, and I did not like to say how disappointed I was in case they misunderstood me. When I reached Daddy's studio, he was very pleased with the singers but felt that the orchestra had not played as well as they could. He was cheerful, though, despite the sad opera, and full of enthusiasm for the work itself.

"Debussy is such an exciting composer. Isn't it a magnificent work? Did you enjoy the production?" he asked.

I jumped up and hugged him almost to death. "Yes, the music was beautiful. Thank you so much for bringing me. But next time can we have an opera with a happy ending?"

Daddy smiled. "I'll see what I can find."

We went home in the hire car, the chauffeur in front with his glass window closed, allowing us our own special intimate world as we sat reliving the performance. I told him I thought that Pelléas and Mélisande really did love each other but that Golaud loved her too. He agreed with me.

"And now, my little one, it is time for you to audition for the Conservatorium High School."

"But I am not quite eleven yet," I said frantically, fearing I would never be good enough, "I'm not ready yet. I've only had a few hours of violin practice and no real lessons. Donie says you have to play at least two instruments really well. I'm not good at all, really I'm not. I could never pass. They wouldn't accept me."

"Enough of all that now. I'll find you a good teacher. You're a Goossens and you can do it, just as we all did. And, who knows, at the end of your studies you might even go in to opera yourself, either into an orchestra, on the production side or as a singer. It is just a beginning. We all had to train, we weren't born with our skills, although people seem to think we were."

This was the longest speech I had ever heard from Daddy. He sounded so interested in my future, so understanding, even sympathetic. There was no choice but to succeed for him. To be a Goossens. Daddy made me feel very proud. I had always felt scared about the responsibility of 'being a Goossens', knowing how famous my father and his brother and sisters all were, and realising that to live up to them would be very difficult, if not impossible. It seemed that my role in life was cut out for me: to be a person Daddy could be proud of, to live up to expectations and above all, to enjoy being part of his life.

As long as I could live up to the expectations, at least to some of them, then I felt as if I really belonged and was worthy of him. It was only when I was part of that musical world that I felt close to him, for at other times he seemed to be in quite a separate sphere to which nobody else could aspire.

Stepmother was part of that world, and this must have been what united them. She was involved in rehearsals, sitting in the lovely old Town Hall and moving around to various spots to check for 'balance' and to let him know how everything was going. He valued her judgment musically and respected her opinion. She was also a gracious hostess to overseas guests and this must have been important to his career. People admired her dress sense and she was often featured in magazines and newspapers for her good taste and cosmopolitan style.

My new violin teacher taught upstairs at the Conservatorium in one of the smallest turret rooms. You walked through the draughty buffet restaurant to reach it, past groups of students gossiping over a cup of tea and sticky iced buns and lukewarm sausage rolls. I felt very important to think I might join them one day, though I was worried and scared about the new instrument and learning to play it properly.

A motherly-looking European lady with a pretty face, soft accent and sweetly elegant clothes accepted me as her violin student. She demonstrated her own instrument, making the most beautiful of sounds.

"I won't be able to play as well as you do. Ever," I told her, my voice all embarrassment. "Please don't expect too much, will you?"

She was a reassuring sort of person, friendly enough to enquire about my cats. It was impossible to dislike her. Her face broke into smiles almost every time I spoke.

After my first lesson I did not imagine I would ever be any good. The violin lessons made the piano all the more attractive, specially *the* piano, the beautiful pale green instrument that

Stepmother had bought in the antique shop. It had the true rich Bechstein tone, but what startled people most was its beauty, and its setting. Although she had apparently received no formal training, Stepmother's artistic eye would have made her brilliant as a stage set designer.

I hurried my piano exercises, worried away at the sonatas, and passed fifth grade quite decently for me, receiving a mark of ninety. At this age I was very uncertain, and when Daddy remarked "Is that all?", no doubt being proud of me, I failed to understand his praise and mistook it for hopes of a better performance. One of the examiners noted on my report, "Pity this child has never mastered the use of the pedals." Thankfully, the examiner failed to realise that I was shaking so badly that my legs could not even find, let alone master them. The prospect of the fiddle caused me even greater concern.

"Daddy, do you think I could practise out in the laundry?" I asked after supper one evening during the first week. My head was filled with visions of dripping sheets and misery.

"Why ever would you want to do that, child?" he replied, puzzled.

"Well, it's out behind the kitchen, a little further from your wing of the house. That way you won't have to hear me till I get a bit better. I'm making quite awful sounds now. I can't bear them myself."

"If that is what you would like to do, you practise wherever you like, my girl, as long as it's half an hour *every* day."

The laundry was the most miserable place I could have chosen. It made me laugh at myself. I took out an old alarm clock we had collected on our travels. Nobody missed it. I even cheated with myself. I would set the alarm for half an hour ahead, then wind the hand forward until my practice became a mere ten minutes.

"Have you really been gone for thirty minutes?" Nell would ask, her voice indicating disbelief.

"That's what the clock says," I would reply. We laughed

conspiratorially and she would make me a cup of hot milk and put plenty of honey in it. It was as if she would have liked to sweeten the sounds I had made. Her baby Helen would hold out her tiny arms to be picked up and I loved giving her a bottle before helping put her to bed. Yady was often absent, either with Daddy or out with friends, and Donie would be playing in the orchestra. It was good being at home with Nell.

"Did you do all this music practice when you were little, Nell?" I asked.

"Not me," she answered scornfully. "I am not, what do you call it, a music type. More too lazy for all that. You do music. I cook. It is the way of things. We cannot all make the music."

To my amazement I passed the audition, and the most enjoyable time of my childhood began at the Sydney Conservatorium High School. It was a very different school then, with just sixty girls and nine boys. A voice teacher on staff was called Renée Goossens, but she was no relation of ours. It was a very strange coincidence, and such fun to tease new students by telling them that I was the voice teacher who gave lessons after school.

There were obligatory lessons in theory and harmony for everybody. On my first day one of the girls in second year said, "Are you coming to Mozart?" That wasn't what she said, really, but 'Mote's Art', for Mr Mote was the teacher. He was a funny short man whose glasses did not fit, so he used a monocle which he had not quite mastered, and it kept on falling down. His lectures were amusing, and as he could not see too well, he asked students to write the notation on the board for him. It was rather a good way of teaching. We loved him and felt sorry for him, so we did exactly as he told us.

Everybody's favourite teacher was Miss Betsy Brown. I felt immensely privileged for I knew her well by now, having shared many secrets in the past four years since our first meeting. It had been a fortunate event, when Father had mistakenly hoped to enrol me those years before. He had later asked her to see me down to the train after music lessons, then I would chat away to her until she got out at Roseville and then do my homework until the train reached Wahroonga. To begin at school having my own special friend in a teacher, and one I admired and respected, was a wonderful experience. I had confided in her, over many journeys, my hopes and aspirations and my fears that I could never live up to my family. She in turn had comfortingly reassured me that she had no doubt that I would be everything I should be.

Miss Brown was still very thin and birdlike. She really knew how to talk to children, whom she treated as miniature adults. She made us feel grown up by making us feel responsible for what we were doing. I felt she would always understand me and listen to my point of view.

My father was particularly busy, putting the finishing touches to his opera *Judith*. He spoke excitedly about the soprano he had engaged to sing the title role.

"Joan Sutherland is one of the most promising voices I have ever heard," he declared. "She will become famous, she deserves to. But she will need to go overseas."

Joan was a really nice person to meet, not at all difficult, with a sunny temperament in rehearsals, even once when she fell off the bed in a supposed moment of passion. "Clumsy old me," she said, picking herself up and laughing, although I suspected she was possibly embarrassed but being brave.

When I met her after opening night she was the easiest person to like. She asked me if I was very proud of my father for his opera.

"Very proud of him," I said, adding, "You were good too," as one might say to a friend at school rather than to a star. She hugged me and said she was glad I had enjoyed the opera.

My wildest dreams were to be fulfilled in 1967, when I returned, myself a member of staff at the Conservatorium, to

teach French to opera singers. Then, to my great joy, Joan Sutherland and Richard Bonynge came back in 1974 for a season
including French opera and I was privileged to be chosen as
French coach for the company, on loan from the Con. Joan was as
friendly to me as she had been when I was a child. As I had not
known Richard then I called him, I felt with correct reverence,
'Mr Bonynge', but he laughed and insisted I should call him Ric. I
never managed to do that, but joined the rest of the company and
called him Richard. It was unbelievable to be in the position of
correcting the person who was now one of the world's greatest
sopranos. How easy she made this task, and how warm and
comfortable was our friendship throughout those five happy years.

As part of our school's training for entry to the musical world,
we were assigned to the opera school for practical experience.
If we could sing, we went into the opera chorus. This meant an
easy introduction to friendships with students from other classes,
and we generally had a very good time. Advanced instrumental-
ists were placed in the orchestra. My first year of violin lessons
had not prepared me for that, so I joined the chorus in various
productions, beginning as a street urchin in Moussorgsky's *Boris
Godounov.*

The tenor lead was Alan Ferris, the man I had idolised in *The
Mastersingers*. This time he was Dimitri, pretender to the throne,
the man planning to destroy the Tsar Boris. The stage was set
with a ramp raked at a steep angle so as to cause a dramatic effect,
particularly as he entered on horseback. Unfortunately Mr Ferris
decided that his role would be enhanced by a display of villainy
and he achieved this on the spur of the moment by kicking me
down the ramp during the dress rehearsal. I was not physically
hurt but I was humiliated, particularly by the act of the man I
had previously adored. My adoration ceased.

However, I recovered quickly from the insult of being kicked
downstage by my hero, and there were more performances of
Boris with scope for further disasters. I was chosen to be the
urchin who kneels at the Tsar's feet in the coronation scene, the

two of us centre stage, the chorus supposedly, in the distance, though only a couple of metres behind. Daddy was the conductor, as usual, and the performances were sung in English.

Boris sings, 'I have attained the highest power', in an aria which is largely unaccompanied. However, this was not the case on the press night. Kneeling at his feet, clad as a ragamuffin child, I developed hiccups.

'It was a pity that the main aria of the Tsar was marred by the hiccuping of the conductor's daughter', read part of the review in the *Sydney Morning Herald.*

Not even being sent to my room without the cats equalled the mortification of such a mention. Daddy thought it was rather funny, but Yady was furious with me.

"There's nothing anyone can do to stop hiccups," Donie remarked kindly, and she patted me on the back at interval and told me it probably would never happen again. Perhaps I should keep a lump of sugar to suck in my pocket next time, she suggested. To give me no opportunity for further disgraceful disruption, I was pushed back into the chorus line and another child was given my place.

"Your time will come," Daddy said to cheer things along.

In so complex a medium as opera, I was caught up in its excitement and I loved the comedy of things going wrong. In *The Bartered Bride* when Majenka was embraced by her fiancé Jenic, her luxuriant blonde wig caught on his waistcoat button. As he turned to leave her, scarcely missing a beat of his top note he dragged the blonde pigtails with him, revealing her own short black hair. Responding to the applause of the audience, he untangled the wig and threw it, with a kiss, to Majenka. We thought him most stylish but pitied the hapless bride.

There were further productions. In *The Bartered Bride* I was one of the children in the chorus, and in *Roméo et Juliette* I played a stage musician, miming to sounds of an orchestral violinist. These were family events, with Daddy conducting, Donie playing the harp and her husband-to-be, John Young, playing a monk as

Varlaam in *Boris Godounov* then later the Friar in *Roméo and Juliette*.

Dressed in full costume and make up in the final dress rehearsal as the Friar, John received a phone call at the Con to say that his mother had suffered a heart attack. Utterly distraught, he excused himself to my father, leapt into his tiny car and headed across the bridge to her bedside at Royal North Shore hospital. He wound down the window and paid his toll at the toll gates.

Minutes later a police car was in pursuit, having been warned, due to the redness of his nose and his monkish outfit that there was 'a drunken villain on the road'. When the uniformed officer stopped his car, John explained his situation. The police were understanding and sympathetic and offered him a siren escort all the way to the intensive care unit. Happily, his mother was out of danger. John was mortified at having to walk back through the crowded waiting room in Casualty. He drove back and the rehearsal continued as if nothing had happened.

The very first article I wrote entitled 'Dress Rehearsal', was published in the *ABC Weekly*. I was thirteen; I adored every moment of being on stage in the chorus, and described the tensions and the excitement. It was thrilling to see my name in print.

Lessons at the Conservatorium High School included normal school subjects: history, English, maths, geography, history and art. I hated maths. Music lessons took place before school, at lunch time and after school. My violin lessons had brought me past second grade, the piano to sixth.

All children must study three instruments by the end of first year, I was told. Three! And I had considered two to be challenge enough!

Daddy happily reminded me how much I had seemed to enjoy Bach's *St John's Passion*, recently performed in St Mary's Cathedral. Perhaps I had made an innocent remark about the sound of the cello being magnificent. What had captivated my interest was the handsome appearance of the principal cellist. Nonetheless, I had to admit to a weakness for the cello too, considering its deeper sound less likely to offend than the dreaded violin.

Daddy took me to buy a cello from Paling's music store, right next to Wynyard station. The one we chose was a beautiful instrument, the wood shiny and reddish, the shape most perfect with its black bridge holding the four strings so tightly. It looked much more friendly than a violin, and considerably more impressive.

Including its bulky case, my cello was just about as tall as I was, and presented more than a little difficulty in transportation. My new teacher, Mr Gladstone Bell, was down-to-earth, practical about lessons and I was not at all afraid of him. His little studio in the Con was also in one of the castellated turrets. He had stuck some attractive travel posters on the wall, from a travel agent's, he said. I liked the one of Nice, reproducing a Dufy painting of the harbour. It reminded me of St Jean Cap Ferrat, so I told him all about my time there and Uncle Charlie.

He sat down beside me, each of us with a cello pressed to our knees. "Copy the way I hold the instrument," he said, then stood up and adjusted the angle of my cello.

"You hold the bow nicely, anyway," he commented, and gave me a quizzical smile indicating hope rather than approval. "That's a good start. Some people never do get the hang of it. Now try to play a scale. Just work it out for yourself the first time, moving your fingers about until you get the right sound."

I was happy to discover I managed a scale almost immediately. A look of distinct relief was added to his smile of encouragement. The cello was going to be quite fun. Mr Bell told me as much. Perhaps I would even be quite good at it.

"You realise you'll need half an hour's practice every single day," he told me.

"That means over ninety minutes as well as my homework," I protested. It was a miserable realisation, and of little comfort to know that all my classmates faced the same problem. Perhaps they had a better attitude.

Penny did not come around to play any more, having been sent to boarding school at Ravenswood, although it was only ten minutes by car from her home.

"I don't mind being a boarder," she told me on the phone. "Nor would you with five brothers like mine. Imagine living with Bruce, my horrible little brother, five times over, especially as the others are much worse. Just be glad you haven't even met the others. Absolute pests they are! My friends say my time will come when we're older and they begin to bring their handsome friends around. Let's write letters and visit each other in the holidays."

Making new friends at the Con happened naturally, as I was thrown instantly into chamber music groups, or chorus rehearsals, and so I never felt lonely.

The Conservatorium opera season took place twice a year and it was marvellous to be involved. Sometimes I was so happy I simply could not believe my good fortune. Being in an opera, in however minor a capacity, brought me a whole new world, into which I became totally immersed.

We put on our costumes and make up in the small hall, with the grownups, then sat in the main hall waiting to be called. Most of us did our homework until the lights dimmed for the piano dress rehearsal. We were terribly busy. "A busy child is a happy child," Miss Brown used to say when parents worried about us having too much work. She was quite right too.

Recovering from the shame of my hiccups, and no longer in disgrace, I was nevertheless surprised when Yady called for me after school. "Let's go home on the train together," she said in a friendly manner. "My car's in at the mender's. Something about a big end blowing."

I led her down Bridge Street to Wynyard, realising it was the first time she had been on a train with me. We chatted happily, she about the difficulty of finding a man who understood Fiats, and I about how to find time for my geography essay.

It was a crowded carriage, being the rush hour. We sat knee to knee, Yady's head against the glass partition on the inside of the standing room area. I put down my cello firmly in front of my knees. There was a shrieking sound from the lady opposite. The cello's long metal spike had not been properly secured and had punctured her sandalled foot. Blood was shooting upwards, she was yelling, "Look what you've done, you careless, irresponsible child!"

I looked at Yady quickly, surprised at her silence, as I watched the frightened, yelling woman jump up, smashing her head against the glass panel behind her. Glass rained down and blood seeped over the poor woman's face.

There was nothing to do but to sit very still, having retracted my cello spike, innocently, as if it did not really belong to me. The woman, pointing towards me, limped off the train, her bloodied foot leaving an impressive trail. Several men muttered sympathetically to her. Yady said nothing at all. I felt very frightened at what had happened. I think her silence was the worst part.

At Wahroonga station we got off the train. Only then did she speak. "You are the most impossible child anybody could have to put up with. All I can say is this: no more cello. I will take it back to the shop tomorrow."

I was no good at replying when people were cross with me, preferring silence to making things worse by saying the wrong thing. This was interpreted, usually, as churlishness on my part but was really due to the fact that I was completely terrified. Yady seemed quite calm once she had declared 'no more cello', and as she did not refer to it after supper when Daddy returned, I crossed my fingers and hoped she might forget the matter altogether.

The following day after school we were to sing in a Bach chorale then attend a diploma concert, which meant arriving home after eight. Nell made me a snack and I set about my practice. Piano first, then get the violin over with, leaving the best till last. I looked everywhere for my cello.

"Have you moved my cello, Nell? I can't find it anywhere."

"No. The cello he is not here. Mrs G, she took him into the town, to a Palings I think. Said you had been a very stupid girl and did not deserve it. I no understand her. She really madder than I ever see her."

Surely there must be a chance of regaining my cello, if I promised never to leave my spike out again? Anyway, we needed to play three instruments to stay at the Con High School. I planned an appeal to Daddy and awaited the right moment.

At the weekend things seemed peaceful, and I had rehearsed what I would say in explanation about the spike incident. The chance never came, for Yady said once again, "We're going to France. Not all of us. Just Renée and me. It's time she had a second language. That dreadful combination accent of hers, neither American nor Australian, makes her sound so uneducated. I will take her myself and she shall benefit from a sophisticated European education."

"But Daddy," I appealed, "I love being here in Sydney. I am totally happy at school. I know I've been a bit hopeless. But I'm not really bad, and I promise to try harder. I never do anything bad on purpose, honestly! I will try harder, really I will."

Daddy looked uncomfortable and for a moment I thought he was about to agree that I was not all bad. Instead, he looked me firmly in the eye.

"Marjorie has decided upon your future. I shall be away frequently due to my touring commitments over the next two years. Donie is busy with her own life. You will do much better in a boarding school."

"Couldn't I go to boarding school here? My friend Penny does. Maybe you could ask whether her mum could look after me in the holidays if you are away."

"We will discuss the matter no further." His voice was angry, his mind apparently on something else.

"But I don't even speak French. I do it at school, but it's not what you could call speaking French, it's just strings of words which we muddle and mangle. I couldn't make myself understood. It would all be absolutely miserable."

"That is quite enough! I went to boarding school when I was about your age, to Belgium. It did me no harm," Daddy proclaimed.

"But were you happy?" I asked, pleading both on my own behalf and on his.

"Goodness, child, nobody is happy all the time."

He must have been unhappy too, I thought, but I did not suppose he had been allowed to admit it. It was difficult to think of him as a child. Why could he not protect me now from a similar, unnecessary experience? It was utterly hopeless.

It was not until 1967 that I learned from Betsy Brown that Daddy had tried to intervene, asking her if she and her sister Barbara could move into the Wahroonga house to be my guardians once Stepmother left for Europe. It was heartbreaking to know that he had wanted to shield me from the pain of leaving, by asking them to do this and worse still that I never had known how much he loved me. Of course, a busy headmistress, as Betsy was by then, and her sister who worked full time for the government, could not possibly have left their lives for me, but it was marvellous to know he had wanted this for me. Later I blessed him for it.

And, of course, it would never have suited Stepmother to have me cared for by the Misses Brown. I was her passport out of Australia, a socially acceptable excuse to leave Father. Not knowing or understanding this for several years, I merely saw myself once again as that wilting pot plant, lacking nutrition, just being moved from garden to garden, and in this case from my own paradise to what would become purgatory.

We packed; Stepmother joyously, looking forward to her European adventure. I was not permitted to take more than two suitcases, three winter outfits and two for summer, boring underclothes, night dresses and shoes. I was allowed to take my essential Kobbé, and a hastily assembled collection of photos, Donie, Daddy, Nanny with me in New York when I was five, George with Pelly and Melly on the veranda, Trilby digging up the tennis court, and Daddy in a publicity photograph for the *ABC Weekly*.

Arrangements had obviously been made prior to the announcement. I said goodbye to my classmates and teachers at the Con, hugging Miss Brown and asking her to write. Last of all I phoned Penny's mother to explain what was happening and promising to write.

Three days later, Stepmother and I were on yet another ship bound for England, and thence to Paris.

PARIS

I was to go to a boarding school. Such an establishment had yet to be identified, but ideally it was to be in Paris, or so I was led to believe. I addressed my captor, as I regarded her, no longer as Yady but as Stepmother, and although she did not like this, she seemed to understand that I was angry about being taken away from Sydney. She seemed to have no idea that I was desperately unhappy, deeply resentful and trying to imagine a way of escaping back home.

The ship we boarded was a cargo liner with twelve passengers, all adults, and to me they seemed stuffy, ill-assorted people. I wondered why they had forsaken the luxury of an ocean liner with its promise of entertainment, films and libraries, to travel in this uncomfortable manner.

We dined, as we always did on sea voyages, at the captain's table, an honour that Stepmother accepted as customary. This privilege, however, caused jealousy and rivalry among the other unaccompanied females. Those invited to join us appeared to be allocated on a rostered basis, so the presence of others was predictable and unavoidable.

The ship's doctor was a cheerful man whose anecdotes became swiftly of the category referred to in whispers as '*pas devant les enfants*'—an allusion to which I took great exception, particularly as there were no other children on board. He was, nonetheless, the most entertaining of the table guests.

The good doctor possessed a melodious speaking voice, tinted with the Irish lilt my nuns had shared. He used fantastic gestures to illustrate his tales, most of which they would never have approved of nor understood. It was not unusual for him to use the table napkin as some form of costume, either on his head, or as a cummerbund around his waist, when assuming the voice of a shy teenage girl, a drunken sailor, or even a Wagnerian soprano. His impersonations of Rasputin, complete with heavy Russian accent, were particularly successful. His presence enlivened each meal and he obviously enjoyed his captive audience.

However, when his stories contained sexual innuendoes, I was despatched to my cabin. This afforded me an opportunity to learn to type on an old rattler of a machine, the gift of a handsome young Italian officer with an enchanting accent who fancied Stepmother. To be truthful, to me he looked scrumptiously fascinating, but I knew I was too young for him even to notice. No doubt he assumed his chances of an early conquest of Stepmother more likely if kindness was bestowed upon me. He was apparently to be disappointed.

"Keep that dreadful man away from me, child, won't you? But let him teach you to type. He left this book for you, a *Pitman's Guide*, something which has diagrams of the keys. It will teach you how to use the right fingers," she informed me.

"I suppose it must be rather like the piano fingering for a sonata," I remarked.

"Hardly as skilled," she said imperiously.

"Can you type?" I asked.

"Heavens no, but there's no reason why you shouldn't."

Within the first week my speed was quickening. Using the stopwatch Daddy had given me when we timed musical programs together, I discovered that on reaching the Suez Canal I was batting along at forty words a minute. By the end of the seemingly interminable voyage, I had reached a dazzlingly useful fifty-five words a minute. It was more fun than playing the piano in the airless hold, and what else, in five weeks, was there to do?

When travelling on such a journey time passes slowly, and apart from reading, learning to type and practising the piano, I made the most of observing those around me and their different or strange behaviour. There was one 'personality' who amused us all by her extrovert behaviour. Her name was, or perhaps was not, Miss Grace Anodyne. She was as fascinating to observe as a star of stage and screen, for she was both attractive and affable. She was as curvaceous as an egg-timer, her hips as sinuous as a snake. Her crowning glory was coiffed into a nest of shiny blonde curls of a texture resembling acrylic carpeting, positively gleaming, as polished as a piano lid. When the Barbie doll was invented, they could have modelled it on her.

Her attempts to inveigle the younger officers into her cabin offered an education equal to none. I found Miss Anodyne most amusing. She was the most vital person on the whole ship.

The high point of the voyage was to be an excursion to see the Pyramids. On our previous journey back from France, our ship had been diverted to Eritrea to take on board a group of displaced persons, refugees from violence and torture. On that occasion, one unfortunate victim had perished from typhoid. As a result, we had all been placed under quarantine, and nobody was permitted ashore to see the Pyramids or to visit the towns. This time, surely, we would manage to cross the sands to one of the great wonders of the world.

Who could believe that there was an accident within the Suez Canal the day we entered it? Nobody was allowed to go ashore, all leave permits being cancelled for the crew as well, as we awaited our tug boat to guide us through the narrow canal. A ship had hit a bridge and caused a narrowing of one of the sections. I was extremely disappointed to miss the Pyramids again.

"I was going to the Pyramids with the first officer," Miss Anodyne chanted at dinner, indiscreetly, but with immense satisfaction.

The temperature was over a hundred degrees fahrenheit, with not a single cloud in sight. The local people in their boats were pestering us constantly, clamouring beside the ship's nets, yelling their bargain prices, wanting to climb aboard to sell their trinkets.

The impressive sight of grappling men was not as powerful as the ascending odour of unwashed, overheated bodies, uncured leather and rotting fruit from the boats below. The noise was deafening as ropes were lowered and merchandise was hauled up for us to inspect or buy.

Several passengers bought souvenirs, leather wallets, miniature Pyramids, copies of busts of Egyptian queens, all beautifully coloured. I wanted one of Tutankhamen, but the merchants had none left. I disappeared to do my piano practice but as the temperature rose the airless, stifling hold became intolerable. The piano became more out of tune with each hot day, the humidity increasing as if in a shower room. Even Mozart lost his sparkle and sounded positively asthmatic.

After docking in England we went by train to visit my Uncle Léon, Aunt Leslie and their two daughters Corinne and Jennie. Uncle Léon was Daddy's brother, a famous oboist. He had a friendly, round face, a great sense of humour, and was welcoming and smiling most of the time with me. Leslie was slim and pretty, a former ballet dancer. Although they were family, I really did not know them and felt very out of place.

They lived in a beautiful country property in Sussex. The house was freezing, the weather incredibly cold. After enjoying the sunny warmth of Australia, when the winter came upon us in early October I could not believe the darkness of the evenings and the sudden chill that crept throughout the house. It was a cold which seeped into my very bones and the only way I ever felt really warm was when immersed in hot water. The bath was an antiquated affair with a gas contraption above it which made the most terrifying, volcanic, explosive sounds when it was in use.

I was to stay with them 'for a while'. Nobody told me how long that would be. Corinne and Jennie were welcoming and kind, introducing me to their friends, and even taking me to school with them. It was difficult to fit in, with subjects taught in a different syllabus from that I had known in Sydney and I felt awkward and backward. My accent advertised me as 'a colonial' and it was strange to be regarded as a curiosity. Girls would offer me their sweets, so I obliged by speaking, realising that quaintness had its virtues.

I did not learn anybody's name, a defence against the fact that I knew it could only be a matter of weeks before I was despatched somewhere else, with all the loneliness and confusion that that represented. My isolation was immense.

Many years later, in what seemed another lifetime, in 1994 I returned to England to visit my Aunt Sidonie, who was then 93. She arranged for me to meet my cousin Corinne. The same age, as adults we developed a firm friendship that I hold dear to this day. To discover at last a relative, one who would correspond, come to see me, speak on the telephone, and share discussions of the past, validated all that had happened to us both in life, and gave me great comfort. Corinne, a grandmother, friendly, sensitive and beautiful, I know will continue to be there for my son Philip one day, as part of a family once more. He and I both needed so much to feel part of a family, as most people do.

It soon became obvious that my presence in the household was an unwanted intrusion. Stepmother was not liked, for she was considered to be a 'user' who only contacted family when she required a service or a favour. Aunt Leslie considered it unfair to be 'lumbered' with me, as I overheard her telling a visitor. I felt like a parcel abandoned in a left luggage locker. The respite was temporary, but it did nothing to secure a feeling of family. A family could not be created as a convenience, and there was not time to adjust or to try.

Uncle Léon had come to Australia once in 1954, on a brief concert tour, and stayed with us at Wahroonga. But I didn't really know him at all. He had been very popular in Sydney, a wonderful raconteur at Daddy's parties, but my school exams were demanding and I seldom stayed up late. The audiences loved concerts with Daddy conducting and Léon as the important solo artist 'from overseas'.

Programme notes I read at the time in Sydney told me more about the family than I had known before. I learned that Daddy and Léon were two of the five children of Eugene Goossens, a conductor. Grandfather was the chief conductor of the Carl Rosa Opera Company. My grandmother Annie, whose maiden name was Cook, was a contralto. Daddy's two sisters, Marie and Sidonie, were famous harpists in England, celebrated and renowned.

Aunt Marie did session work as well as playing in various orchestras, and Aunt Sidonie played with the BBC Symphony Orchestra and took part in recordings of radio shows, including the *Goon Show*, among many others. They both played for musical comedies and in the theatre too.

There had been another brother, Adolphe, a talented French Horn player. Tragically, he had been killed in World War I, in northern France.

I had asked Daddy to tell me more than the programme notes revealed, and he filled in a few details. It was comforting to hear him say how much he adored his parents. Being in a family of famous musicians, I realised how important it was for me to achieve excellence or to play nothing at all.

In England and meeting more of the family, I felt humbled and useless. It would never do for me to fail. I wanted Daddy to be proud of me for doing something really well, even if it was not in music.

The loveliest member of the family was, without a doubt, Aunt Sidonie. She lived with her husband Uncle Norman in a seventeenth-century farmhouse also in Surrey. He was an arts administrator who worked for Sir Thomas Beecham. He spoke with a beguiling Scottish accent. In addition to their musical life, their home, on several acres of land, was part of a working chicken farm. Sidonie used to take boxes of eggs to her orchestral friends. They grew all their own vegetables and had established a beautiful flower garden. Squirrels, deer and rabbits could be seen from the house.

Sidonie travelled to London each day from Betchworth by train, then by tube to Maida Vale to the BBC rehearsal and recording studios. I had never met anybody as attractive, as much fun, as loving, as agreeable in my life as my aunt Sidonie. I wished she could have been my mother. Unfortunately for me, she and Norman were also two of the busiest people, with overseas touring contracts as well as their London work.

In any event, other plans were afoot to move me on. It seemed there was nowhere for me to stay without causing inconvenience to somebody.

After only a few months in England, arrangements were made for me to stay with Stepmother in a Paris apartment. Aunt Leslie put me on a boat train for Paris and gave me some money to tide me over. I felt very frightened about setting off alone. What may have seemed an exciting excursion to others filled me with fear of the unknown and dread of the imagined.

Stepmother was there to meet me, and on this occasion I was almost grateful to see her. Time had not helped me to grow fond of her, but being so alone, I tried to consider her as family.

We took a taxi to the Rue des Saints-Pères, not far from the Louvre. In the pouring evening rain, I scarcely noticed France's beautiful capital. The American friends who had lent her the apartment had gone away, so we had the apartment to ourselves.

We received only one visitor, a man I was asked to call Uncle Sigmund or even worse, Ziggy. He was Polish, a count, and well versed in the art of name-dropping.

"We often dine with the Countess Oppenheimer. We frequently go to hear the famous baritone Tito Gobbi," he would gush. "You can't imagine the difference it makes to be with a person of such quality, such education, such taste." The fact that the 'royal we' included Stepmother gradually dawned on me. He was not a person I liked. Could he be the reason we had come to Europe? There seemed to be no one else who occupied Stepmother's time.

It slowly became obvious to me why I had been taken from Sydney—to provide an alibi for Stepmother's chosen other life. This I was unable to comprehend for, as I had observed, she had seemed to live her own life in Sydney also, in whatever way she wished, always managing a trip overseas 'to avoid Sydney's winters'. Perhaps there had been disagreements about this between her and my father, but I never knew of them. Now, of course, she could do as she liked, on the pretext of 'looking after little Renée'.

The apartment had five bedrooms, windows onto little balconies that didn't open, and tall, painted shutters to close out the wind. There was an imposing 'salon' and a large separate dining room. A pervading air of opulence was created by ornate gilded antique furniture; massive, densely piled Chinese rugs on polished parquet floors, large mirrors everywhere and heavy royal blue velvet curtains.

The place looked like a stage set. Some of the rooms would have been useful in a production of *Tosca*. Nobody could describe it as cosy. For all its opulence it lacked the style of our Wahroonga music room. The leather-bound books in the bookcases had nothing within their covers but blank pages, as I found to my amazement when I opened a volume labelled 'Shakespeare'.

"A tricky business, decorating, when you have an apartment like this but travel constantly. One must not leave valuables here, yet still make it appear luxurious for rentals," explained Step-mother.

"Are we renting this place, then?" I asked, afraid we might be staying.

"No, certainly not. But we may use it whenever my friends are away. We could never afford a place like this. It belongs to old friends of mine from Pennsylvania. They kindly offered it to us."

I breathed a sigh of relief. "Is there anything here that I might borrow to read?" I enquired.

Stepmother glanced around, discovered nothing for me to read and offered to go out to buy me a magazine and a book. "Want to come too?" she asked, with friendliness in her voice.

We walked towards the Seine, crossed the Pont Neuf and headed towards the Louvre, where we spent most of the day, looking at exhibitions that caught Stepmother's interest. We saw so many things that they all began to merge into one meaningless blur.

"We'll have a pleasant meal, then go home," she said. My heart almost stopped at the idea as I realised her idea of home and mine were entirely different.

We had left Sydney in the brilliant sunshine of September. It was mid-term there, and she had incorrectly planned that we would settle in France after Christmas for the new academic year. Semesters begin in September in France, so I knew I would be out of pace with the other students, particularly after the wasted time in England. Not yet fifteen, I could not imagine how I would fit in anywhere.

We attended a few concerts, and tried to buy tickets for a production of *Faust* at the Paris Opéra. The tickets were sold out, but Stepmother asked if we could have a tour of the theatre. Just as I had been overwhelmed with the beauty of the Louvre, I adored the building and found it magnificently opulent.

The Paris Opéra looked like a temple or even a palace. The interior made me feel we were part of another era and that we were very important just to be inside. That is how I imagined people should feel when they attend a performance combining magnificent music with exquisite singing. On such rare occasions, the audience is truly privileged. I admired the plush red seats, the splendid velvets, the curved tiers of seating, the domed ceiling and the delicate sculptures around the ornate walls.

"Isn't it exciting to imagine a performance here?" said Stepmother, pleasantly lost in her own thoughts, and unaware of mine.

"You really are a most difficult child!" she had said before, I did not quite know why. Maybe in her mind my very presence was an obstruction to following her own path. I had not, of course, wanted to be there, and must have shown this by my lack of grace and enthusiasm. All I wanted was to return to Sydney, Daddy, Donie and what I viewed as my own life. I had no wish to be part of whatever she clearly had chosen for me to suit her needs.

Perhaps I was a nuisance, but she possessed as little idea of how to manage me as I did of pleasing her. I decided to eat as little as possible in the hope that I might grow dangerously ill and require immediate return to Australia. Doctors call the condition *anorexia nervosa*, although I had no idea of that or of its meaning. Regardless of its name, I was doing it to show how terribly unhappy I felt, and was hoping she would notice there was something wrong.

"Paris is a beautiful city. Just look at the buildings. Here you will see history. Everything you have learned will mean so much more to you. Imagine what it must have been like here, in the time of Marie Antoinette," Stepmother said, trying hard to capture my imagination as we set out on a seemingly endless tour of museums and cathedrals.

My morose company must have tried her patience. Then one day, unexpectedly, she said, "You are to be auditioned this afternoon by the great Nadia Boulanger. You are very lucky, for she is a famous composer and pianist who has one of the most prestigious schools in Europe." Indeed, not only was she all these things, but I knew my father and his sisters had worked with her in London before I was born.

My heart sank. "I haven't practised since we were on the boat on that awful out-of-tune piano. You know I am not very good, even when I work hard. It will be a disgrace to Daddy. I don't want to audition."

We went to Madame Boulanger's imposing home by taxi. She was an ageless lady of regal deportment who dressed like a fashion model, yet possessed the most friendly and gentle face I had ever encountered. There was something about the way she moved which suggested she would be kind, her graceful arms moving with a fluidity, touching me gently on the shoulder to guide me into the room. She must have been in her late sixties or early seventies. It was not what she wore that impressed me, but her inner beauty that gave reassurance that everything was going to be all right.

"So this is *la petite musicienne*?" she enquired, welcoming me, continuing her conversation in rapid French which I could not understand. She indicated to Stepmother that she should wait in the salon, led me towards her music room and bade me sit at the piano.

The room was not as beautiful as ours in Sydney had been. It lacked colour, and its centrepiece, an enormous Bösendorfer Concert Grand, was forbiddingly black and threatening.

"*Ma petite*," she began, continuing in English. "You will learn the language, do not fear. Here all I need is to hear how you play. First, a little sight-reading."

She brought out a bundle of immaculate music sheets, such as we seldom saw in Australia. I missed the dog-eared music books to which I had grown lovingly accustomed.

The first piece was by Jacques Ibert, 'The Little White Donkey'. A recent examination piece, it was one of the few pieces I had committed to memory. If I played it now as a sight-reading test, Madame Boulanger might imagine me to be proficient and gain false expectations. My thoughts raced.

"I cannot do it. I cannot play the piano. You see, my parents *want* me to be good, like them, but I have no talent. I really must go back home to Sydney now. I would be useless to you and a disgrace to my family. Please understand." I could not restrain my tears.

Madame Boulanger came and sat down beside me on the piano stool, as my friends used to when we turned pages at each other's concerts.

"Would you not play just one piece for me? That way, your mother, she could hear you had tried. I could explain that my standards were too demanding for one so young. That would maybe save the situation."

I could have kissed her.

There was one movement of a Mozart piano sonata in C major which I knew I could play passably well. I smiled at her and launched into it, introducing sufficient wrong notes to make even this lovely music excruciating, laughing as I did so. She put her hand on my shoulder and gave it a squeeze.

"It will be our little secret," she promised, stroking my hair and smiling at me. "Leave it to me. Be happy somewhere, my child," and we walked out into the salon together.

"Madame Goossens, I am afraid, the little one, she is not ready for my school. A good child, but much too young. Let her develop a little. We will say *au revoir*. Perhaps we shall meet again in a few years' time."

Stepmother was gracious, stoical and not even unkind to me after this event. Shaking from the experience, I could not forget the incident with the cello. "We'll find somewhere," she assured me, cheerfully, but there was a hint of panic in her voice. She made me feel that by now someone should have taken me on, more to relieve her of the burden than to find any particular teacher for me. She made it clear that this business of finding somewhere to put me was taking far too long. It was obvious by now that I should stay almost anywhere so that she could get on with her own life, preferably without me anywhere near.

"I don't want to be a nuisance. I don't mind going back by

ship on my own, really I don't. And with practice I might be okay back at the Con. Nell could look after me, I won't be a bother, really." But my pleas were to no avail.

Christmas was spent at the flat of the Americans. They came back to spend the festive season with us, a tall, thin monocled man with a mean moustache and his wife, a short rotund lady who oozed out of her dresses and waddled as she walked. Her shape was emphasised rather than embellished by a quantity of rings, bracelets and necklaces dangling everywhere. She looked like a small, fat military officer drowned in medals. Or perhaps a miniature Christmas tree.

Our hosts paid scant attention to me, ignoring me in conversation as if I did not exist. "We aren't good with children," I had heard them say to Stepmother.

Christmas was a miserable, grey, cold, foggy day. I missed the sunshine and warmth of Sydney, the visits to the beach, and above all friends my age for company. The women gave each other expensive jewellery, impressing each other and not wanting to be outdone.

"What an absolutely fantastic pair of diamond earrings!" gushed Stepmother.

"We bought them in the Rue St. Honoré," replied the couple in unison, as if rehearsed.

Stepmother gave the woman who waddled a silver bracelet in a box marked 'Cartier'.

"What an impressive gift," said the American.

"Just a little something to thank you for letting us use your apartment," explained Stepmother, who had shown me the receipt so I would realise it had been excessively expensive.

The man with the moustache was given a pair of gold cufflinks. He thanked Stepmother, taking out his monocle to inspect them. He then put them into his pocket, admiring the box, also from Cartier, almost more than the contents.

"We'll just love showing people back home where the jewellery came from."

The American couple had bought a wonderful landscape painting by the Impressionist Sisley. It seemed odd to me that anybody could afford to buy a real original. They must have been terribly rich.

The man I had to remember to call Uncle Ziggy arrived with a stylish pearl necklace for Stepmother and a ghastly marcasite brooch for me which I absolutely detested. It was gaudy, looking like something one would expect to find on the coffin of a deceased, elderly person whose clothing indicated they had little taste. It gave me the creeps. It looked like a scorpion or perhaps a centipede, some evil insect designed to sting and harm.

"Isn't that lovely of Uncle Ziggy?" insisted Stepmother.

Politeness and anxiety forced me to utter gracious words of thanks.

The Americans gave me a book about cats which I adored, a most thoughtful gift. Stepmother thanked them in the kitchen and I overheard her saying, "That's exactly the sort of book I meant you to buy for her. Well done!"

I received a card from Australia with a picture of Sydney Harbour Bridge, which said, "Hope you're settling down nicely, Love Daddy." It made me so sad. I missed him dreadfully. There didn't seem to be any reason for me to be with these people I disliked, in a place in which I did not belong.

A long letter came from Penny who had met a boy in the holidays but did not want her mother to know. It was also wonderful to receive a beautiful silk scarf from my darling sister Donie. There was a little gift card with a delicately hand-drawn angel on it. "Missing you. Hope you're having a lovely time in France. Write and tell me all about it."

I wondered what they were doing for Christmas in Australia. It would be hot. Daddy would probably be having a break from the orchestra for a few days. Donie was now married to the baritone John Young, and they were both working and performing, although I hoped they'd have a break for Christmas itself. Penny would be having a marvellous time at the beach, although she would be complaining about her brothers. How I longed to see them all.

We went to midnight Mass; Stepmother, me and the name-dropping trio of the Americans and the Polish count. I even had a fantasy about the count with Stepmother as his countess walking down the aisle together, she dressed more beautifully than ever. Mass was celebrated at a large Greek Orthodox church with wonderful music.

Only one more week of official school holidays remained before I was due to be sent to boarding school. If one could be found.

We went to the Eiffel Tower, Montmartre, places tourists visited. It wasn't an I-am-going-to-live-here sort of place.

MORTEFONTAINE

"Tomorrow we are going out into the country. There is a place called Mortefontaine run by some wonderful Dominican nuns. They may have a place for you." The dreaded words were uttered when I least expected them.

Between excursions with the adults, I had studied French, from an instinct of self-preservation rather than interest. The words *Morte* and *Fontaine* were clear enough and the idea of attending a dead fountain was ominous rather than appealing. I looked it up in our guide book; Stepmother had told me it was near the *forêt de Senlis*, about sixty-five kilometres east of Paris. It might as well have been at the end of the world.

Stepmother hired an oppressively grey Renault and managed driving on the wrong side of the road without incident, reminding me that she came from America where they also drove on the right. At this moment I wished she had remained there.

In an attempt to divert me on the journey, she had bought a baguette with my favourite pâté and a runny Brie, planning a picnic in the woods en route. Misery and gloom overcame me. The woods reminded me of the stage setting for *Pelléas and Mélisande.* This time I would join Mélisande in my own particular nightmare of unhappiness. I suspected that Stepmother was going to leave me behind and probably for some time. It would have been so much easier for her to send me back to Australia. Her conversation was sparse, although she frequently made reference to the count. The idea that my education was the excuse for her absence in Europe froze me to the bone, more profoundly than winter's chill wind.

"The convent is an impressive building, you'll see. It used to belong to Bonaparte's brother Joseph, so it must be beautiful. Isn't this exciting?" she asked, trying to keep the atmosphere buoyant and light-hearted.

We approached the chateau through unfriendly black ornamental wrought-iron gates. A man with a bent spine was there waiting for us. He unlocked the heavy chain slowly and solemnly. Did this mean we would be locked inside? It was an impressive building, awesome and unwelcoming. Inappropriately, yet obsessed with keeping warm, I asked if the heating would be adequate. Stepmother smiled in a satisfied manner but made no reply. It was a look which increased my fear.

Mother Superior greeted us, gracefully descending the curved marble steps to do so. She instructed us where the rented car should be parked. Her manner was dismissive and unfriendly, but she wore her Dominican habit to great advantage, her deportment as stately as that of a queen in an opera. If only this were a scene from opera, safely removed from real life, I could have enjoyed it.

"I understand you wish your daughter to learn perfect French," she intoned in exquisite English, which gave me hope of future comprehension. Arrangements continued between the two women in French. Pieces of paper were exchanged—a cheque, I suppose— a deposit in return for me. It was obvious from the expression of relief on Stepmother's face that something satisfactory had been arranged. Her unwanted parcel had finally been accepted, and this was to be my new left luggage compartment.

Smiling, she turned to me, "You may as well stay now. Pity to go back to Paris and become unsettled again. They have a place for you and term is well under way. You have four weeks of work to catch up on as it is. I will say goodbye now."

"But Yady," I pleaded, hoping my use of her more friendly name would move her, "I haven't brought anything with me, no books, no clothes, none of my pictures of Daddy and Donie or my friends or Wahroonga."

"You will not be needing photos here. Mother Superior says she has your uniform and bedding waiting. She will provide all the books you need, too. You can make a new start. I may see you in the school holidays. If they don't fit in with my schedule, I am sure the nuns will find some family who can take you in."

Unable to grasp all that she meant, all I could do was protest spontaneously about the immediate arrangement. "But I don't want a new start. I want to go back to Sydney, and Daddy and the Con and I hate it here and it is going to be absolutely awful." My speech was as rapid and long as it was ineffectual.

Stepmother planted a perfunctory kiss on my forehead, looked firmly at Mother Superior and nodded, and moved away as speedily as her elegant legs could carry her.

There had been other moments when I had felt miserable: Nanny's departure, being lost and leaving Sydney. But this was the most frightening and desolate moment of my life. I considered running away, escaping somehow, through those large black iron gates, hitch-hiking back to Paris, to London, and stowing away on a ship. My mind raced forward but my body stood transfixed.

"*Venez. Il faut rencontrer les autres filles,*" said Mother Superior, in the only language I was now to hear.

The first month was the hardest, with the cold dormitory never warmed by heating, fourteen to a room, only cold running water, and broken windows replaced with cardboard and sticking paper. My background had failed to prepare me for the austerity of postwar Europe and I hated every single moment of it. The familiarity of Latin for Mass and the rituals associated with the Catholic liturgy were the only things that helped me to feel part of its world. But even so, it was a world devoid of music.

The other girls had never heard of Australia and could only assume it was a place I was mispronouncing. This was a very French reaction and geography lessons did not enlighten them further, concentrating on topical land formations, industry and Europe. Our textbooks, carefully selected by the nuns, never took us abroad. We were totally insular. The daughters of wealthy industrialists and minor aristocracy, the girls had been brought up to value money and what it could get for them as the sole reasons for existence. Music and art were both absent from the curriculum and, apparently, did not feature in home life. It was considered socially unacceptable that my parents never came to see me. Obviously they could not be very important, or so the girls decided.

Gradually I made myself understood, and did my best to make a few friends. At Easter I was told Stepmother was busy and there was nowhere for me to go for the holidays, so at assembly an announcement was made: "Can anybody offer a home to the little Australian for the holidays?"

Marie-Jeanne obliged. Her family were not particularly pleased to receive me, but treated me with diffidence rather than unkindness, allowing me to enjoy their picnics, feeding me beautiful patés and cheeses, and laughing merrily over copious glasses of red wine.

They lived in the Dordogne, a journey of six hours by train which occupied the first and the last day of our holiday, leaving us just one week to relax and get to know each other.

Coming from Australia, I was extremely interested in historic buildings. In Sydney I had loved 'quaint old buildings' but had had no comprehension of architecture, merely an admiration for beautiful things.

It was wonderful to see the ornate churches and chateaus of France. The Dordogne valley was full of picturesque villages in honey-coloured stone, the broad flowing river and walnut plantations contrasting with the stark, sheer rock face of bare cliffs. It reminded me a tiny bit of the Blue Mountains but was not really the same at all; it was my mind playing tricks to comfort me.

Marie-Jeanne's family took me to see Rocamadour. She said it was the second most important tourist attraction in France. When I asked about the first she said it was Mont Saint Michel, but she had never been there and believed it was in Brittany. Built within the rock face of the sheer cliffs were sanctuaries and on a lower ledge the single narrow street of the village lay, before the landscape dropped to the valley below. The view was dramatic and expansive, if forbidding.

Visiting the Rocamadour shrine required considerable physical energy, with over a hundred uneven steps to reach it. We were young and strong so it was easy for us, but when we were told pilgrims had climbed them on their knees, often in chains, I thought they must have been in considerable pain. Marie-Jeanne and I agreed between ourselves that it also seemed an utterly idiotic idea. This made us laugh, and we had no desire to try it ourselves.

This was our only excursion, apart from picnics in the nearby park, as the family was not the sort to enjoy touring. They took me to Rocamadour only so that I would have something different to remember, which I did. It was kind of them, but they gave me the impression that they did not want to be too friendly in case they were saddled with me again.

Marie-Jeanne was a tall, well-built girl with a sense of mischief that would lead her into more trouble than she quite imagined. She confided that she had been to bed with her soldier boyfriend Nicholas from the army base close to Mortefontaine.

"How on earth did you manage to arrange that?" I asked, pleased that my French was becoming so fluent as to make such bold enquiries.

"With the sheets, it was easy. When you're all asleep, I take the spare sheets from the cupboard, knot them together, like I once saw in a film, and out I go, shooting down beside the drainpipe. Nicholas waits for me and takes me on his bicycle back to the barracks. There we make love."

"What do you mean 'make love'?"

"First he kisses me, I will show you how, with his tongue and everything. Then slowly he takes off my nightdress, much quicker than clothing, and in no time, his hands are everywhere. He rubs my nipples, kisses them, and I did not quite know at first what to do with his enormous *sexe*. But he soon showed me. Sometimes I put it in my mouth. Sometimes he pushes it inside me. It is the most wonderful feeling on earth."

I thought she was probably making it up, for Marie-Jeanne was known for her inventive tales, but it made her glow with happiness telling me about it and her mood changed totally. Being with her made me feel that I shared in her happiness.

"Have you ever done it?" she asked.

"Heavens, no," I told her, blushing at the idea. My life had been very sheltered, and as to discussing sexual matters, that had been totally a closed shop. At fourteen I think I was very far behind my peers, even in a French convent.

Back at school, the nuns had their own peculiar rituals for dealing with burgeoning sexual awareness. Sister Marie Perpetua was on night duty and came around the dormitory tapping us on the arms if our hands moved down from our shoulders. We had to keep them folded across our chests as in a religious painting, but it was terribly uncomfortable and the moment we dozed off, our arms would drop. Then, tap tap with the stick, waking you up abruptly.

"They do that to stop you fiddling with yourself," explained Marie-Jeanne, tittering. I had no idea what she meant.

Stranger still were our washing arrangements. Once a week we traipsed across to the main heated building where the nuns lived. We took it in turns to shower. There were ten cubicles for eighty girls, so it was a time consuming activity.

Sister Marie-Josephine was in charge of showering. We used to laugh at her name, remembering that this very chateau had once belonged to Napoleon's brother and had been a luxurious shelter for the Emperor and his wife Josephine in good times and bad. We used to talk about them and fantasise about their lives, knowing that they would have had hot water, comfortable beds, servants, and no broken windows. Now, unsmilingly, this distinctly unregal nun stood at the entrance between the hall and the shower cubicles with a pile of folded material across her arm.

As I approached, she handed me one of whatever it was, saying, "Now you put this on yourself and you shower under it. *Sous l' imperméable.*"

I knew the word for raincoat but was not certain about *sous*. Perhaps I had it wrong. "*Merci, ma soeur*, but how can one shower *under* a raincoat?"

She showed me what you did with the cape. The idea was to cover yourself up, then splash the water up under the garment, "So you do not see yourself, my child," she explained.

I became accustomed to this unsatisfactory arrangement which, although impeding cleanliness, was useful for excluding draughts.

Baths were another proposition. These were not offered frequently, perhaps once a month, like a special in the supermarket. We did not all go, of course, only in bunches of twos or threes, and never together, always alone.

To my surprise, there she was again, Sister Marie-Josephine. This time she offered us no capes, but square tins. Surely it could not be talcum powder! Nothing as luxurious as that, in this most spartan of establishments.

"Do you know what this is for, *ma fille*?" she asked.

Of course I knew what talcum powder was for.

"Yes, *ma soeur*, you wash yourself, dry yourself, then sprinkle it all over to make your skin smooth."

"You have no idea, do you! *Pas du tout*," she proclaimed. "The talcum powder, it is for sprinkling *over* the water, so you do not see yourself through the water to be tempted."

This was 1954, Paris, France. When I wrote to Penny to tell her all about it, she would have been sure I was making it up. But she never received my letters; Stepmother had already given instructions to stop my mail, I did not discover till much later that this was another of her plans to isolate me from the past.

It was a desolate place, Mortefontaine. Our routine was strict, up at six, wash in basins of cold water, walk in the freezing cold to the chapel, pray till seven, breakfast in silence. Breakfast was tea or coffee. Tea was made in an urn where the leaves went in first, then water, then milk, then sugar. This concoction was then boiled together for an hour or so.

The coffee, apparently bitter, smelt absolutely disgusting. The girls said it was made from acorns due to postwar shortages. I was not very interested in knowing its origins or tasting it, so I chose the tea. The baguettes, however, were baked on the premises and were delicious. Those who brought butter or jam did well until they ran out, and those of us who failed to bring such luxuries enjoyed the baguette just as it was.

The routine was occasionally interrupted by the presence of parents who visited their children on birthdays and feast days. My parents were noted for their absence. There was a romantic rumour about me that I was an orphan and that Stepmother was a very kind lady who paid my board. As to my parents' place in society, people neither knew nor wished to know. We were rank outsiders.

Lessons were conducted by a nun from a blackboard. When I failed to grasp the basics of mathematics, I was told to sit in the back row of the class, to read a book, a French classic, or a play by Molière or Racine. My vocabulary increased, gradually, and these times became useful as I rather enjoyed reading.

Lunch was in the main refectory hall, a vast stable block with high ceilings and exposed beams, everything conspiring to make it exceedingly cold. The duty sister of the day, from an engraved, raised wooden stand, would give voice to holy readings from a variety of liturgical books. We were not to speak. The food was reasonable; meat, salad and fresh fruit. A vinegary, bitter wine was served, *vin coupé*, half red wine diluted with water, in pitchers. We were told to drink this, for it was good for us. It was not an easy taste to acquire.

Lessons continued in the afternoon till four. We had no sport, music, or physical education. Instead, we were sent on a long walk each day whatever the weather. Then came warm baguettes with two pieces of dark chocolate, all deliciously melting inside. For girls ordered by their parents to slim, there was an orange. Homework was to be done till seven, and the evening meal was so austere that we were grateful to have eaten the baguette and chocolate.

Some nights we were given a boiled egg followed by three or four sticky dates. At other times there could be noodles with oil, followed by a pot of yoghurt. The best offering was vegetable soup and bread. It was not much to last us through the following twelve hours.

Excruciating pains in my stomach made me report to the infirmary where I told the nursing sister that I was ill. She put me to bed for a couple of days. My temperature was taken every four hours with a large glass object about five times the size of the thermometer with which I had been familiar in Australia. I put it in my mouth and it was very uncomfortable. The nursing sister came in and laughed.

"But, *ma fille*, it is to go in your rear end." Her choice of words was prudish and correct. I must have been mistaken about the glass object. But why would it be placed in my rear end?

"Like they do for horses?" I asked, hoping to give a quaint colonial touch to make her like me a little.

"It is not *comme il faut, ma fille*, for young ladies to know about horses."

When my cramps became more severe, a doctor was summoned. He diagnosed suspected appendicitis and sent me to Paris, by ambulance, to L'Hôpital des Enfants Malades.

Stepmother was my official guardian. This meant that the

nuns were compelled to contact her for permission for me to have surgery. They learned from the concierge at the address she had supplied that she had never lived there. This delayed permission for surgery and caused the nuns great inconvenience. They even had to telephone the police, who contacted the passport control division to determine her whereabouts.

There were other difficulties concerning my admission. Due to a shortage of beds as well as the absence of accommodation for teenagers, I was put in the babies' ward. The only concession was a full-sized bed, but with no curtain to go around it.

During night duty, I heard a doctor and a nurse talking to each other in an excited, amorous manner, and to my surprise, he persuaded her to remove her uniform. He took down his trousers from beneath his white coat, leaving on his shirt and tie, and climbed into the other single bed across the row from mine.

"*Cheri, je t'aime,*" I heard the nurse squeak.

There followed a cooing noise and much sighing from the man as they lay under the sheets.

"*Toujours, toujours à toi,*" she said, sounding like an operatic heroine.

The man was out of breath as he began to pull on his trousers. A baby was crying in the cot next to my bed.

The girl's voice said something about seeing to the baby, the man's said not to worry about it. Another baby began to cry.

Then, suddenly, another nurse rushed into the ward with her torch, first going towards the sound of crying, then stopping, seeing movement in the bed, pulling off the sheet and screaming abuse at her colleague. "*Salope!*" she yelled.

The doctor punched her in the face, took away the torch, blamed her for waking the baby, then abandoned his naked girl-friend, whose clothing had fallen to the floor under the bed where she could not reach it. There followed a fight between the two girls, and from what they said I discovered that the doctor had previously been making puffing noises with the second nurse as well.

I kept very still, but unfortunately the baby next to me kept crying, and when the second nurse came closer she saw me. She burst out laughing, saying I would be a useful witness and that she was glad I had received an early education in sexual shenanigans.

The doctor who inspected me in the morning in no way resembled the young swashbuckler who had graced the bed opposite mine. He was one of those short, obese, pompous physicians who despise the nursing staff as inferior, resent the patients for wasting their time and loathe working in hospitals. His name was, forgettably, Dr Oublie and his personality did not inspire confidence. He examined me and confirmed the earlier diagnosis of suspected appendicitis, then demanded to know where my parents were. The nurses explained the problems.

"Most unsatisfactory," he proclaimed. "This child requires urgent surgery and the parents are not to be found. Where is the father?"

Upon learning that he was in Australia, the doctor laughed, considering Australia to be so distant that no postal or telegraphic service could possibly save me.

Later that morning came a call from Mortefontaine to say that Stepmother had been contacted in Spain. She had demanded that I be transferred to a private hospital. She would pay for my treatment.

Things had become so interesting in the ward, despite the visit of Dr Oublie, that I rather regretted the prospect of a change, but my stomach cramps had increased and I wondered if anybody would make time to look after me in between their sexual encounters anyway.

I was taken to the American hospital in Neuilly and Stepmother came to see me. A doctor considered surgery imperative. He was angry that the nuns had not been given permission to act on my parents' behalf. Stepmother was furious at the entire incident, agreeing with the doctor, defensively, "They could have given permission. I paid them enough."

The operation took place, and the appendix had not been enlarged, which made Stepmother even more furious. Her holiday in Spain had been disrupted and she had found it embarrassing to be tracked down. She told me that the count had been more than a little put out.

"I am sorry that I am sick," I told her, honestly. "I did not mean to spoil your holiday. Are you very fond of the count?"

"That is none of your business," she replied, adding, "and you are not really sick, you are simply very disturbed."

"I am very unhappy," I said.

She summoned my surgeon, spoke briefly with him, then announced that I was obviously a most disturbed child and insisted that a child psychiatrist be commissioned to examine me.

"You seem very unhappy," declared the psychiatrist. He spent a generous amount of time with me discussing the possible causes.

I told him how much I missed my father, my sister, my friends, my home.

"Do you like your stepmother?" he asked.

"No. But I have to pretend I do because she's all that I have here in Europe."

The psychiatrist looked at me sympathetically and replied, "It is quite all right for you to say that you dislike somebody, even to say that you hate them. Sometimes it can be good for you to express your feelings frankly."

"I wouldn't be able to say I hated her, because that wouldn't be fair. She has really tried terribly hard with me. I just don't like her at all. At first I tried, but I was so angry when she brought me to France that I have never really been able to forgive her."

"That's not an inappropriate way to feel," he said, reassuringly.

"I think we had better make some different arrangements for your care," he said, writing something down in his notes.

"Couldn't I just be sent back to Australia?" I pleaded.

"Things are not usually as simple as that. For one thing, there's the fare to be paid. Why don't I see what I can do for you?"

I believed there was a tiny grain of hope. Perhaps the kind doctor would persuade Daddy that I was old enough to look after myself, at Wahroonga.

EAU VIVE

Apparently my school fees had not been paid at Mortefontaine, so the nuns, not unreasonably, refused to take me back. My sessions with the child psychiatrist continued. He told me that in his opinion my parents were unable to look after me, and with my father in Australia and Stepmother not resident in France, I would need to be made a ward of the French court. He mentioned something about Stepmother being 'an unfit parent', but I cannot recall the exact terminology. He introduced me to a colleague, a man he considered suitable as my future *Guardian ad Litem*. I cannot recall any ceremony involving my presence. My guardian's name was Dr Thompson. I liked him immediately.

He was an Englishman of about five foot eight, (173 cm) solidly built with silvery grey hair. His eyes were of a most unusually intense pale blue, like the sky on a cool European day, but they were kind eyes. He was a calm man, the type I imagined to be the perfect father. He had all the time in the world to listen to whatever I had to say, even on our first encounter. We walked in the park rather than in the hospital setting and he never gave me the impression that I was wasting his time.

Until meeting Dr Thompson I had believed I was unlovable and that the fault must lie entirely with me. He explained that until we learned to forgive ourselves we could not understand others. This was difficult for me to comprehend because I had, to date, blamed first myself for everything, and then Stepmother. I never blamed Daddy because I sincerely believed he had tried to save me from France, but had failed.

Dr Thompson also said I had to learn to think about all these things differently, firstly to forgive my parents and above all to stop blaming myself. In his eyes, there was no question of blame. We had to build from that forgiveness and plan for a positive future. Lost, away from my country, I had had no notion of a positive future. Now I felt there was a chance, somebody was going to repair the damage for me, by taking control, by looking after me in a way I had not felt looked after for some time. Dr Thompson reconstructed my life for me as best he could. From basic arrangements such as somewhere to live, something to do, financial provisions, he wanted to teach me to establish the foundations for self sufficiency. He celebrated my fifteenth birthday with a special meal made from vegetables he had grown in his garden patch and a delicious goat's cheese he had made from the milk of his precious and much loved white goats.

Dr Thompson arranged for me to go to a convent where the nuns took in paid boarding guests. I was to attend university in Paris, a Catholic one, L'Institut Catholique, not the Sorbonne, commuting each day. I would pay for my keep by peeling vegetables four mornings a week for the meals shared by the nuns and their paying guests.

Le Couvent de l'Epiphanie was at Soisy-sur-Seine, on the Corbeil-Melun line, an hour from the Institut Catholique where, despite the fact that I was only fifteen, I was accepted for *Etudes Supplémentaires*. This was a diploma in French studies.

The other residents at the convent were Catholic women who

were seriously ill, disabled, or who had retired and had nowhere else to go.

It was not a merry place, and everybody kept to themselves, retiring after meal times to their cell-like rooms. There were two long corridors on the first floor of an eighteenth century building which lacked charm or warmth, the wooden frames of the doors of each room the only decorative relief. At the top of the stairs was a plain Crucifix; a sad, cruel, empty cross. To me, it presented an image of fear and oppression rather than comfort.

The nuns were self-sufficient, growing their own vegetables and surviving on home-made cheeses from the milk of the goats they kept, fresh produce and meat which they exchanged with local farmers. Apart from gardening and cooking, most of their time was spent at chapel praying for those of us for whom they considered intercession was seriously required.

Sister Léo was the only nun I began to know. Many years previously, she told me, she had won a major art prize, the Prix de Rome, and had planned to marry and settle down to family life. When her young man was killed in an automobile accident, young Léonie became so distraught that she had attempted suicide. Her family feared more for the safety of her soul than for her life, as suicide was considered a mortal sin. They brought her to the Dominicans and asked them to look after her.

After six months at the convent, Léonie decided that she had a strong religious vocation, requested consideration to join the group as a postulant, and then became a nun. She took the religious name of Sister Léo.

I was glad she was there, for she had sufficient knowledge of the outside world to converse knowledgeably on many subjects. She had much to teach me, particularly about art. She could describe paintings so vividly that they were as real to me as if they were on the wall before me.

"You must miss your music," she said to me one day.

"I miss it dreadfully," I confided. "Why are you not permitted to have records and to listen to the radio?"

"It all started with the privations of the war. I don't suppose you know much about the effects of wartime on Europe. We had to sell the gramophone in order to pay for horticultural equipment. What was so sad was that the sale provided us with nothing very grand, just a simple wheelbarrow. Not many of the nuns had studied music, although one of them used to play the piano."

"What happened to that?" I asked, hoping a piano might be stored somewhere, although I had never heard it played.

"The piano had been lent to us by a villager. When times became hard, she asked us to return it as she needed to sell it. To my dismay, I later learned that, unable to raise any money for the instrument, she had chopped it up for firewood."

It was shocking to hear that, so I asked Sister Léo to tell me more about wartime. Her revelations astonished me.

"I didn't even know about rationing," I told her, realising how fortunate I had been.

"I believe you were born in America, was there no rationing there?"

"Not really. But I do remember that Nanny said we couldn't buy any butter. At the grocer's we bought a packet of margarine, which was white. We were given a little twisted wax paper parcel of colouring, so that we could add a yellow dye to it to make it look like butter. It didn't taste like butter at all, but it was all right in cakes and biscuits."

"*Mon Dieu*, we never had anything as luxurious as a cake or a biscuit in wartime, even if we cooked it ourselves."

I realised how much I had to learn about life in Europe. Perhaps it had been a good idea of Stepmother's to send me away from my happy, sheltered life in Sydney, although I hardly appreciated her motives at the time. My heart was too fragile to allow for goodness in her and it took me many years to realise how difficult my presence must have been for her. What puzzles me still is why she took me on in the first place—other than as an alibi to leave Sydney. Would it not have been easier, or certainly more honest, simply to ask for a divorce?

The winter of 1956 was one of the coldest on record. The temperature fell to minus eighteen degrees Celsius. I could never have imagined how cold that was. Dressing up warmly in snowboots given to me by my beloved Dr Thompson, borrowing jumpers, scarves and gloves, I set off by train and métro to the Institut each day.

To watch the snow falling from the cosy, snug warmth of my cell-like room gave me great pleasure. When I was five, Daddy had given me a paperweight containing a snowstorm. When you shook it, white flakes flurried around the Empire State building. I had loved the snow then.

Now, as I watched the snow falling from inside the smallness of the room, I felt as if I were inside a paperweight myself. I wondered if it was snowing for my mother. I hoped she thought about me sometimes and that she was happy, wherever she was. Daddy would be warm, even hot, in Sydney. The falling snow made me think of Daddy all the more, and Donie.

When I was first captivated by *La Bohème* in Sydney, I was seated beside my sister in the old Tivoli theatre box, next to her harp. Act Three begins with the snow falling by the gate to the city of Paris. Puccini has written the music so that the harp accentuates the falling of each flake. The sounds and images are breathtakingly beautiful. Every note came swiftly to mind as I sang it silently to myself now.

I closed my eyes and willed myself into the drama that was *La Bohème*. Immense gratitude for the gift Daddy had given me overwhelmed me. The joy of music was something nobody could ever take away. How I missed him. How I loved him for the gift of music.

But I was grateful for my substitute family, Dr Thompson. As my legal guardian, he was to be given a sum of money twice a year by Stepmother for my upkeep. Predictably, she did not honour the commitment. However, being under the protection of a man considered by the villagers as a modern-day saint, I did not concern myself with the shortage of finances, being certain everything would work out, even if I was unable to consider how money might be found.

Dr Thompson lived across the road from the Couvent de l'Epiphanie in a Catholic community centre called Eau Vive, with the English meaning of 'living water'. How contrasting and extraordinary it was, not only in name but in atmosphere, after my fortunate escape from Mortefontaine (or dead fountain). It was at Eau Vive that Dr Thompson brought up two orphaned German boys he had adopted, Heinrich and Johann. They had both known inconceivable suffering.

Heinrich had been found in an attic where he had been locked for two weeks. Bound to a table, he had been forced to watch his parents tortured and killed. The soldiers had then abandoned him in the room to relive the horrors he had witnessed. The dead bodies of his parents lay uncovered before him. He was eight years old. Little Heinrich had acquired a look of haunted pain that even now, as a medical student, would never leave his eyes.

Johann was blind as a result of an explosion that had killed his parents and his brothers and sisters when he was a baby of eighteen months. That had been in 1943. Now, in 1957, Dr Thompson and his two sons were loved and respected members of the little community. The boys had grown into fine young men. I was particularly impressed by Heinrich, who was tall, blond and blue-eyed, extremely good-looking and, as if that were not enough to win the heart of a young girl, his nature was both compassionate and genial. Occasionally we went by train to Paris together, he to his studies, I to mine. Not often, because he started very early in the mornings when I worked in the kitchens.

Johann was studying to be a physiotherapist, and was less communicative than Heinrich. I admired his attitude and the way he overcame his blindness in so positive a way. He enjoyed music very much and liked me to tell him amusing anecdotes from happier days in Sydney. It was a relief to be able to talk about music again, and to have somebody who seemed quite happy to listen to my prattling.

Johann was accepted as a paramedic on a government medical team organised by the Red Cross to travel to Africa on a mission. He was overjoyed at the prospect and Dr Thompson was very proud of him as we waved him goodbye. Heinrich was due to leave shortly as well. His appointment was to the Faculty of Medicine at Toulouse. So my two new friends quickly disappeared from the scene. It was a difficult feeling to describe. People of whom I grew fond always disappeared. I wondered if I would ever see them again. It provoked a feeling of great isolation once more.

It was so cold in the winter of 1956 that the Seine, normally a swiftly moving river, had frozen solid. The ice was so deep that it was safe for motor cars to drive across it. Motorists found it saved them hours of travel. The métro was warm, overheated. The poor and the homeless congregated in the tunnels by day and by night, sleeping on the platforms.

One morning, as I walked up the staircase at Montparnasse-Bienvenue, the change in temperature of the piercing outside air was so great that I found myself on my knees. My feet and legs felt as if they were frozen. A young man helped me to my feet. "*C'est le froid, mademoiselle*," he said.

Travelling by métro had its drawbacks. It was very crowded in the rush hour, and every moment was an opportunity for would-be Casanovas to pinch the bottoms of attractive women. I was filled with admiration as I watched an elegant Parisienne retaliate by firmly stamping her three-inch heel into the foot of a man with wandering fingers. It reminded me of my cello incident.

Textbooks were costly. Fortunately, the Institut library kept copies of most of the references we needed, but the ten copies of *La France au XVIIIième Siècle* had all been issued. The book was too recent a publication to be available second hand, so the librarian told me I would have to buy a new one.

My salary for peeling vegetables was strictly expenses only. The nuns offered me free board and lodging as well as money for my train and métro tickets. They also gave me just enough money to buy a generous baguette with ham in it each day, a few francs. There was no opportunity for saving. The book was well beyond my means.

"I don't really know what to do, Madame Rose," I confided to one of my fellow boarders, a fragile woman in her eighties whose angina confined her to a wheelchair.

"Mademoiselle, I suffer terribly from the cold, as I cannot move about. Allow me to buy the book for you. In exchange you will give me . . . let me see, your snowboots."

I accepted her offer, despite my chilblains. My toes were red, swollen and bleeding for several weeks while the weather was at its worst. The book enabled me to pass my exams, so the ends justified the means. If I ever returned to Sydney, which I certainly planned to do, I knew there would be no more chilblains. How I hated the cold!

The Algerian revolution was at its height. Demonstrations were a daily occurrence in Paris. Street chanting was perpetual, with Arabs clad in white holding banners proclaiming *'Algérie n'est pas française.'*

I varied my journey occasionally to enjoy the streets of Paris as several métro stations were within walking distance of the Institut in Rue d'Assas. One of my favourites was Montparnasse-Bienvenue. I adored the name. The wide boulevards, the tall apartment buildings, the jumbled, varied shapes of the roofs and the trees still bare of leaves but beginning to reveal signs of spring filled me with anticipation.

The seasons were more clearly defined here than they had been in Sydney. Weather changes were far more dramatic. When night fell, it did so gradually, not suddenly as in the Southern Hemisphere, although in winter I hated it being dark by about four o'clock.

At Mortefontaine, when I had been consigned to reading the classics instead of doing mathematics, I had had the advantage of learning about this neighbourhood. Therefore, when I stepped into the Rue St Germain and when I admired the great boutiques around the Place de l'Etoile in the Rue St Honoré, these places represented history and literature to me. Victor Hugo had used these *quartiers* in his vibrant writings, and the paintings of the Impressionists had depicted the atmosphere. So many accurate details had come from my reading and from paintings that I felt I knew my surroundings as if I had been there before.

To my horror, one morning a dead body was spread across the pavement before me. Clad in white robes, the victim must have been an Arab, stabbed, with blood all over him, lying on the pavement. I rushed to the gendarme directing the traffic.

"It is not important, *ma petite*," he told me. "I have thousands of people to get to work on time. After the rush hour, then I will attend to this body, and to the many other dead Arabs from the night. They are already dead, no further harm will come to them."

He spoke to me quite cheerfully, "This happens every day. It is the way of things. Do not concern yourself. *Allez! Partez!*"

I had never seen a dead body except in newsreels. It was a frightening experience and made me shake so much that I found it difficult to cross the road to reach the Institut. This was not to be the only death that week. One of the Arabic students, the son of an oil magnate, was found knifed in the courtyard. As a result, all students had to report to the director of studies. Foreign students were to present their passports, which we carried at all times.

The list was alphabetical, so it was afternoon before they reached my name. I went in, trembling, hoping I could seize this opportunity to be sent back to Sydney.

The director had a cheerful face and stood up to greet me. He shook me by the hand as he took my passport and scrutinised its details.

"But what is this? Your birthday is in August so you are not quite sixteen? We do not accept students under the age of eighteen! There is some mistake. And your examinations, they are only valid for tertiary students."

He sat at his desk, gestured for me to sit on the straight leather-backed chair in front of him.

"How are your studies progressing?" he enquired, inspecting the report cards in front of him.

"Nothing fantastic in your results, except that, given your age, *ma petite*, I think you are doing very well. We will keep it our secret, *n'est-ce pas*? I insist that you tell nobody you are under age. This way we avoid trouble and you pass your exams."

"Perhaps I could fail my exams and you could send me back to Australia," I said, hopefully.

"*Non, soyez sage, ma petite*. Pass the exams. Then you have a better opportunity to plan your future or to get back home as you seem to wish. Discuss it with those who care for you. Something will work out. Meanwhile, you will gain a qualification. Congratulations and *bonne chance*."

I worked very hard, bearing in mind his words about the virtues of a qualification. After I finished perhaps I could get a job and work my way back to Sydney. Following his advice seemed sensible, so I embraced it with great enthusiasm.

"You've worked very hard," said Dr Thompson.

"I've had a word with the nuns at your convent and they have agreed you may stay on there if you like. I can't keep an eye on you any more, although I know I seem to have done so little. There is an interesting position in Oxford which I have applied for, and, if it comes through, I will be leaving in a few months. You can come there with me and I will find you lodgings, and a position so that you can be self-supporting. Or you can stay here. You see, I have been given no money by your family. Letters to your father have remained unanswered. Perhaps he never received them. I don't know where your stepmother is, and my savings have been used on my research project. Although I should be retiring, I will work for a further five years. Let me know what you would like to do."

It was only then I learned that Stepmother had never sent the money which was part of the guardianship agreement. Letters from Australia had stopped, quite suddenly, at Mortefontaine, even before my appendix attack, and there had been no news of Daddy for some time.

It was therefore necessary to make a decision quickly. The idea of losing Dr Thompson was more than I could bear. "I have relations in England but they wouldn't want to be saddled with me again. I would love to stay with my Aunt Sidonie, but she is terribly busy. Dr Thompson, you are the only person who cares about me. Please don't go to Oxford without me. I think it'll be easier for me to work things out there. I really don't want to stay here. Although the nuns have been kind, I feel so alone. Peeling vegetables is not my idea of a future."

He looked at me, his honest soft blue eyes filled with understanding. "I will write some letters to people I know. There will be lodgings for you, I am sure. You can already type, and you will have your French diploma. You'll manage. Rely on me to stand by you, but I cannot help you financially."

The months passed rapidly and we were planning the move to Oxford for the following week.

Sister Léo came to fetch me. "It is your *belle-mère*. She has telephoned to say she is going to come to visit you tomorrow. She has something important to tell you."

My heart sank. To me she was the person who, having taken me from my home and family, had abandoned me. I could not imagine that Daddy would have allowed me to have endured it all, had he known of my circumstances. I had no idea he had received none of my letters.

Stepmother arrived just before lunch and was invited to join us for the meal. Impeccably dressed, elegant and perfectly groomed, she was totally out of place.

Gathered around one immense table were seven nuns and their ten paying guests. As a group we had almost nothing in common. There was little old Sophie fainting from her fits and having to be escorted from the table for her medicine, and

Madame Rose smiling reassurance at me from her wheelchair, her feet snugly encased in my snowboots. Stepmother was tense and ill at ease. She looked distressed, despite her polite exchanges with those around her.

After lunch, Sister Léo offered us the parlour so that we could speak privately.

"I have received a letter from your father in Sydney. There has been some dreadful trouble. With the police. I don't know much about it. The press got hold of my address, God knows how, and asked for a statement. I said I would stand by him, of course. I just thought you should know."

My response was immediate. "That means he needs us to go back. When can we leave?"

"I don't think that will be at all appropriate. It sounds to me more as if he is to leave the country, in some disgrace, and that it is more a case of our staying in France to support him."

The idea of her supporting anybody made me feel suddenly very miserable, totally sceptical, and untrusting. "What could it all be about?" I asked her.

"I've no idea. It's probably something that will blow over. And did I remember to tell you that your father was knighted for his services to music?"

She hadn't told me, and I would have been so proud.

"This means that I am now known as Lady Goossens," she said, her voice filled with pride.

"Well, Lady Goossens," I said, "Shouldn't we be celebrating?"

"I doubt it," she said. "One of the newspaper reports declared that his knighthood might be taken away."

All I wanted to do was run to my father, to be with him, to hug him and tell him it didn't matter what the papers said. I still loved him. The idea that he was in trouble and we were so far away made me feel powerless. I felt angry at being in France, furious with Stepmother for taking me there. How lonely and afraid he must be. I wished so much I could telephone him to tell him how much I loved him.

"I must go back to Spain now. There's a train this afternoon, if I don't miss my connection. I don't want you to make me late," she added crossly, as if she resented the time she had spent with me.

The news I was not told was that in March 1956 Father had been travelling by plane back to Sydney after a musical tour overseas. The police and customs officials had been alerted that he was carrying illegal photographs in his luggage. In Sydney there had been sensational publicity, in England too, but in the depths of a French convent, we never received local newspapers, let alone any from overseas. It was many years before I discovered the facts behind the disgrace and scandal which brought my father's musical career to an end so cruelly, inappropriately and unjustly. He had been forced to resign from his joint positions of director of the NSW State Conservatorium as well as of chief conductor of the Sydney Symphony Orchestra.

In my protected world I would not have understood even the word 'pornographic', and in the context of the permissive society which was to develop in Australia within a matter of a few decades, that which was considered horrific was soon to become commonplace, available on supermarket and newsagents shelves as well as on a new device called the Internet. But all that was in the future. It made me terribly sad that I had not been told the substance of Father's troubles, and was not permitted to comfort him or stand by him. But I was powerless then.

Sister Léo escorted Stepmother to the door, then came back to me, smiling, "That was good, was it not, seeing your family again?"

This was not the time to delude her. Sister Léo had anointed my chilblained fingers, swollen and red from the buckets of cold water into which I plunged the day's potatoes each morning before I went to college.

"To be honest, no, it was not good to see her, and Sister Léo, I cannot think of her as family."

"Do you want to talk about it, *mon enfant*?" she said, putting her arm around my shoulder and walking me outside into the friendly woods. She pointed to the wild strawberries popping their faces through the grass.

Telling my story to Sister Léo was comforting. I wished I had confided in her when I first arrived, instead of being so remote about personal matters. We had talked about our mutual love of music, but it never encouraged me to speak of my family and how I missed them.

After I had told her everything she was silent and obviously engrossed in thought, but when we returned from our walk she took me into the parlour, unlocked a desk and handed me a dozen letters.

"Take these, my child. They are from your father and your sister and from a Miss Brown. The nuns from Mortefontaine sent them here, but they told me that your stepmother had forbidden you to receive mail. I did not know the reason but could not bring myself to destroy them. If you need to talk to me when you have read them, come to me in the chapel any time. I will pray for you all."

She handed me the precious bundle, wiped away my tears with the corner of her sleeve, and said quietly, "God be with you, and forgive me if what I did was wrong."

The letters were old, written monthly, and had stopped in August 1955. It was now March 1956. Poor Daddy, poor Donie and darling Miss Brown. I had been writing letters to them, handed trustingly to the nuns at Mortefontaine, but none of them had been posted.

Then, at l'Epiphanie, I had stopped writing, because I believed they did not care about me any longer. How wrong I had been. The letters were full of sunshine, of love, of music. I wept all evening, with streaming tears of relief, regret and joy.

At nine o'clock, just before the bells rang for the service of compline, there was a knock at my door. It was Sister Léo. "My child, I think you have been alone too long now. You have missed supper. I have kept something for you."

She handed me a plate with three large chunks of cheese, some farm bread, five olives, and a banana. It was more than we usually had to eat.

"Now, my child, will you give me the pleasure of accompanying me to the service of compline? It will comfort you for the night. I will feel better, too, to know that you are all right. Also to know that you have maybe forgiven me."

I hugged her, took her hand, and went into the chapel. There was new music in the nuns' voices and sunlight in the candles.

THE CHATEAU

In the middle of the final term at l'Institut Catholique, students were invited to put their names down for summer vacation positions. I joined the list of those seeking *au pair* assignments. Although I lacked both domestic and child care experience, it was time I learned, I thought. I was eager and more than willing to join a French family.

We were interviewed, asked about our areas of interest, background, previous experience with children, and preferred geographic location. I assumed it was a screening procedure to enable the university to discover more about us prior to contacting suitable families.

I was given a piece of paper on which was written the telephone number and address of a Madame de la Chapelle. I rang the number. Madame sounded friendly and eager to receive me.

"*Prenez le car pour Versailles*," she said. "I will meet you at the bus stop."

Only the French would call the coach *le car*, but it was

comforting to know she would meet me. I would recognise her, she said, by the four children accompanying her.

The coach was comfortable, the journey less than one hour. The constant chatter of two elderly women behind me was irritating, and I was nauseated by a steady stream of smoke emanating from several *Gauloise* smokers, but thankfully one of the other passengers opened the windows. The breeze was pleasant on a hot, stuffy day. I had read as much as I could find about Versailles and was looking forward to being there.

The coach sped along swiftly, the sun flashing intermittently through the sturdy poplar trees. One moment it was as if a great veil of gauze had been placed across the road, and then through this mistiness would flash a bright light, and then another. There was an excitement to it, like erratic stage lighting, as if I were happily ensconced in the storm section of *The Valkyrie* which my father had presented at the Conservatorium. The coach was late arriving and there was nobody to meet me accompanied by four children. However, an attractive woman held up an envelope with my hand writing on it so I knew it must be Madame.

Appreciating her pleasant smile and relaxed manner, I wondered how any woman could remain so beautiful after rearing four children.

"You know this is only the first part of your journey, don't you?" she told me to my surprise, "Because in two weeks time we will all be going to Brittany." She helped me unload my case from the hold of the coach.

I was touched when Madame carried my case for me, leading the way. We walked through a wide square leading to a narrow, cobbled street. She used her key to open a shiny blue door, an impressive entrance to what was revealed to be a shabby interior.

"*On ne prend pas l'ascenseur*," she told me, carrying my case up a short flight of stairs with a spring in her step. I already knew it would be an *ascenseur* instead of a lift, or even an elevator. A sign on the iron bars of its cage notified us that '*Il ne marche pas*'.

Paintings of Botticelli angels resembled Madame. Her face was enhanced by abundant auburn curls. Her frame was slight beneath her wisp of a delicately flower-embroidered muslin dress. She was probably in her early thirties. On her feet were the lightest of espadrilles, with ribbons laced up to her knees as if she was a dancer.

Thinking she might have been a dancer made me wonder if the university staff had tried to find me a family with a musical background. But it was soon apparent that the only thing the family knew about me was that I was from Australia. Even when I had the opportunity to tell them of my father's work as a conductor, it was evident they had never heard the name. I had supposed our surname would have been well known in France, given that my father had received the Légion d'Honneur for his contribution to French music.

One lesson my travels had taught me was that fame was strictly local, that people famous in one country were not necessarily known elsewhere. Generations failed to pass on knowledge of previous artists and even the violinist Ginette Niveu, who had been a favourite of my father's, was not known in every French household and certainly not in this one. Being in so musically privileged a family during my earlier years, I had been accustomed to learning about artists of international reputation, reading about them, finding out more, as if my very life depended on it. But, of course, this was not the case everywhere.

The apartment was welcoming, not only in its furnishings but in the happy laughter with which the children greeted me.

"*Bonjour, Mademoiselle de l'Australie,*" chanted three voices, while the babe in arms cooed enchantingly and extended his arms. They looked too good to be true.

"What a beautiful chair, Madame," I said, not daring to sit on the armchair she offered me.

"It has been in the family always. It is from the time of Louis XV," she told me without seeking to impress. "Please make yourself comfortable. That is the purpose of a chair, no?"

I sat, without comfort, as one of the chair legs was shorter than the others, so I lurched uncomfortably to the right. Across the room I noticed that one of the table legs had a book under it to keep it straight.

"We never repair things. But my husband will be here soon. He will see to such matters."

The children bustled around me, particularly Monette, who climbed up on my lap, squirming with laughter. "You will come with us to the chateau, won't you? We always have such fun there," she asked.

Madame told me that once Monsieur returned from his position with the Army '*aux Indes*', he would be joining us for a month. She never explained if this was India or the Indies, but he was clearly a long way away most of the time. Life must have been difficult for her without him and I wondered if she missed him terribly.

"It will be good to have you with us, *ma petite*," she continued enthusiastically. "I can't manage everything on my own away from this house without my mother's help."

Grand-mère came into the salon to announce "*Le souper est servi*," and led me to the dining room, where a plate of hot soup with fresh bread and an assortment of several cheeses awaited. There were brie, camembert, bleu de meau and chèvre, as well as Petit Gervais, a soft cream cheese that was the children's favourite.

"*On mange à midi*," Madame said in explanation, which made me wonder what extra delicious items might be included at lunchtime, evidently their main meal.

The children sat quietly at the table, helping themselves to their bread and cheese, spooning their soup quietly.

"If we're quiet we can eat as much fruit as we like," whispered Robert, who siphoned his soup so rapidly his mother exclaimed that most of it was going down his shirt. "*Pardon, maman*," he said in a contrite voice. Madame appeared to have things well under control.

After supper, I helped her to bathe the children.

"You've come on a bad night," she said, pouring water from a kettle into a large cast iron bath on wheels in the middle of the kitchen. "Friday night is bath night. We only go through this performance once a week, because it is so difficult. As we have no water heater, we have to heat huge kettles, pour them rapidly into the bath. It takes at least nine fillings, then we add the cool water till it's the right temperature. The children pile in, one on top of the other, which they seem to enjoy."

A boisterous happiness among the children demonstrated she was right. Philippe, aged nine, was in charge and first in, stirring a metal sieve that contained remnants of soap ends, until frothy bubbles appeared in the water. Next came Robert, who was seven. He decided to keep on his underpants in front of me, so he wore them into the water.

"Take those off, you silly boy," said his mother. He refused. Then four-year-old Monette, all smiles and wearing a bikini, announced proudly, "This is my new costume. For wearing to the beach. I like to get used to it in the bath first." On her little round face was a coquettish grin to match the voice. Her dark brown hair was cut in a pudding basin shape with a very straight, heavy fringe. I adored her from the moment of our very first meeting.

Madame wore a mixed expression of beatific acceptance combined with an air of discipline, which made her smile unusual, uncertain, like that of the Mona Lisa.

The bathing took half an hour, until Philippe proclaimed, "That's enough now. We're perfectly clean. And the water's getting cold."

He led the team out, *grand-mère* appearing again with small bath towels, one for each child. She rubbed them down efficiently, then departed, telling me she'd get them ready for bed.

"You, *ma petite*," said Madame, "will stay here please to help me empty the bath."

As there was no sign of a plug at the bottom, or a hole with a pipe, I discovered that the bath required emptying with saucepans. It was rather like being in a sinking lifeboat, bailing out, excepting the fact we were in no danger other than of exasperation. It didn't seem to fit with the Louis XV furniture, but then perhaps it did, if you are strict about historical accuracy.

A visit to the toilet brought me even more fiercely into France and away from the Sydney of which I still dreamed. For there, hanging from a long string, were hundreds of pieces of a chopped-up telephone directory covered in heavy black print for the wiping of the bottom. I regretted the economy of it all, and realised how easy it was to take such apparent luxuries as toilet paper as a matter of course.

An urgent voice at the door squeaked, "*Je dois faire pipi,*" so I hurried to let Monette take my place. "Wait for me," she asked as she climbed onto the toilet seat.

I wondered where the children were meant to wash their hands. She showed me, dragging over a wooden step and climbing up onto it to reach the kitchen sink, turning on the taps, rinsing her fingers, then clambering down again, looking for a towel and, not finding one, wiping her hands on her skirt.

"*Voilà!*" she said breathily, leading me to her bedroom, introducing me to the doll Poupette and asking me to read her a story. She held my hand throughout, difficult though it was, whilst squirming into her pyjamas, fetching the book, and turning down the sheet.

"You will stay the whole time, won't you?" she asked in an anxious voice. The story, by Antoine de Saint-Exupéry, was *Le Petit Prince.* She told me it was her favourite. "Because of the sunflowers," she explained, "and we have lots of them at the chateau." She fell asleep quite suddenly, at last allowing my hand to slip away from hers.

Despite the genuine Louis XV antiques, there was a distinct sensation of poverty and lack of comfort in the apartment. All the available money must have gone on beautiful meals, for we ate the great French dishes at midday, such as I would have expected to be found only in expensive restaurants. Most of the cooking seemed to be done by *grand-mère.*

The first day she offered us a home-made paté, followed by

boeuf en croûte with a pastry so light it melted in our mouths. I couldn't resist the camembert, ripe and runny. Tiny pastries with cream and a mocha filling was the dessert.

If a chair had a broken leg, one simply avoided it. If a door did not close, it probably never would. Broken window sashes made for difficulties with opening and closing. The beds were uncomfortably soft, the mattresses lumpy relics of generations past. The sheets were soft as silk, some almost transparent, all many times darned, with embroidery from *grand-mère's* trousseau and the letter 'B'—for Bernhardt, she told me as she ironed one day.

"So you are related to the famous actress Sarah?" I asked enthusiastically.

"You'll understand what I mean when I say, 'on the wrong side of the sheet'," she replied with what seemed to be rather a proud smile.

"Do you like music and the theatre, madame?" I enquired.

"Yes and no. Theatre is exciting if you can afford the prices, and music is something I have loved since I was a little child. Most of my records became broken when we moved them to Brittany for one holiday. We had a marvellous old wind-up gramophone, very beautiful with a huge brass piece for the sound to come out of. Now we only listen to the radio occasionally, to hear symphonies and *concerti*." I noticed her use of the correct Italian plural and remembered how insistent Daddy had always been about such linguistic details.

"What type of music do you enjoy, *ma fille?*"

"I love opera. Is that something you like too?"

Grand-mère shook her head vehemently. "That was the undoing of *Grand-père*. It was shameful, really it was."

"Would you mind telling me about it?" I asked.

"My husband was a viola player. He was neither particularly talented nor well paid. He was a freelance musician and earned money for the family as best he could."

"My father is a conductor," I said, puffing with pride. However, it was obvious that the family had no knowledge of mine, or of their importance in the world. When I used the French term *chef d'orchestre* I realised what a descriptive term it was for his role. It made me chuckle to myself at the very idea of Father as a chef in the cooking sense, but he was indisputably a leader.

"*Vous voyez*, my husband once played in the orchestra of the Opéra de Paris. However, that's where the problem started. He became enamoured of a certain soprano, and before long they became lovers. He used to go to her dressing-room in that special half hour before the curtain rises. She considered that *l'amour* made her sing particularly well. Can you imagine, making love then? They did it, with her in full costume and make-up. He used to find it very exciting. So exciting that he left home after a performance of *Tosca* in which she played the leading role. I can't bear to hear Puccini any more."

It seemed unfair to blame Puccini, but I comforted her by saying, "I can understand that, madame. It must have been a great shock to you."

Wishing to remain on the subject of music, I continued, "How about concerts, symphonies, *concerti*, do you appreciate them still?"

"Oh indeed, yes. I adore Brahms, Beethoven and Bach. None of this modern work, though, I can't abide Stravinsky, not that his odious works are played much here. Do you like modern music?" she asked me.

"I share your love of the three great composers beginning with B. Daddy has introduced Stravinsky to me, so I didn't really find his music odd. He told me the story of the ballet *Petrouchka* before I heard the music, so I suppose it made more sense. But some modern music is very difficult, I agree."

"How did you manage to sit through concerts if you didn't always enjoy them?" asked *Grand-mère*.

"I never thought about it very much, as I enjoyed watching my father at his work. But when the music was really awful, I used to count the organ pipes in the Sydney Town Hall. I knew the music would stop eventually, because the musicians would have to go home. It's an amusing way of coping, don't you think?"

"I like your attitude," she said, "but unfortunately you won't be hearing any music during your stay. For one thing, there's no electricity at the chateau, and although we had that beautiful gramophone, when my records got broken, I gave it away."

Grand-mère seemed particularly friendly after our talk, and often used to ask me about my life in Sydney.

Madame came out thinking I might need rescuing, but looked rather pleased that we were getting on so well.

The children were happy and passably well behaved. Madame was consistent. "If they are naughty, smack them. Never let them get away with grammatical errors, either, none of this *vous disez* instead of *vous dîtes*. Remember that I forbid rudeness at all times. Be strong with them and they will respect you," she advised on the very first day.

"Can we go to the park?" asked Robert.

"I don't see why not, do you mean the Parc de Versailles?"

We went, taking *un bon goûter* of chocolate, *petits pains* and a bottle of milk for the baby. I pushed the pram while the others followed along beside or gambolled in front of me.

Near the entrance gates were brightly coloured vans festooned with balloons where ice cream vendors encouraged clusters of hopeful children.

"No ice creams. Your mother has given me a picnic for you. Don't keep asking."

There was a hurdy-gurdy man under the shade of a huge tree. His intriguing device played music by Chopin, and delighted groups of hand-clapping children were gathering around him. It was amusing to realise that the children lost no enthusiasm whether the music changed to a funeral march or a polonaise. We wandered over to join them because Philippe said the hurdy-gurdy man usually had a little monkey with him.

The monkey was dressed in a romper suit with a rather incongruous Charlie Chaplin hat on its head. The children clapped as the tiny creature came around to take coins from their hands. We didn't have any money, so Monette began to whine. Robert, just seven, slapped her on the arm and she started to cry.

"You dare!" he shouted in a voice of great authority. She stopped crying and wiped her eyes on the skirt of her dress, took my hand and then laughed at the monkey as if nothing had upset her.

I was heartened that they seemed such agreeable children who played happily, chasing one another around while I sat on a park bench to rest.

To miss Versailles is to miss one of the most beautiful sights in the world. My great regret is that I was unable to explore my surroundings with any eye for detail, as the children were so energetic it took all my attention just to keep them with me. This was my first experience of having children in my sole charge and I was nervous lest they become lost.

The park itself was breathtaking, with its smartly trimmed hedges; its mathematically ordered beds of perfect plants in a variety of spectacular colours; its manicured lawns, lavish fountains, tiny footpaths and immense trees. Even from the outside, the main chateau was vast and impressive.

As well as the miniature chateau Le Petit Trianon, a short distance away by the lake was the charming Hameau de Trianon, known as La Maison de la Reine. It was fascinating to see this cosier, homelier building where Marie Antoinette used to enjoy what she referred to as 'simple country living'. It was the kind of simplicity I could find more than satisfactory, I considered.

Philippe was the rascal who climbed to the top of an oak tree, hanging upside down and waving to us, frightening me nearly out of my wits lest he fall and break his neck. Just as I had persuaded him to come down, Robert climbed into one of the fountains, jumping up and down, encouraging Monette to join him.

I parked the pram safely under the shade of a tree, ran over to the fountain pool, pulled out the drenched boy and was about to congratulate Monette for being a good girl when she sat on the side, laughed gaily, then lost her balance and fell in.

We had set out quite late, around half past four. I had not taken my watch but imagined it to be around six when I summoned them for our return home via the exit gate.

To my horror, it was locked. A notice informed us: "Closed at 19.00 on Mondays." It was obviously much later than I thought.

Panic filled me. The children were whining and hungry for their supper. I searched anxiously, hoping to find a keeper to let us out. I traced a hosepipe enthusiastically, imagining it might lead to a gardener watering the beds, but found to my dismay that it led merely to a fixed sprinkler.

Monette yelled out, "Look, there's a man at the other side of the gate. Let's all shout to him for help." Without awaiting my reply, she led the others into a screaming match of "*Au secours!*"

The man on the other side of the gate called back. "What's the matter? Can't you find your way out? Are you locked inside?"

When we shouted our reply, he said, "I'll go and fetch the *gardien*. He'll let you out. Don't worry!"

Madame had come across the road towards the park, looking for us, and appeared just as we were being escorted out of the specially unlocked exit with a gruff keeper shaking his finger at me.

"*Ma pauvre petite*," she defended me, reached into her handbag and giving the angry keeper a tip. He walked away contentedly and she gave me a hug. "*Ne vous en faites pas.* I should have warned you, it is early closing on a Monday. Usually they stay open until nine."

I was relieved she was not in the least bit cross, but glad to see her children climbing all over her and shouting excitedly what fun it had been. She wasn't even vexed about the wet clothing. Baby Henri yelled relentlessly, as it was well past the time for his next bottle.

The journey to Brittany by train was exciting. Madame's main preoccupation was the perpetual need to keep us all together, holding the baby firmly on her hip, grateful that Monsieur had joined us.

If Madame were a Botticelli painting, then Paul de la Chapelle was Clark Gable. I found him a devastatingly handsome man, perhaps five years older than Madame. He treated her as if she were a queen, spoke to her with great kindness and affection, and managed to control the children despite their habitual excitement at being so briefly reunited with him.

A farmer with a small van met us at the train and carried our bags. He assured Monsieur that the *deux chevaux*, which they regularly used in summer, would be ready the following day. He apologised, "Please accept the inconvenience of travelling in my van today."

We clambered into the uncomfortable conveyance, an unpleasant odour greeting us.

Philippe exclaimed, "Pig swill, is that the smell? Is that what you had in here this morning?"

His mother rebuked him. "Don't make a fuss. Just be grateful we don't have to walk the five kilometres with our luggage."

The chateau stood on a gentle slope, both imposing and dis-integrating, strange combination as it seemed. The rugged stones of its exterior were old and crumbling. Monsieur told me that generations of his family had lived here since the fifteenth century, although parts of the building had needed reconstruc-tion over the years.

There was a pretty tower to the right which Madame told me was a *pigeonnier*, a dovecote. White doves still nested inside it, and Monette and Robert rushed towards it, declaring they would play hide and seek.

Madame told them this was not the moment for games, and to wait until we had settled in.

The stone framed windows of the chateau contained segments of glass, as opposed to actual windows, many of which were cracked or completely broken. The interior walls had been white-washed unevenly and the distemper was peeling around the doorways. The ceiling of exposed beams led to an attic with few floorboards. A hazardous cast-iron spiral stairway spindled its way upstairs to five bedrooms.

The kitchen, with its old coal-burning stove, a stone sink with cold running water and a large scrubbed wooden table in the centre of a cobble-stoned floor, was just as it must have been hundreds of years ago. There were eight chairs surrounding the immense rickety table. Copper pots grown green with time and lack of polish hung from hooks on the ceiling and a bucket of coal stood beside the stove. The ventilation was provided by a small broken window above the sink.

"Welcome to our chateau," said Madame, beginning to unpack provisions for our late lunch. Her mother had prepared us a sumptuous collection of *charcuterie* and six fresh baguettes, cheese, olives, butter and two bottles of red wine. There was fresh lemonade for the children.

"We're having a picnic!" shouted Robert, clapping his hands with delight. A merry meal continued well into the afternoon after which the children dispersed to explore and the baby went to sleep.

It was in this kitchen that I unexpectedly received my first experience of sexual awakening. I was standing at the sink peeling the vegetables for the evening meal. Madame was in the garden playing with the children, when I felt two hands encapsulate my waist. They slid gradually up to stroke my breasts, as Monsieur kissed my neck gently, then directed my hands to the front of his unzipped trousers, inviting me to stroke him.

It was extremely exciting, forbidden, enticing, amazing and scary as he turned my face towards him and kissed me passionately. Then, hearing the voices of the children, he ran and quickly sat down on the sofa in the next room, hiding himself behind a copy of *Le Figaro*. As he left he said breathlessly, "There will be many other opportunities, *ma petite*, do not fear," his voice hoarse with lust and urgency.

I remained at the sink, preparing the vegetables as though nothing had happened, but inside I was overcome with emotion. What a terrible thing to have allowed him to do. The worst thing was that I rather enjoyed it, and had wanted him to continue. Then my Catholic upbringing brought home to me the realisation of the sinful deed I had committed.

That evening, ashamed and embarrassed, I went to my room after dinner and burst into tears. Madame must have known what had happened, for she followed me in.

"Do not feel embarrassed about Paul. He cannot help himself. The moment he sees an attractive woman, whatever her age, he cannot resist temptation. I will tell you what to do. Go ahead if you like, discover what it is to enjoy sex, for my husband is a fabulous lover. I do not mind, but be careful. It would be a tragedy for you at your young age either to fall in love with him or to fall pregnant. It would be a terrible responsibility and I would feel I had played a part in it by agreeing to your behaviour. What I mean is, it would not hurt my feelings. There is much I have to tell you. Tomorrow I will arrange for Paul to take the oldest children fishing. You and I will stay behind, with the baby." She hugged me and assured me she understood everything. "*À demain*," she said, leaving the room.

The next morning, as planned, Monsieur took the boys and Monette fishing, Madame declined his invitation for us to join him. Cooking tasks beckoned, she explained.

"Have you had any experience of sex?" she asked, coming straight to the point.

"No. Heavens, no. The nuns were very strange about anything concerning our bodies, almost denying they existed. But there was one girl who became my friend who did tell me some rather amazing things. Nothing ever happened to me until last night."

Madame sat down at the kitchen table. Beside her was a pan of peas to be shelled. She handed them to me, walked over to the stove, quickly made us both a cup of coffee, then settled down again. " Let me tell you all about it then, *ma fille*. Some men seem to need more sexual comfort than others. My husband is one of them. He adores women. His needs have changed the course of our family's life. You see, his posting was to India, where he works under permanent contract. He has not lived there alone, as you can now imagine, for these past five years." She looked extremely sad and I thought she had finished all that she wished to tell me. But I was fascinated by the story and hoped she would continue.

"It did not take him long to find a beautiful native girl. They made love, and before long, she became pregnant. Knowing that his tour of duty was to be for ten years, and that he loved her, he decided he would make her his wife there."

"But, Madame, what of you and your marriage?" I asked dumbfounded.

She smiled wistfully before replying. "Everything is all right now. I am not telling you this from self-pity. It is a relief to talk about it, but I think you will understand the situation better if you know the truth. He has three children now, over there, by Leila, such a pretty name. From her photographs I can see that she is a lovely woman. She is faithful to him and cares for him well. At least while he is in her care, he does not seem to be getting up to any other mischief."

"Did he tell you about it himself?"

"Not of his own accord. I found a photo of a beautiful woman and two children when I was checking his uniform pockets before sending it to the cleaner's. I asked him who they were. He looked very much like a child who had been found out. First he hugged me, told me he loved me, then he explained how it had all come about."

"*Ma pauvre Madame*," I said, touching her on the shoulder.

"Yes, and no, and I thank you for your concern. I am only telling you this because I know he finds you very pretty and would like to make love to you. It would not, however, be a good idea for you. It would not make me jealous but I would be concerned for you as a young girl in my care. I have my four children and, God forgive me, I see to it that there will not be a fifth. I go to confession after we have used the devices, and tell the priest it is necessary for me. It is a silly business, this Catholic belief in natural family planning. No wonder half the world is starving. I look after myself."

She looked totally serene as she said this, not remotely as if she were the injured wife.

"Now," she said, "I will show you how to cook a wonderful lobster dish."

Lobsters were plentiful and inexpensive, bought from the market close to Concarneau and just a few kilometres from the chateau. We brought them home and they squealed in their wicker baskets in the back of the little *deux chevaux*, crammed with children and provisions, Monsieur driving as if without a care in the world.

"But how do we cook them?" I asked.

"It's a question of courage," she said with a wry smile. "You have to decide, is it better to boil up a pot of water and hurl the poor things immediately into it, so that they die quickly? Or will you put them in a cold pot where, unaware of their fate, death will come upon them slowly, without realisation?" She crossed her fingers for hope as she made the last remark. "That is what I usually do."

She took two lobsters, put them into an empty saucepan and poured cold water into it from the tap, putting them on the stove and beckoning to me. "Now, don't laugh either," and she took me by the hand, closing the door after her, turning the key as she left and putting it into the pocket of her professional apron.

"Why the key?" I asked, amazed but laughing too, and feeling very sorry for the lobsters.

"You never really know what they might do in revenge, do you?" she replied.

Madame had a girlish smile, a sense of fun, and it was as if none of the sorrow she must have endured affected her now. She treated me as if I were a beloved older daughter and set about the business of teaching me the domestic skills which had been lacking in my upbringing.

Before long, I learned to make *mousse au chocolat*, several types of *risotto*, a very good curry, assisted by Monsieur—his arm around me, a kiss on my neck, but nothing more. Perhaps Madame had spoken with him.

Madame specialised in superb *coq au vin*, *moules marinières*, a wonderful creation with chestnut purée, and endless batches of meringues. The baby had an egg yolk added to his cereal each day, so whites were plentiful. Madame made the preparation of each meal a pleasure and its consummation a joy.

"I'm going to ask a very special favour of you, now that you are such a good cook," she said, to my great surprise.

I expected we were to have some kind of dinner party, such as Stepmother might have held in Sydney. But there were never any visitors at the chateau.

"As this time is so precious to me and Monsieur, I am going to ask you if you will look after the children here by yourself for a week, so we can have some time alone together."

I was amazed at the request, realising Madame was unaware that I had only just turned seventeen. She probably assumed I was eighteen, as I attended the Institut. I did not dare to tell her, remembering my recent promise to the director that I would reveal my age to nobody.

"You may refuse if the idea frightens you, but you are very capable, the children adore you, and I will give you my mother's number in Versailles, and my sister's. They would come here if anything went wrong."

"And may I contact you if there is a problem?" I asked, anxiously.

"No. The idea is for us to have a complete holiday from the responsibilities of the family. This is the only month each year I see Paul, and I feel at a disadvantage as Leila has him eleven times as long. Would you be kind enough to render us this service?"

There really seemed to be no choice. I agreed, reluctantly, filled with fear lest something terrible should happen to the children in her absence. With as much enthusiasm as I could muster, remembering my mother's farewell to me, I reassured the children that we would have fun. We clustered around the door to wave the parents goodbye.

The idea of coping alone was terrifying. Four children. The baby still in nappies and requiring a bottle, spoon feeding and total attention, particularly now he was crawling. Madame managed to do everything with him in her arms, securely nestled in by her left hip, her left arm holding onto him while her right arm was free to do the cooking. I was glad that I had observed her so carefully. There were so many things which might go wrong. I was terribly worried.

"Can we go on excursions while our parents are away?" asked Philippe, the eldest.

"Only if you make yourself responsible," I challenged him.

We went to Mont St Michel by coach, the five of us, scrambling into a little ferry at high tide and planning to walk back to it, with Henri in his push chair, later when it was low tide. An English couple on the boat were intrigued by the sight of us.

As little children will, Monette always called me, 'Maman', and there was a vibrant exchange of conversation amongst us as we crossed the water. The children shrieked with delight at the lapping of waves and the occasional splash of foam into the boat.

"Oh look, James, that poor young woman, she can't be more than twenty, and she already has four children. These Frenchmen really are quite disgusting!"

As we disembarked, I smiled at them both. "As a matter of fact," I replied, also in English, "I am only seventeen!" I could not resist it. The look of horror on their faces was most amusing. The excursion had been a success, the children were totally exhausted and ready to go to bed. Only six more days to go.

The following day the baby fell against the leg of a chair on the kitchen floor and split his head open. There was blood everywhere and I was sure he was going to die. I had no idea how it had happened and was shaking at the thought that everything was now up to me. My feet propelled me forward faster than my thoughts as the poor little mite screamed with pain and fear. Monette stopped playing at the sink, Philippe pushed Robert over as he dashed across to see if he could help.

"Philippe," I ordered, "You are in charge. Collect your brother and sister immediately. Follow me."

Startled by the urgency in my voice as I picked up the baby, cradling his head, wrapping the wound in a makeshift bandage of two teatowels, the children rushed with me to the house on the hill. The chateau was within a small hamlet, not even a village, what the French call a '*lieu dit*', which means simply a 'designated place'. There were only five houses within a kilometre. I chose the closest. It was quite a long walk, and I had no idea who lived there, what reception I might receive, or whether anybody would be at home.

I knocked at the door and a woman answered. I said breathlessly, "Please look after the children for me. The baby has cut his head. I have to take him to the hospital. I'll be back as soon as I can. Sorry we haven't met you before and that I don't know your name, Madame. This is an emergency."

The neighbour, who apparently had never spoken either to Monsieur or Madame, was stupefied. Ten years previously she had come to the conclusion that they were nobility and above her station. However, she instantly accepted her role of guardian angel, hurrying the children to the kitchen to help her to prepare some food, as she said undoubtedly they would be needing some lunch.

The twice-a-day bus was dragging itself up the steep hill so slowly that I was able to run after it, waving and screaming, "*Au secours!*" The driver must have looked in the mirror and seen me stumbling up the hill with the baby in my arms, trying to attract his attention. He reversed the bus down the hill towards me so I would not have to run so far, and one of the passengers, a cheerful young man, helped me up the steep step with the baby.

"To the hospital," I told the driver, realising I had not as much as a coin in my pocket and no purse. He generously dismissed the need for money, gesticulating excitedly which made me fear for our safety, his hands were off the wheel for so long. Once we arrived in the town, he directed me efficiently and in detail the shortest route from the bus stop to the hospital. "*Bon courage*," he added.

The baby's head wound required four stitches. A solicitous doctor checked him thoroughly and kept us for a couple of hours to rule out concussion. He did not initially consider an X-ray necessary, but after what appeared to be an argument in the background, it was decided that this was essential. To my great relief, there was no hint of a skull fracture. The baby was smiling but I was crying from anxiety and relief. As soon as the result was known, a nurse warmed up some milk for Henri and gave him a bottle, cuddling him and saying how lucky I was to have such a beautiful baby. I laughed and explained the situation. She reached into her pocket and brought out an apple which she gave me.

"You have been here for four hours so you must be ravenous. Here, take this, I am sorry but it is all I have."

As I thanked her, she hurried to boil up a kettle, prepared me some instant coffee, then excused herself as another patient had arrived in casualty.

Decades later I would have need to call upon the services of the French health system many times. Although the government had almost broken their budget on health, the facilities were excellent. Private insurance was unnecessary as legal residents were covered for all medical care. You paid the general practitioner for his services, about one hundred francs for a visit to his surgery, and then reclaimed 75 per cent of this from the government offices. If you required a home visit—and in country areas these were made willingly—you paid 20 per cent more. Most consultations were around thirty to forty minutes and doctors were numerous. A visit to a specialist was quickly arranged, and hospital admission was uncomplicated. Patients with spinal injuries were transported, for safety, by private ambulance, also paid for by the state.

A couple of curiosities existed. The hospital charged fifty francs per day for meals, and served a quarter litre of wine with lunch and dinner, and you had to provide your own towels. Most hospitals had single-room-only facilities, on the grounds that patients did not like sharing, although old hospitals had only shared bathroom facilities. These were updated gradually from the 1990s onward, with *en suites* for each room. The standard of health care was certainly equal to that in Australia and in far better shape than the National Health Service in Britain.

By the late afternoon we were back with the neighbour, who was reading stories to the children. She made me a cup of hot chocolate, gave me a baguette with jam and said if I needed her she would always be happy to help us.

"*Ces petits*, they are beautifully behaved, and so amusing," she told me and I felt proud of them, taking the compliment upon myself. She even walked us home, "to be sure the little ones are all right".

Monette now slept in my room, spoke often in her sleep, and would awake crying, need reassurance, and snuggle into my bed with me. One night I heard her little voice beside me, "Don't worry, I am here. Don't be afraid," and it was her turn to comfort me. I'd been having a vivid nightmare that Monsieur and Madame would never return, but of course I said nothing about it to the children.

When I took the children to church on the Sunday, Monette kept grabbing at my skirt to attract my attention. Hushing her was useless, so I bent down to ask her what the matter was. She pointed to two loudspeakers in the corners of the church. The sermon was on full throttle, the priest absorbed in his lengthy discourse. "Look, look!" she cried vehemently, determined that everybody in the church should know. "It's *le bon Dieu* trapped in those boxes and he is trying to get out."

Even the more staid members of the congregation could not prevent themselves from laughing. I told her not to worry, God was safe and sound and it was only the priest's voice in the boxes. She was unwilling to accept my explanation.

When the week was over, I breathed a huge sigh of relief as I saw Monsieur and Madame puttering towards the chateau in their little *deux chevaux*. We all embraced each other. Tears rolled down my cheeks as Monsieur and Madame expressed their gratitude and thanked me for allowing them to spend seven precious days together. Monsieur brought flowers for me and chocolate for the children. There was a spirited clamour of reunited voices. The following morning Monsieur returned to his overseas posting. We all went by train together to Paris where the children hugged and kissed him and pleaded with him to stay. It was very sad. Madame had tears in her eyes for most of our bus journey to Versailles.

There were only two weeks of the school holidays remaining. *Grand-mère* was pleased to see us, spoiling us with every delicacy she could muster and begging us to tell her about every minute of our time at the chateau. Madame appeared to settle back into her life alone and the boys were eager to return to school and their friends. Monette was looking forward to her first day at the *école maternelle*.

The merriest months I had spent in France were coming to an end. In that short time Madame had taught me much about love, and by her example I had experienced the warmth and solicitude of a family who found the best in each other, despite what others might have considered intolerable odds. The idea that this special family would no longer be part of my life was very sad. It was time to move on again, because it seemed the only sensible thing to do. Dr Thompson would take me to Oxford within the next week. Madame promised to write but, as I had no address to give her, I promised to send her a postcard and to keep in touch.

We did lose touch for a few years, but once we regained contact, we have corresponded at least four times a year. Her children are now grown up. Monsieur predeceased her, having taken early retirement at the age of fifty-five, so they enjoyed some fifteen years of happiness as a united family. Now the proud grand-mother of nine little ones, she sees them regularly, still spending summers in Brittany but wintering in a small studio apartment in Versailles. She suffers from terrible arthritis and writes a great deal about her pain and loneliness. Our letters are a comfort to us both. To me they are particularly sweet for they have brought continuity to a life that had hitherto experienced many departures and the loss of friends I had held dear.

OXFORD

My first sight of Oxford, with its magnificent colleges, elegant church spires and sense of history, appealed to me greatly. Students bustled around the town on their bicycles, some wrapped quaintly in academic cloaks which flapped in the wind, whilst others rushed efficiently about on foot or stood chatting together in sheltered doorways. There was a liveliness, a sense of purpose and an energy which I responded to and longed to join.

As promised, Dr Thompson had arranged for a Catholic family to offer me bed, breakfast and dinner. They had another lodger too, a priest, who intimidated me greatly at first but later broke the ice by telling wicked Irish jokes at dinner. Although the family were not amused, I considered them very funny. I was to pay for my room as soon as I secured a job. They said they could manage for a month until I was organised. My adult life was beginning. Although only just seventeen, I felt very grown up and excited.

Beech Lawn Tutorial College had accepted me as a student.

Through them I would be able to take the Oxford Board exams and then University Entrance. I really wanted to obtain a degree, probably in French, but I had no particular idea as to what else might interest me. As long as it ultimately secured me a passage back to Australia, I would be completely happy. As I needed to earn money, I would attend lectures and tutorials only part-time. The challenge appealed to me.

One of the colleges required a part-time secretary. I was interviewed and accepted the job. With some deft juggling of my schedule afforded by the flexibility of my tutors, I was able to fulfil all my obligations. I enjoyed everything about my new life.

My college secretarial work demanded unusual feats of planning and discretion, for my employer was the bursar, a woman who enjoyed her whisky. The solution was for me to arrive as early as possible, do my work before lunch and bring it to her for discussion and signatures prior to the striking of the midday bells. For that was when the bottle came out, and her exceptional efficiency of the morning was rapidly transformed into a sea of disastrous confusion.

This was my first experience of a person out of control from alcohol. Its effect upon her usually quicksilver wit and clever use of language was frightening. Her steps became staggered, her speech slurred and she used Spoonerisms amusingly, without realising—'mattending to the ail', instead of 'attending to the mail', 'sooting on the pamp' for 'putting on the stamp'—rendering communication difficult.

I studied Russian with Lydia Slater, the sister of Boris Pasternak whose work had recently received much attention through the publication of the controversial novel *Doctor Zhivago*. The lessons were informal and unusual, with afternoon tea around a massive samovar, conversation rather than grammar. Being with Mrs Slater and her children gave me the impression of living in a different era, perhaps even in Tsarist Russia.

Other subjects that made up my self-imposed curriculum were French, maths, biology, and English literature, so that I could sit for University Entrance, as my former education had afforded me no recognised school leaving certificates.

Luck brought me to the examiners' attention and I won a scholarship to Somerville College to study French and Russian. Such scholarships were means-tested. I supposed there would be no problem, as I had no parent present to contribute. The position that had brought Dr Thompson to Oxford involved considerable medical research. Unfortunately, this necessitated his departure to America as the source of finance was an American drug company. Research money in England was very scarce. He took me to a farewell dinner in an Indian restaurant. Knowing that he was leaving made me feel so forlorn that I could scarcely eat. His encouragement of my plans and his words of praise for all I had achieved were a comfort, yet once more I felt totally alone. He promised to write.

It seemed to me, once more, that someone who had cared for me and for whom I had cared was going to disappear, probably forever, as indeed was the case. He might have written, but if he did the letters never reached me. I had learned from previous experience that letters did not always arrive and it did not always mean one was forgotten. But we lost touch, and one more of the foundations which held me together was pulled from under me. This feeling has made me act impulsively over many years, seeking love and understanding.

I had received no letters from my father, even though I had written to him many times after Stepmother had told me of that wretched scandal in Sydney. Perhaps he had never received my letters. Perhaps he had already left Wahroonga. All I could do was to keep on doing my best academically and saving money so as to return home to Australia as soon as I could.

There were other unexpected hurdles to overcome. Unknown to me, my father, forced to leave Sydney in 1956, had arrived eventually in London. It came as a shock to him to receive a letter from the university, care of his publishers, requesting him to meet one third of my scholarship fees. It was some weeks before I was to learn how unwelcome this request must have been. I had no notion of his present financial circumstances. In the past, he had supposedly earned more than the prime minister in Australia.

It was not until I read Carole Rosen's book in 1993 that I learned of my father's poverty, of his great financial loss, of his inability to obtain the work that he deserved. This was very humbling, and I so wished that I had been more grown up, or that people had spoken to me as an adult and allowed me to understand how hard things were for him. Only then could I have been a comfort to him in some small way. It was sad that neither he nor any other family member was able to discuss our finances as they really were. There was always an air of pretence, as if everything was all right. Keeping up appearances. I have never believed in that; within a close family circle I would prefer honesty and frank disclosure. I discovered later how much my father had suffered from the Sydney scandal and how his musical career, not only in Australia but in England, was ruined. His only engagements were in eastern Europe, bar the occasional concert in England itself. Such a tragedy, such a waste. How he must have suffered.

When I finally learned of his refusal to pay that small portion of my fees, I found it difficult to understand. I was extremely angry, as if the unfairness of having a parent suddenly outweighed any possible advantage. He had not been there when I needed him, and now his arrival in England threatened my hope of a better life. What I would have to do was learn to make the most of things, to work out how to gain an education without his help, as I had done hitherto.

Of the events surrounding my father's misfortune, I knew nothing. The university had given him my address and I was confused and upset when he wrote to invite me to visit him at his rented St John's Wood flat. Arriving at the imposing building, going straight to his expansive lounge room, the setting, if not scrutinised with care, belied his circumstances.

He greeted me warmly, giving me the sort of hug I had loved

as a child. But he had no strength in his arms. "It's lovely to see you again. I am sorry that I can't help out with your scholarship," he said hurriedly, adding, "things have not turned out too well for me."

"I'm really sorry about that, Daddy," I said, hoping he would explain more, so that we could discuss my scholarship seriously. I wanted to see if I could make him change his mind about it.

Instead he continued, as if not really listening, "I hear you no longer study music."

Did I note a glimmer of disappointment in his voice? I could not help wondering whether it might have made a difference. His voice was thin, so unlike the confident, powerful and important tone I remembered from Sydney.

"I couldn't study music in the convent in France. It was dreadful to be in a world where music was never played, no instruments, no radio, no records, no concerts. It was something I found very difficult to get used to."

"So, are you going to start your instruments again?" he asked with more interest, but apparently unable to grasp the emptiness of what I had just told him.

"Daddy, I have no money, except that which I earn myself. I don't know many people here, and it isn't as simple as that. It's quite a different world from Sydney and I don't feel part of it at all. My French and Russian are going well, and I hope you will be proud of me."

He gave me a great bear hug, but once again it had an empty feel to it.

"Things are very different for me, too, little one."

In the large, high-ceilinged and cold rooms, he looked like a stranger who did not belong. I began to take notice of the flat and to see that it was poorly furnished and not very clean.

"Stay the night and come to a concert with me at the Royal Albert Hall. It's the wonderful young German baritone Dietrich Fischer-Dieskau. A recital. *Lieder*. It's a stunning programme. He'll be one of the world's greatest singers in a few years. Come and be part of that legend. I've been given free seats by an old friend."

We had never paid for seats to concerts. The idea seemed odd now, that Daddy should ever have to pay. I was glad he had a friend who could let him have free tickets.

"We shall eat at the Colonnade. It's an old family hotel. The food is a bit dreary, but it's reliable. They never serve a bad meal. I have an account there and I think you will like it. We can get taxis around, save getting cold on the tube. You have a bit of a cough, haven't you?" he enquired, concern in his voice.

"I've had this cough for weeks, can't seem to shake it off. All I need is some sunshine." We smiled at each other in agreement, as if we dreamed together of Sydney again.

Daddy helped me into my student duffel coat, second-hand from Oxfam. He pulled down a woollen scarf from a peg in the hall, went to put it around his neck, then lovingly put it around mine instead. I reached up and kissed him on both cheeks, tears rolling down mine as I did so. How could I possibly be cross with him? He was certainly more sinned against than sinning, I thought.

"This is all very strange, isn't it, little one?" His voice reflected his sadness and aloneness.

"Do you think we will be able to go back to Australia soon?" I asked.

"I've had a really bad time there. I loved it and wanted to dedicate myself to the new Opera House, you know the site I wanted was finally chosen, but they were taking so long to organise it." He broke off from what he was saying, looking as if he was thinking about something else, and muttered sadly, almost to himself, "I had thought people respected me."

"Daddy, they did! You had so many friends in the orchestra who adored you, and your diploma students. Surely it will be all right again soon. Surely people don't change."

"Things happened that I don't want to discuss, or to worry you about. But I don't think I am going to be able to go back there. Not for a long time, anyway. You, my little one, would find the atmosphere very changed."

"I'd like to know what happened, Daddy. It would help me to understand what you're going through."

"I'm no good at talking about personal things. Leave it at that. Things will work out."

Daddy had never been one to discuss personal matters, nor had anyone in his family, his brothers and sisters had kept their discussions, in front of me in any event, to musical matters, to the weather, but never to relationships or sorrows, joys or pleasures. It was as if they were unable to communicate at that level. It was many years before I had the pleasure of knowing my Aunt Sidonie more closely, but even then she was reluctant to refer to the scandal. Certainly she had no wish for the matter to be 'dragged up again', and when I did ask questions, they were politely rebuffed.

I felt a sympathy and a closeness to him such as I had not experienced before. However, he never wished to discuss the scandal, and I learned not to ask. It meant we had a further immense gap in our relationship. I could not understand his position, and he did not wish to share his problems with me, nor did he seem to have any concept of what he was causing me to lose. Compared to his loss, of course, it was nothing. For I had my youth and my health.

Beneath my desire to understand his problems, however, there burnt a rage that his arrival in the UK (meaning that I had a parent who could be held responsible for me) and his new-found poverty was depriving me of my university scholarship. Although I felt ashamed at my anger, it seethed and caused a great unhappiness and resentment to well up within me. He seemed to have forgotten our discussion, as if everything was all right. We were playing what I had remembered while I was so lonely in France as the 'happy famous family photos' sessions.

Even back at Wahroonga between 1949 and 1954, when Stepmother and Father had been leading totally separate lives, we would be assembled, with Donie, for photographs for the newspapers and journals, to show what a happy famous family we were. Now we were neither happy nor famous, and we had ceased to be a family a long time ago.

The Royal Albert Hall recital attracted a full house. It was my first visit to that beautiful concert hall, although I knew my family had performed there for decades.

Unfortunately for me, Daddy's friend had given us seats in the second row centre, which brought us into immediate view of the singer. This should have been ideal, until my cough took hold. Once I began, I could not stop, using Daddy's scarf to muffle the loudness, almost choking with the effort of silencing my barking sounds.

At interval, Daddy said we were going to see Mr Fischer-Dieskau. As we walked into the green room, he rushed forward and shook Daddy by both hands.

"Sir Eugene, so kind of you to come to my recital."

To my eternal mortification he turned to me, "And this little lady, she is your daughter, no? And with a very bad cough." He smiled and addressed me directly, "I will give you a pastille to suck. It will help the soreness in your throat."

He handed me a Zube, then changed his mind and gave me the whole packet.

I was speechless with embarrassment, then, remembering my manners said, "Forgive me. Your wonderful recital is being spoilt by my coughing. Would you prefer that I did not return to the hall?"

He smiled again, his young round face friendly and enthusiastic. "The most important thing for a singer is to have an audience. It is not your fault you have a cough. Please go back to your seat now, and forget your embarrassment."

He asked his pianist to fetch a glass of water, gave it to me, and also poured himself some water, taking a separate glass. I supposed he was afraid of catching my germs.

The treatment must have worked, for I did not cough even once during the rest of the programme. At the end of the performance, he came forward to take a bow, and his special smile first to my father and then to me is amongst my most treasured memories.

Although I had no choice but to accept that Daddy could not contribute towards my fees, I was devastated. I resented the fact that he had returned to London. Why could he not have remained out of contact like my mother, so that I could have been considered an orphan for the purposes of the scholarship? I had been without parents, so it seemed, for most of my adolescent life, so why had he appeared now? I wished him away, angry and disappointed and unable to come to terms with the unfairness of it all. And yet, inside my heart, I was deeply ashamed for feeling that way.

I would have to recover from this resentment, I knew, for I also wanted to try to get to know my father. Fortunately I was able, as the months went by, to value the occasional times he would invite me to see him in London, always generously remembering to enclose thirty shillings for my fare and expenses. As it wasn't going to be possible for me to go to Somerville College now, I could see no recourse but to abandon my studies.

When I found a full-time position as a secretary, my income became more respectable. Various advertisements in the *Oxford Times* offered flats too costly or bed-sitting-rooms too squalid. Under the heading 'Share Accommodation' was a phone number answered by a girl with a delightful Welsh accent. Her name was Bronwyn Thomas, she was a hairdresser's assistant, and she agreed to interview me.

The flat was in The Cornmarket, close to St Giles Church, above the hairdressing salon.

"I'll wait for you outside because the shop will be closed, so don't be late, seven o'clock, if you can manage it." Her voice sounded very confident.

"How will I know you?" I asked.

"You know the way people recognise each other in spy movies?" she asked. "Why don't I carry something, I know . . . a magazine, it's a glossy and it's called *Hair*."

Her idea appealed to me. When we met she shook my hand and hurried me inside, away from the cold.

Bronwyn was a tall, slim girl with a perfect figure. Her shoulder-length hair was pretty, brown and naturally curly, which I could tell because it had been drizzling and the rain made her hair kink upwards.

Bronwyn spoke in a high-pitched voice but she sounded very positive in her opinions as we closed the door behind us, leaving the noise of the traffic behind. Her acceptance would open a new door for me. Independence. For the first time, I would have a place almost my own, sharing with a person I had chosen rather than someone chosen for me.

"You always have to walk through the salon to get upstairs to my place, as there's only the one door. You'll find the smells from the shampoos pleasant, but the stuff they use in the bleach don't half knock you out. Right brings tears to me eyes," she told me, leading the way.

"It's a large space," I remarked, feeling rather out of place as we pushed chairs back on the chequerboard linoleum floor.

"Black and white is the theme this year, quite the rage. Last year it was yellow with pink. Absolutely frightful! Here we go, just fifteen stairs and you're home."

It was a chilly sitting-room, with an unlit gas fire in a brick chimney.

"Got any coins for the meter?" Bronwyn asked.

I shook my head.

"Never mind, I'll go down and rob petty cash. I do it all the time. As long as I leave an IOU note, Mrs Keffoops doesn't mind."

"Who on earth is she?" I asked, not believing the name.

"Of course that's not her name really, it's something foreign, Greek, I think, I never get it right, so to be polite, I usually just call her Mrs K. She'll have to check you out if you like it here, because it's her place, this flat. Not that it's much, but she always says it'll do her nicely if the old man don't treat her right."

I wasn't accustomed to grammar like that, but I liked Bronwyn's vivacity.

In the sitting-room, with its sagging sofa covered by a brightly coloured Indian bedspread, were two metal chairs with a plastic covering in pink and yellow.

"Left over from the salon disaster last year," she said as she showed me into one of the bedrooms.

"This one's mine. Don't mind the curtain, there isn't one, which is why that old grey blanket is hanging by a safety pin at the window. It keeps the cold out, and me mum's given me loads of warm blankets for the bed. Plenty for you, too, if you need any."

There was nothing else in the room apart from the bed, a heap of books on the floor and a bedside lamp without a shade. Cigarettes spilled over from an ashtray and a dirty mug of half-finished coffee stood on top of the books. All from the library, their shiny plastic protective covers revealed they were thrillers and romances.

We walked into a second bedroom.

"This is the better room. And of course there's no mess yet. It's nice to see a room before a person puts themself into it, I always think, but then on the other hand, it looks kind of lonely."

It was a larger room. The single bed had a patchwork quilt on it and there were pink and yellow curtains at the window, ceiling to floor in a pathetically thin fabric, protecting the interior from neither light nor cold. An old battered wooden school desk had a chair beside it, and the light globe in the ceiling had no shade. A small window gave onto the back of the adjoining building, but one could glimpse a pretty church close by.

"Where do you keep your clothes, blankets, towels and things?" I asked, surprised at the spartan arrangements.

"Don't laugh. I keep them all in the larder. There's hanging space where people used to keep brooms, just right for dresses and coats. Spare blankets can go under your mattress, and I've only got the two towels, one in use, one waiting to go to the laundrette. Anything else goes on the bottom shelf under the dried milk, baked beans and bread."

In the kitchen was an enamel sink with a filthy wooden draining board which had grown some kind of green mould. There was a rusting plate rack. For cooking there was a Baby Belling stove, just the one ring.

"Mrs K lets us have the electricity without extra charge. Same for the hot water. It's only the gas fire we need the coins for. Wait a mo, and I'll go get some money for it and we'll have a chat and try to warm up."

Before going downstairs Bronwyn filled an old metal kettle with water and placed it on the Belling ring. This gave me time to inspect the rest of the kitchen. On the table was an oilcloth, mercifully clean, in green and white check. Three chairs, a stool, and over the sink dangled greasy, yellowed muslin net curtains shielding us from the gaze of the flat opposite.

I opened the larder door and found it much as she had described, but cleaner than I had expected. It was particularly quaint to see a fur coat hanging beside the feather duster. Despite the shabbiness, the little flat had an airy of friendly homeliness about it.

A match was struck, Bronwyn lit both the fire and a cigarette, and brewed tea served in two cracked, tea-stained mugs from the sink. Some instant milk powder from a tin made nasty glutinous lumps on the edges.

"Don't you have a fridge?" I asked.

"Hardly needed here. It's always freezing in this flat. Anyway, where'd you put one? On the sink! Tiny, isn't it?" she observed.

I liked Bronwyn. She was straightforward and energetic. I could imagine she would be good company. And I would get used to the grammar, although I found it hard not to correct her.

"What do you like doing when you are not at work?" I asked.

"I go dancing with me boyfriend. He's called Thomas and I never call him Tom. From Wales too, so I only see him once a month when he comes by coach. You may have seen the fur coat. He gave it to me last Christmas. It used to be his gran's, but she died and his mum didn't want it, nor did his sister. It made them cry all the time, so he said I might as well have it. It's not smart, but ever so warm, I often put it over the bed."

This didn't explain what we might do together of an evening, with Thomas only coming once a month. She proceeded to tell me.

"I like to go to the cinema, listen to the wireless, the rest of the time I read. Do you like reading? There's ever such a good library at St Aldate's, just five minutes walk away. I adore it."

"But here's me going on about meself and never a word about you or whether you'd like to share. Do pardon me, I'm sure. The rent's ever so cheap, only £1 10s a week and I'd like to have you here. It'd be company. And after all, a home is just where you hang your hat, me mum says."

I told her about my new job as a secretary at a clinic where they treated children with problems.

"Just like we do here, only it's not official. Everybody's got problems, you can't imagine what they tell us!"

We smiled at each other. "I think I'd quite like it here, if your Mrs K says it's all right," I said.

Bronwyn told me about her plans to marry Thomas the following year and to have five babies, one every year. She loved hairdressing but wanted to have her own part-time business while the children were growing up. She planned to stay in Oxford until they married, and was saving up for a double bed for her old room. Her parents had said they could live with them at first. Every detail was planned.

I had to give a week's notice at my digs. I thanked them for their kindness and they wished me well. When Mrs K agreed to my tenancy, she told me there was just one condition. Our meeting had gone quite well, I had thought. But she had the same critical look in her eye I recalled from Stepmother, judging a book by its cover.

She looked me up and down. "You're a nice dresser, no doubt about that. But that plain and dreary hair! Dear child, you will be walking out of my salon every day, and coming in at night. What *will* people say with it looking like that? It's hardly an advertisement. You've got quite a pleasant face, nothing special, but you'd make a good model for the apprentices. You are to have your hair done here at least once a week. And you're to help out if we need you for modelling at the London shows. There'll be no charge, of course."

I must have winced, for she added, "There's many girls out there who'd give their eye teeth to have a free hairdo each week, so mind there's no complaining."

Mrs K bustled out then, as swift and breathless as her sentences.

The flat, despite its coldness, was a reasonable starting place and Bronny, as she asked me to call her, became a good friend. She never listened to music other than pop songs, had never attended a concert, but enjoyed some of the same movies as I did. It was lucky that the movie theatre was just three doors away, and the price most affordable.

I had no records or music of my own yet, but I listened to her radio when there was classical music on and she was working late. As long as I could listen to music occasionally, I was happy.

Being a secretary at the Child Guidance Clinic was my first full-time job and I loved every moment of it, looking forward to arriving in the morning, to welcoming the worried mothers and keeping the children entertained whilst they saw the psychiatrist and psychologist for whom I worked.

The consultant psychiatrist was beautifully spoken and extremely courteous, but left me in no doubt as to who was the boss. My first meeting with him had been amusing.

I had found an advertisement in the *Oxford Times*: 'Wanted:

Grandpa Goossens (Eugene II)
the family patriarch

Photographed in New York
in 1945, aged four

Arrival in Sydney, 1947. From left: Donie, my father, me, Marjorie

My mother, Janet, as Flora. Photographed in New York by my father.

My stepmother Marjorie.
Photograph: Max Dupain

My father when
conductor of the Sydney
Symphony Orchestra

Donie, the youngest
member of the Sydney
Symphony Orchestra, 1947

My father in front of the house at
Wahroonga. The window to his study is
immediately on his left. My stepmother's
rooms were in another wing of the house
on the right.

With Donie and my stepmother in the
garden at Wahroonga

A new student at the
Conservatorium of
Music, 1952

*"OH, WHAT A LOVELY
DAY!" sighed 12-year-
old RENEE GOOSSENS
at the Town Hall last
night. "Swimming in
the morning and two
concerts in the one day."
Renee, who is a student
at the Conservatorium
High School, was among
the 1,500 children who
attended accompanist
Gerald Moore's special
matinee recital for
children during the
afternoon. In the even-
ing, pretty as a petal in
her pink organdi dress,
she was at the orches-
tral concert, conducted
by her father, Mr.
Eugene Goossens.*

Marjorie and my father on the beach

Father and Marjorie at Rose Bay, Sydney, late 1940s. They were probably photographed as they were boarding, or leaving, the flying boat. Courtesy ABC Document Archives

My father with tenor Allan Ferris and contralto Florence Taylor. Courtesy ABC Document Archives

My father's design for Sydney's opera house, sketched by Bill Constable in 1955

With Madame and baby
Henri in Brittany, 1956

The photograph of Philip, aged nine months, that kept me alive, 1962

With Philip at Terrigal, north of Sydney, 1973

Christmas in July, Sydney, 1976. From left: Norman Ayrton, Isobel Buchanan, Geoffrey Bell, Huguette Tourangeau, Richard Bonynge, Caroline Lill, Rosina Raisbeck, Philip, Joan Sutherland, June Bronhill, me

Philip with Betsy Brown at the award of
his Honours degree in History and English,
Sydney University, 1985

Philip, Aunt Sidonie aged
100 and me in Sussex

On my scooter in
Somerset, 2000

Medical Secretary, must be adaptable and able to work on own initiative.' I telephoned for an appointment and a time was made after the clinic closed for the day. When I knocked on the door there was no reply, but I heard an incomprehensible, rather cross muttering inside. Then a voice said, "Come in."

I went in.

"I'm Dr Ounsted," he said, kneeling down on the floor surrounded by metres of recording tape. "If you can sort out this muddle, take dictation from it, and put up with me, you can have the job."

It took me half an hour to sort out the jumble.

"I must have pressed the wrong button or something," he said sheepishly, his pale blue eyes looking at me as if for approval. Dr Ounsted was a handsome man, resembling the actor Peter Finch. He was a neuropsychiatrist with an international reputation. Had I known how important he was, I would have been terrified at interview and completely overawed.

As it was, there were several chairs scattered about the waiting room, and so I brought them in and used them to wind the tape around. Dr Ounsted showed me the electric typewriter, gave me some sheets of paper and asked me to start working from the tape, now connected to a dictaphone. I had never seen such a contraption before, but it didn't take more than a moment to work it out.

"I'm happy to pay you, don't worry. It may take you all evening."

The tape translated into fifteen letters to general practitioners, replying to their referrals concerning children. There was a medical dictionary on the shelf behind me and I extricated the more difficult pharmaceutical spellings, then took in the letters for signing.

"It looks as if you are my secretary already. That is absolutely marvellous. When can you start?"

"I'll have to give two weeks' notice at the College, but then I'll be able to come immediately, if you wish."

"Done," he said, extending his hand, "Let's shake on it."

As an afterthought he said, "Find out the going rate. I'll pay you ten per cent more, will that be in order?"

Mr Akhurst, or 'Ak' as we called him, was the psychologist in charge of the Schools Psychological Service. He was also my boss as he had administrative responsibility for the clinic. He, too, was very good-looking. His sense of humour was far keener than Dr Ounsted's, his only drawback being his absentmindedness. It wasn't unusual to find an empty tea cup in a filing drawer, or the filing cards in the fridge. He had good intentions of putting things away, but something more pressing inevitably distracted him en route.

Mrs Tow, an Australian about fifteen years my senior, was the psychiatric social worker. She wore pretty, feminine clothes, looked after us all like a benevolent mother, and was wonderful at sorting out the most desperate of home circumstances. Her long work and home visiting hours, sometimes till ten at night, made her appreciated and loved by all who enjoyed her care.

Everybody made me feel part of the team, and the four of us lunched together, often worked late into the evening, and occasionally shared a pub meal down by the River Isis or at the Trout Inn. They all looked after me, but they also made me feel useful. I wanted so much to be like them; professional, organised and able to do something of service to others.

Dr Ounsted told me that I was wasted being a secretary and that I should consider instead pursuing a career as a teacher in special education. I was perfectly happy in my work and had no desire to change, certainly not yet, anyway.

The clinic treated children with emotional disorders, interviewed parents and relatives, and provided a supportive environment as well as referral to one of the very first special schools on the ground floor of the premises.

Dr Ounsted was always horrified when he detected that babies were being physically abused. He would make special arrangements for their care and protection. They were listed as 'battered babies', the term then in use. Those considered particularly at risk were sent as in patients to the Park Hospital for Children, where he was medical director and principal consultant for the Oxford region. For a man in his early forties, he had done really well.

His wife was also a doctor, but devoted her time to their four children. She also kept a close eye on her husband. One day she phoned me at the clinic. "Just pop in and see what shoes he is wearing this morning," she asked me.

"But he's seeing a patient, I never go in then," I protested. "May I phone you back?"

"Take him a cup of coffee or something. I have to go out now and it really is quite urgent."

I knocked on the door, coffee in hand, placed it on his desk and glanced down at his footwear. Beneath his impeccable three-piece pin-striped suit were white socks and tennis shoes.

When I explained this to his wife, she laughed. "Just as I supposed, they're the ones he was wearing last night for squash. I usually put his clothes out for him in the morning, and if I don't have time he just puts on whatever comes to hand. He has an important lecture to give tonight, at a medical convention on autism. I'll bring him over some black socks and shoes. Just make sure he puts them on, won't you?"

There was an unexpected side to the good doctor as well. He asked Mrs Tow and me to collect odd saucers for him whenever we went to fêtes or jumble sales. These items cost but a few pence each and he would always reimburse us when we bought them. They were to be stacked in a pile in the provisions cupboard where we kept our tea and coffee.

From time to time he would announce at lunchtime, "Why don't you ladies go out and get yourself a sandwich? I need to do work privately here alone."

We would return to find Dr Ounsted looking very relaxed, and a pile of broken crockery on the floor. I would sweep up the pieces and put them in the bin for him.

"There is nothing on earth as satisfying as breaking a pile of saucers when you're tense about something. I'd recommend it to my patients if they wouldn't think I was completely cracked myself. I've done it since my childhood," he explained, the look of a mischievous cherub spreading across his face.

The hair business was a great trial. I had never enjoyed looking at myself in the mirror, finding far too many faults, as teenagers will, and so hid behind a book while the combing, cutting and colouring took place. The experimental effects included tinges of pink, blue, red and even mahogany. My own mousy colour made it easy to become blonde, an uncomplicated transformation which people seemed to like, and so did I.

I had been taking driving lessons again. The reason for it being *again* was a disastrous failure six months previously in London when I had had ten lessons with an instructor who had proved more of a would-be Casanova than a teacher.

While staying with Australian friends of Daddy's near Piccadilly, I had enrolled at the British School of Motoring. Daddy was away on lengthy conducting engagements in Prague and Budapest, so it was good to have people I knew in London with whom I could stay, and it was always fun to talk about life 'back home' in Sydney. Daddy had secured little work during this time, but when he went away, it was usually to eastern Europe. I treasured the few postcards he sent me, but they never revealed much: perhaps details of the concert programmes, the artists, or the hotel at which he was staying. What I really needed to hear was if he was happy, if he was in good company and profession-ally satisfied. But I never had any idea of his true highs and lows.

My driving lessons were booked for a two-week period between five and six on weekdays. The instructor was tall and gaunt, his skin greyish in tone, and his clothing over-colourful, I thought, eyeing his tweed jacket, red-and-blue striped tie and green shirt. His fingers were cigarette-stained, and he exuded a powerful odour of nicotine.

The first lesson consisted of driving the vehicle out of the parking lot into Piccadilly, checking the mirrors, learning the gears and being reminded of the Highway Code, which I was supposed to learn word-perfect by the next lesson. All this to a ceaseless repartee of ingratiating compliments as he tried to win me over. I detested him.

At seventeen, any compliments caused me great embarrassment and I had no idea how to put him in his place. He was totally odious, but I had paid my money in advance and wanted to complete my lessons. It was too mortifying to have to explain to someone in the office my desire for a refund.

I mastered steering with my right hand while fending him off with my left, except when changing gear as we approached the Trafalgar Square roundabout. London's rush hour never allowed us to journey further than this, nor to advance beyond second gear. He always made a point of taking over, using the dual controls, when we approached the roundabout. My first test was taken in a different car, with an examiner who positively rushed me over to Isleworth, insisting on thirty miles an hour.

The examiner, tense and anxious from my uneasy kangaroo-like advance from second to third gear, shouted: "Turn right here," at the next roundabout. Obligingly I turned right into the roundabout, thus moving in a direction quite opposite to everybody else. Tears streamed down my face as my whitened knuckles clutched the steering wheel. After ten minutes a lapse in the traffic permitted an exit. His voice shook as he gave the next instructions.

"I'll drive us back to Piccadilly now. You will not be surprised to learn that you have failed. I've never been so frightened in my thirty years as an examiner. This was a disgrace. Who taught you? Why? How?"

Once I recovered from my failure, I realised I should start all over again, and signed up with a very pleasant family man who taught me, carefully, correctly, to drive. With my confidence gained after a series of a further ten lessons, he suggested I book a test, which was scheduled for the very next day.

Thursday night was my having-my-hair-tortured night. I was engrossed in a paperback thriller when it came to my attention that someone was sobbing behind me.

I looked up into the mirror. "Whatever is the matter?" I asked the girl with the fancy French name which nobody ever remembered.

"It's you that's the matter. Can't you see?"

I looked to see what I might have done wrong. Nothing seemed out of place.

The girl screamed at me before collapsing in tears on my shoulder.

"It's gone green. Bright flaming green. Look! I must have mixed up the wrong chemicals. See what it says? 'Do Not Use this product on hair that has been previously coloured.' Oh dear, just look at you now!"

I looked at myself in the mirror, deciding it did not matter much. The hair was set better than usual, I noted, once it emerged from the drier, and if you didn't look too closely, the colour didn't seem to show. I gave her a hug.

"Stop worrying, you can fix it another day, and Mrs K will never know, because I'll be gone well before opening time."

I arrived at the driving examination centre with my head wrapped in a scarf against the cold and the wind. I had almost forgotten there was another reason. Bronny, full of sympathy, had lent me her best Lanvin original, all black, white and grey circles with the designer label showing ostentatiously.

The man at the desk had his head down, his ear to a phone, concentrating on his appointment diary. Without looking up he directed me to the waiting area, suggesting that I revise my Highway Code. A short, elderly gentleman in a most correct grey suit, white shirt and sober tie introduced himself.

"I am the examiner," he announced in a voice of doom. He sat me in the driver's seat, made certain I was familiar with the position of the mirrors, the gear lever, and how to adjust the seat because I was shorter than the previous victim.

It was half past eight and the winter's sun was shining brightly on the muddy windscreen. Forgetting my green topping, I took off my scarf and threw it on the back seat in a cavalier manner as if I did it every day. Then I took out a handkerchief, spat on it, got out of the car and cleaned the windscreen with a sigh of satisfaction.

When I got back into the driving seat, the examiner, exposed to the full horror of my grass-green hair, looked as if he had seen a creature from outer space. He told me to turn right, then left, go down to St Aldate's, round and up the Broad, and through the Cornmarket. One emergency stop. One three point turn. Back to the Centre.

"You've passed," he announced, rapidly writing me a certificate.

I looked at my watch. The entire process had taken less than ten minutes. I wouldn't be late for work after all.

When I reached the clinic Dr Ounsted looked at me. "Why *do* you do it?" he asked, as if some dreadful crime had been committed.

"Morning. What have I done? Lost a file?" I asked cheerily. "I'm early, you know, because I passed my driving test."

"I'm not surprised," the good doctor replied. "The poor examiner is probably having a nervous breakdown. Look at your hair!"

"Oh, yes, that. I'm so sorry, I'd almost forgotten," I remarked brightly. "The girl mixed up the chemicals and got it all wrong. Don't worry, she'll fix it."

"Thank God for that," he said. "I thought you were doing it to be noticed, some sort of personality statement."

"Nothing like that," I said. "It's just part of my rental agreement."

AN UNEXPECTED
RENDEZVOUS

I had not heard from my real mother since we left the New York apartment when I was six years old. To my surprise, while I was in Oxford I received a letter enclosed in an envelope from Father's publishers. Daddy had added a covering note. 'Jansi wanted you to have this for your eighteenth birthday.'

Daddy's note put aside, I carefully opened the sealed American-stamped air mail letter, postmarked several weeks previously. The unfamiliar handwriting, addressed to 'Miss Renée Goossens, c/o Boosey & Hawkes', marked simply 'Please Forward', touched me by its sad and distant loneliness.

'My darling Renée,' it began, 'Now that you are eighteen and more able to make decisions of your own, I am hoping you will write to me. Perhaps we can meet. I have so much to tell you. I work in a shipping office and can arrange a special deal with an airline company for an affordable fare. I've been saving since last year. Is there any chance I could come from September 15th till the 30th? I have two weeks annual vacation and I want to spend them with you.' The letter was signed: 'With all my love, Mummy.'

It overwhelmed me. The very idea of meeting my mother again seemed terribly strange.

My relationship with Stepmother had almost ceased to exist. We saw each other rarely, and in strained circumstances, both maintaining our privacy and closing off any possibility of intimacy. I resented her more than ever. She never went back to my father. I neither heard from her nor desired to know her whereabouts.

How often I had wished that my real mother would contact me. It grieved me that she had never written and I had always wondered why. What could I have done to make her hate me so much? Twelve years after I last saw her, I was holding her letter in my hands. Better late than never, but I was apprehensive about the consequences of this belated meeting and uncertain of my ability to respond appropriately.

How could I express my feelings in a letter? Better to say little and await the meeting. I wanted her to receive my reply quickly because it was three weeks since she had posted her letter. I imagined her waiting anxiously, fearing rejection, just as I did. In a month, if she had the confidence to make her booking, I would see her.

'Dear Mummy' — just to write these words was a relief. Being able to write the word 'Mummy' was very comforting. I put my pen down, stopped and reflected. Why had we lost contact? Was it my fault?

Why had she failed to send me birthday cards in the past twelve years? After the horrible experience of having my letters intercepted in France, it was easy to blame Stepmother and imagine she had prevented my mother's letters from reaching me. Perhaps I was wrong. Maybe Mummy had never written at all. I supposed she had started a new life which included no room for me or for my sister.

I continued my letter, 'It was so strange to see what your handwriting was like, to have your address, and to realise that you cared. Yes, please come, and quickly. I need to see you, to hear that you are all right. Forgive me for wanting to know why you've never written before. There is so much to say but I will save it until we meet. I only hope you won't be disappointed when you see me. Give me your flight time and number, and send me a picture so I will know what you look like. I'll come up to London and meet your plane.'

Then, I wanted to write 'love' but, frightened, I finished my letter 'Regards, Renée'.

She received my letter, booked her flight and came. Much later she told me how upset she was that I needed a picture and that I did not sign the word 'love'.

Her flight was to arrive at London's Heathrow airport at four in the afternoon. With my perpetual fear of being late, I left Oxford before lunch, wishing to be there to greet her, imagining how anxious she would be if I were not there. I realised she would have no idea of my appearance, as I had not thought to send her a photograph.

Many times I studied intensely the passport photo she had sent me. I had put it in a frame and kept it beside my bed since receiving it. It showed a woman who once must have been very beautiful. She looked unwell, her face was drained of colour, and she had dark rims around her eyes. It was not a flattering photograph, I was sure.

The airport was crowded and noisy. With an hour to wait, I found the cafeteria and bought a revolting dark cup of warm tea, recalling the dreadful brew at boarding school. Yes, there was much to tell Mummy. The word captured a warmth and cheerfulness for me. I had always saved this name for her alone, never considering it suitable for the outsider who had taken her place.

I went to the barrier where a bustle of relatives and friends waved excitedly as their dear ones came into sight. Then I saw her. My heart almost stopped.

I recognised Mummy from the photo. But she was so fragile, defenceless, and small. She was just over five feet tall with red hair so fine that it looked as if it had been stuck onto her head, not like a wig, but as if patches were missing. Her clothes were neat and comfortable rather than elegant. Her silky pale green paisley suit was crumpled. The fur coat draped over her shoulders kept slipping down, needing to be pulled up again. She dragged her hand luggage along by a lead, its tiny wheels clattering along behind her like a child's toy. She later told me a kind friend had attached them as she had problems with heavy cases. It was obvious that she was a person who needed to be looked after.

I ran towards her as she searched for me, nervously crying out, "Mummy, it's me, Renée."

As I said the words, my fear was dispelled, changing to joy, allowing me to relish the meeting. I felt very small and uncertain of myself, longing for the security of my mother's enfolding arms.

"For twelve years, my little one, I have thought of nothing but seeing you again. Will you let me make up for all those years and can I try to be a proper mother now?"

The idea startled me, and made me afraid again. We could not turn back the clock, forgetting the years of absence. I could not allow her suddenly to become the mother she had not been when I needed her. Trust needed time to develop. The words came surprisingly easily: "Mummy, may we start by being good friends, and getting to know each other?"

The 'just good friends' sounded more like lovers breaking up than a mother and a daughter coming together, so I added, "If that's all right with you. Please can we learn more about each other?"

"Time is so short. I have lost so many years." She looked sad as she spoke and I felt a deep sorrow for her.

We walked to the bus terminal, after collecting her one little suitcase from the carousel. Just one tiny case. I remembered Step-mother and her collection of luggage that had accompanied us wherever we went in the world. I looked sympathetically at my poor little Mummy and she began to talk nervously.

"You see, I have cancer. Now it is in my stomach and they don't give me very long."

Startled and filled with compassion, I took her in my arms and hugged her. Cancer. People did not speak about it then. Nobody I knew had died from it, or if they had it must have been called something else. Cancer was synonymous with death. The idea that my mother was dying opened any barrier that time might have closed. Every moment would be all the more precious. It catapulted me towards a desire to make her visit as happy and wonderful as possible.

"I've booked into a little guest house in the Woodstock Road," she told me. I had been grateful for the letter saying she had not expected to stay with me. I was certain she would have been shocked at the spartan flat. Rather ashamed of it, I did not even want her to see it.

We took a taxi from the bus station. My mother's guest house was about ten minutes' walk from my flat, so it would be easy to spend time together but also to escape at night. It was shameful to admit that I knew immediately that I required time to recover from our meeting. She took me to dinner at the Randolph Hotel, very grand for me, and we went by taxi yet again. I wondered whether she could afford it.

"This will be a treat tonight, but I hope you know other places where we can eat every day."

I could not remember her ever having cooked a meal for us, as we had always employed a cook. Again it set me wondering how she coped in New York, living alone. Perhaps she always ate out, or went to other people's houses.

"A double Scotch, please," she asked of the waiter. It was the first of many doubles that evening. Could it have been due to the strain of meeting me, or the pain of her cancer? It relaxed her and helped her to speak more freely. She smoked all the time, putting out a cigarette merely to eat a little food, then lighting up, sometimes one from another. It made me all the more concerned for her.

"Do you remember much about your childhood with me?" she asked.

Embarrassed, I admitted, "I only remember saying goodbye to you and that you said we would be happy in Australia. My friends remember things from when they were three or four, but I recall almost nothing."

"I shall tell you about everything, then," she said, making me afraid of what I might hear.

She reassured me that she had always loved me, but that she had agreed with Daddy that Donie and I would have a better life with him in Australia than with her in New York.

"You see, although Gene always loved you and Donie, he was not very good at managing his finances. He had no idea about household matters, although he said he would provide for me and both of you. I just think that he wouldn't have been able to remember."

Despite the loss of my scholarship, I felt sufficiently protective of Daddy when she said that he was unreliable that I wanted to defend him. But when I thought dispassionately about what she had said, I conceded that she was probably right. Sometimes Daddy had been so totally absorbed in his music he seemed to forget all about us.

"So, how did you manage? Did you work?" I asked.

"Although I had no qualifications, I managed to find work as a clerk," she replied. "I didn't play the piano well enough to make my living at it, nor did I really want to. My work is nothing very important and isn't very well paid. I moved to a smaller apartment closer to the office, and I've managed to get by. But once the cancer developed it was harder, so my sister Catsie has been helping me. She's married to one of the Boeings, you know."

"I don't really know anything about you, or your family." I felt disconcerted to hear my own words but continued, by way of explanation, "I thought about you of course. But it was not until I began to support myself, by peeling vegetables and other kitchen duties, that I started to wonder how you were getting along, how you were managing financially. Perhaps I was too self-absorbed to worry about you until then. But the worst thing was that I never heard from you, so I imagined that you didn't care."

Mummy's replies became slightly slurred, and her face was pinched with strain. Tears began to fall down her tired face, "Oh, I always cared. I do care. Let's just say goodnight and go to our beds now. Remember that I do care. We'll talk more in the morning."

Although the Randolph was close to her guesthouse, she asked for a taxi, her spindly little legs unable to carry her further. "It's been a terribly long journey," she said. "Forgive me, I am so tired, I must go to bed now. Darling, just know that I love you very much."

She hugged and kissed me as she stepped into the taxi. I stood on the pavement waving goodbye, emotionally exhausted but grateful to have found her again.

Although I had been unable to be close to Stepmother or Daddy, I was grateful that they had never uttered a word of criticism against my mother. Apart from my own hopes and fears this had left me a fresh canvas on which to create a new picture of her.

Her image was imprinted on my sleepless night, her soft and fragile beauty which Renoir might once have been tempted to paint, her delicate pink cheeks, sparse red hair, her porcelain face. Yet beneath this fragility she must have possessed great strength and courage, to come so far to find me, taking such a risk, in the last run of her battle against the merciless cancer.

We explored London together, going up by train, continuing our conversations frantically. I asked her if we should visit Daddy together but she said she did not want that, and doubted that he would wish to see her either. I could concentrate on nothing, almost unaware of my surroundings, wishing to encapsulate these moments and keep them forever. Now that I had found her, it was cruel that cancer should steal her away from me again, and this time it would be forever. This was my last chance. Each evening we would return to her guesthouse to continue uninterrupted our verbal journey of discovery.

She explained tearfully, between gulps of whisky, that she alone had made the decision not to write to me or Donie because she had wanted us both to be free to make a new life, without the conflict of having one mother in America and another in Australia. Her words were defensive.

This was hard for me to accept. I told her that there would never have been such a conflict for me. I told her how much I disliked Stepmother. But most of all I needed her to know how much I had missed having a mother of my own. How at birthdays I had craved the receipt of a card, checking the mail endlessly, aching with the pain of feeling forgotten.

She kissed me on the forehead, then held me very tightly. She lit another cigarette from the one which had not quite yet expired. She averred how much she had missed me, and how much she regretted her decision. On my birthdays, she said, she never forgot, but always cried. By then she was afraid to send a card.

What was she afraid of? Her own feelings? Her promise to herself? To Stepmother? How could a mother be afraid of sending a message of love to her child? I just could not understand, and as she spoke tears streamed down my face. It was beyond my comprehension.

There seemed to be some hesitation in her voice, but she continued, as if trying to reassure herself. She kept saying she did it for the best. To console herself, she then asked me if there was not something I liked once I left New York.

"Yes, there was," I said, then hesitated, aware that whatever I told her would possibly not be what she wanted to hear. Surely she would have wanted me to miss her, even if she had hoped for my happiness. "Our life in Sydney was the best you could possibly have hoped for us. Sometimes I was totally happy. We had music, friends, sun, beaches, a dog and cats. Our house was huge and my friends could come and play. We had the most beautiful music room, I wish you could have seen it! I loved everything about it. I hated being taken away. I'm still very angry about that. I will save up and return one day. You could come with me, if you liked. It's much better than New York. I'm sure you would adore it."

"If only I had time," she replied, and I could see the exhaustion in her eyes. "But I am very pleased you were happy there. So why did you leave?"

"I never wanted to leave Sydney. I hated the idea of being taken away, but there was nothing I could do about it. Stepmother decided I had to go to school in France. She was always deciding to go somewhere, but usually on her own. This time she had to drag me along. Daddy was busy with his orchestra and the Con. I couldn't persuade anybody to let me stay."

Mother looked at me with sympathy, then stretched out her hand and put it on my arm. She took in a deep breath before saying, "There is something important I have to tell you. But first I need to know how you feel about your father."

My feelings were so mixed that it was difficult to find a simple explanation to give her. "Daddy was so often absent and always somewhat distant, you know how absorbed he could be with his work. I wanted him to be close but I don't think he was able to be. I don't know why or even if it was because I was not specially talented. I always had the feeling I was just not good enough, anyway."

"Listen, darling . . ." She looked away from me, her voice faltered, and as she poured herself a glass of whisky, I could see her hands shaking.

"Gene is not your father."

Her words stung me like a whip. "What did you say?" I stuttered and to my astonishment those same terrible words were uttered again. "Gene is not your father," she repeated.

"It's not true!" I wanted to shout, but my voice would not work, mouthing the words silently, unable to release my rage. I did not want her to speak again and I raised my hand to stop her, then put both hands over my ears to be certain to hear no more.

Her words had erased my identity. "What have you done?" I asked accusingly.

She turned her face away so that I could not see her eyes. I gently turned her head back, wanting to see if her eyes reflected the pain her words had caused me. She had invalidated me, like a stamp on an expired passport.

"I am sorry," was all she said at first. She was winding strands of her poor, thin hair around her thumb and forefinger, then she began to bite her lip. She fumbled for a cigarette, took it from her bag, lit it and inhaled deeply. I moved closer and sat beside her, putting my arm around her thin frame. It took some of the loneliness away.

She told me things I had no desire to know, yet despite myself, craved to hear. She and Daddy had drifted apart long before the divorce. He had had affairs and so had she. I did not want to hear that. I wanted to think they were faithful to each other. There was so little I believed in, that every new fact she revealed eliminated my confidence in her and in myself. She blamed Father's concert tours, saying she had felt abandoned. She had been ill and unhappy and was grateful to accept the comforting arms of a lover. The man she said was my father was apparently a Swedish violinist.

I was unready to hear any of it. It was too dreadful to imagine. I had experienced the anguish of belonging nowhere, being nobody, and now I was not even entitled to my own name. She was my mother and I wanted to trust her but I could not believe what she said. The impact of her words choked me. I felt naked and assaulted. I needed her to hold me but I moved away from her, walking across to the darkened window, wishing I were not even in the same room with her.

Her voice was continuing the tale but it seemed as remote as the plot of an unfamiliar opera. I wanted to detach myself from anything to do with her. I wanted her voice to stop, for the words she said to be erased, as if they were merely a false tape recording.

I was mortified to learn that I was just the result of 'a fling'. The violinist had returned to Sweden and they had had no further contact. The confession was one I had no wish to hear. She said she believed she could not fall pregnant, as doctors had diagnosed a benign tumour in her womb as the cause of infrequent past periods. Her explanation disgusted me.

I dragged my mind back from where it was wandering and listened to what she was saying, suddenly aware that this tumour was far from benign, and possibly the beginning of the cancer devouring her now. Sympathy for her condition made me return to her side and take her hand in mine.

She sat looking lifeless and dejected as her voice continued joylessly. She had not even suspected she was pregnant until, at twenty-six weeks, suddenly, she had experienced pain, and to everybody's amazement I was born. I had weighed less than two pounds.

"How on earth did I survive?" I asked in amazement.

Mother looked wistful. It was as if she were describing another person, a person not present. "You were a strong little mite," she said. 1940, she reminded me, was just after the beginning of the Second World War. The tiny village hospital had none of the special equipment taken for granted today. The nurses had wrapped me in cotton fleece beneath the blankets and placed me in a tiny box, oiling my skin every few hours to keep me warm.

As she described this procedure, she seemed sad, yet smiling at the memory as if it gave her pleasure. Then her voice returned to its dispassionate tone, as if neither of us belonged to the story— as if it had all happened to other people, to another mother and an unknown baby. My arrival had been incredibly unexpected. But she told me that the man I had thought to be my father had written proudly to his own parents to announce my arrival. When she told me this, it gave me a ray of hope that I dared not express.

In 1994 Aunt Sidonie gave me the letter Daddy had written to his father describing mother's illness, the suspected tumour, then kidney stones being removed, then finally, to their surprise, the imminent arrival of me.

I had had misgivings about the real nature of Jansi's condition, but as she seemed to experience none of the normal reactions to child-bearing and none of the symptoms, concluded I was wrong, and left Nature to take her course . . . Anyway, a long, rough motor-ride did the trick, and brought on familiar symptoms which even I couldn't mistake. So at 7 a.m. on the sixteenth I telephoned for the ambulance to Biddeford (10 miles away) which whisked Jansi and myself into hospital there—only just in time—and ten minutes after arrival the doctor emerged to say that I was again the father of a girl. It was born 2 months too soon, but the incubator has done wonders and she is almost the appearance of a full grown baby. A fine, sturdy youngster who refused to give in, and though Jansi is back home (arrived yesterday) she—the baby—is remaining in hospital for another ten days before she is handed over to Nannie who is returning with her to Cincinnati to the house . . . so that Jansi and I may remain here till the 20th—Jansi to get thoroughly well and I to be with her and finish the finale of the quartet.

If only I had been shown that letter decades before, much of my insecurity would have been non-existent! It seems strange that my father would describe such a premature bundle as having almost the appearance of a full grown baby, but that must have been the way I seemed to him.

"I must have been a specially strong baby," I said to my mother, trying to belong to the moment of my arrival. How did she expect me to react? Was I to be angry or sad, sympathetic or dejected? It was like being in an opera and not knowing the plot. I wanted to run away from it all.

My mother moved closer. "You are strong, you always have been. You always will be. I don't know how I have managed without you."

Her words confused me. I did not feel strong now, but lost, forlorn and apprehensive. If her words had been intended as praise, they also implied a demand that I was expected to be strong. Mother sobbed quietly, sipping her Scotch, smoking yet another cigarette and occasionally wiping her eyes with a soggy handkerchief.

Questions crowded into my mind. Why had I been taken away if I had not been his daughter? Why did he want to take me from my mother? Was it because he cared for me? Because he loved me? Because she did not? Why?

I had told my mother how much I hated Stepmother and how unloved and unwanted I had felt; how she had made it clear to me that I was a nuisance, an intrusion upon her social life. I had needed my mother to understand how lost I had felt except in my life in Sydney. And now that security, which came from being my father's daughter, was ripped away from me. I was devastated.

Mummy did not register my utter desolation. She did not seem to grasp that her words made no sense to me. I asked provocative questions, tempering them occasionally with belated concern for her. When she kept repeating that she had only wanted the best for me, I was irritated and began to doubt everything she said. With that one sentence, the fragile web of developing trust had been destroyed.

"Mummy, children don't want big houses, tennis courts and hire cars, they want parents to love and hug them, parents who are there." It was hard for me to explain what was important to a child. I told her of the awfulness of Nanny disappearing from my life. But the more I spoke, the more I realised she seemed incapable of absorbing what I meant. It seemed she did not wish to hear what I was saying any more than I had wanted to hear her terrible confession. She looked shocked and hurt, but for herself rather than for me.

"Marjorie promised she would let you keep Nanny," she said defensively, a defiant look in her eyes.

"Tell me more about when I was born," I said softly, needing to know about those private first moments, facts only she could tell me.

"When you were born, Gene was absolutely thrilled and he accepted you as his darling little youngest daughter. I could never have guessed you would have been so unhappy. You must not blame me for that."

Stepmother was the person I had always blamed. She alone was the person I held responsible for my isolation and unhappiness. I thought now, why had my mother not defended her right to keep me? She had let me go. But perhaps I could begin to accept the possibility that it was nobody's fault. My mother could not be expected to shoulder all the blame. There was nobody to blame— my mother did the best she could, and that's all anyone can ever do.

"I am sorry, Mummy. I should not blame you. Things seem to have been so miserable for such a long time." And then I became the baby I needed to be, lying down on the little single bed in her room with my head on the pillow. I cried as if my world had come to an end. But then something wonderful happened. Around my shoulders came a little, thin arm, and a fragile hand began softly to stroke my long hair.

"Cry, my darling girl, because at last I am here with you. I am so sorry you have felt so unhappy and abandoned. Now I can see how wrong I was and how it is all my fault."

As my mother said those words, immense relief swept over me like an ocean wave. At last someone was accepting responsibility for what had happened to me.

I was at last able to absolve her, as I sobbed, "It wasn't your fault, because you didn't mean to do it to me." There had been no intention. How did such a comforting idea come into my head? It must have been something the nuns had taught me, or Pascal, Descartes, or something I had read.

"Mummy, I don't want to upset you. I am terribly confused and I need you to understand me. It was wonderful when you stroked my hair. I have needed you so much."

When she hugged me I felt uneasy because her arms were so

thin and spindly, I was afraid she would break if I embraced her in return. I had to be very childlike to admit my feelings. When I felt braver and more grown up, I would stop being a baby. It was a blessed relief to give in to my emotions, even for a moment. It was as if one minute I was three years old and the next a hundred and three. I needed to keep showing how strong I was, fearing lest in my dependency I might be abandoned again.

I also needed to know about the man Mummy said was my father. She said that his name was Erik Karlssohn. She was uncomfortable about telling me, but she also understood my need for answers. She avoided reference to the intimate side of their relationship, for which I was grateful. She also made it clear I was to harbour no illusions of a romantic attachment or devotion. It was only a sexual fling, she explained, to bring her comfort at a time she and Father were not close. The idea made me shudder. My curiosity was centred only on this man who had apparently made half of me.

Erik, she said, was tall, well over six foot, with tight curly short silver-blond hair, startling jade green eyes, a pale but healthy complexion. He neither smoked nor drank. He read important books, she said with a hint of admiration, by philosophers like Kierkegaard and also Heine, Plato, Socrates and Descartes.

"Was he an intelligent man?" I asked eagerly, needing to know. Suddenly my resentment soared as I remembered my lost scholarship and I was furious at the deprivation, particularly if my father was not really my father. There was no logic to my thinking, only disappointment and seething rage.

"He was much brighter than some musicians," she laughed, breaking the mood of sadness which had enshrouded us like a dense fog.

"Did you admire him?" I asked, hoping so much that she did.

"I guess you would like me to invent a father figure for you who was both Adonis and Shakespeare."

Her words made me angry because I was very proud of my own father, the only man in the world for whom the name Daddy was reserved, and I considered him as handsome as any Adonis and as talented as Shakespeare.

Unaware of my thoughts, she continued, "But I really didn't get to know him very well in two weeks. I could invent a rosier picture than the true one, but I will not do that to you. He was just a pleasant person, of course good-looking, healthy, certainly vigorous and full of fun."

She seemed to cheer up as she said this, briefly enjoying the memory. "He was an easy person to be with, light-hearted, sincere and uncomplicated. There is not much else to tell."

Intrigued rather than shocked, I suggested that if I were half-Swedish, perhaps it would be easy for me to learn the language. It was a positive idea to grasp during another sleepless night that followed. The next day I took Mother to my favourite bookstore, Blackwells, in the Broad. She wanted to pause and admire the window display, but I was upset and needed to talk.

"Mummy, I must tell you how I won a scholarship and then lost it," I explained breathlessly, before launching into the whole story. I needed her to know how angry I was with my father for coming back to England at the only time I would have been better off without him. I raged at the new irony she had created by her revelation.

She told me once again she was sorry, taking my hand and squeezing it. We wandered into the bookstore together and I showed her my favourite sections. When we reached the language shelves, we were beside the Russian books I had searched through so often. I lingered there regretfully for a moment.

"I am sorry about the lost scholarship," she said, her voice quieter in its sincerity.

It was comforting to hear her express regret over my loss, even if there was nothing she could do about it. So I stalked around, anxiously seeking out Swedish books. "Here we are, *Teach Yourself Swedish*," I announced jubilantly.

Mother bought it for me. It cost only three shillings but I was touched because it was her first proper gift to me, and something especially personal, our secret. The book had a shiny cover in light blue and yellow, like the Swedish flag. I even imagined that if I wore those colours they would suit me. My vivid imagination raced ahead. My head was bursting with positive emotions and excitement. My mother was beside me, and in my handbag I had a book that was the key to this amazing new language I would undoubtedly master overnight, due to my origins.

Coupled with this new-found eagerness for learning was a gnawing, hopeless knowledge that Mummy would disappear again in only three days' time.

Everything that she said had been between the two of us alone, nobody had verified one word of it, and maybe none of it was true, I thought suddenly. I felt such despair that our farewell that evening flickered by like a silent movie in slow motion. I walked back to my flat feeling empty, isolated and desolate.

The remaining days passed quickly, as remote as a dream. It was all the more heartbreaking to have my mother there and to know she was glad to be with me. If only time could stand still. Two weeks were far too brief a time in which to reconstruct the missing years.

Inevitably 30 September arrived and we made a dismal journey to the airport. Our conversation had become detached, mechanical and superficial. There was still so much I wanted to ask and to say, but it was too late. She never told me whether Father knew the secret of my paternity. As the moment when she would disappear approached, I clung to her, hoping she would not leave. Finally I let her go and as I waved her goodbye, my emptiness overwhelmed me. The sense of foreboding was a repetition of my abandonment at Mortefontaine.

As the plane disappeared, I imagined how lonely and scared Mummy must feel. I realised I knew almost nothing about her, not even if there was a man in her life. All she had given me was an address. And a Swedish language book. There were no photographs, no images of her life in New York, of how she spent her days. She had spoken of no friends, no music, no concerts. Now that she had gone I wondered if she had even been real. Was she a fabrication of my imagination? She had promised to come to visit me next year. I had no idea if I would ever see her again.

Her departure left me feeling more alone than ever. She had undermined the little confidence I had possessed in the past. Only one person could help me now. That was the man I still wanted to believe was my father. On my bedside table lay my new Swedish book. I searched longingly through its words, hoping they would reveal something significant, that something would magically be engraved on my mind. "*Ja elska day*," I read phonetically, the Swedish words for 'I love you'. These very words were not new to me. I had heard them before, on the ship which had brought us to Sydney. It was Sven, who came to work for Father, who had pronounced them. That was twelve years ago, but it seemed like a lifetime. I murmured the sweet words once more. "*Ja elska day*." These were the words I wanted to entrust to somebody who would say them back, and truly mean them, in any language.

I wrote to the only father I had ever wanted to know, at his London flat: 76 Hamilton Terrace, St John's Wood. I had not been there more than twice, and had not really felt I knew the place, nor taken in much about it. Now I was desperate to know more.

> Dear Daddy,
> I have just spent two weeks with Mummy. She tells me that I am not your daughter. I feel devastated and confused. May I come up to London to see you? I really need to know.
> Love, Your daughter, Renée

Father phoned me as soon as he received the letter, his voice crackling on the line. "Dear child," he said, "what is all this nonsense about? Yes, by all means come up and see me. Will the day after tomorrow be all right?"

His voice reassured me. I grasped at the possibility that everything my mother had said was a total fabrication. Father had never rejected me. So why should I believe my mother? If she was lying, if she had invented the story for some reason of her own, I would never trust her again. I was frightened about what my father might say and could scarcely wait to see him.

Arriving at Hamilton Terrace, I rang the doorbell. Father kissed me on both cheeks as he opened the door, then led me into the drawing-room. The hall carpet was threadbare and there was a musty smell everywhere, as if nobody ever opened the windows. It was dismal and dark, with the heaviness of the grey skies outside permeating the room with their gloom. One of the long velvet curtains had partly come off its railing and was hanging down. The settee was in need of cleaning. A shabby, faded carpet had dirty fringes which were curled up at the edges. I worried in case my father might trip and hurt himself. Cobwebs, dangling from the ceiling cornices, shivered in the draught. Everything appeared neglected, dilapidated, and in need of a woman's touch. It was so different to our home in Wahroonga. There was not even a dedicated music room.

I stood beside the man whose answer would be so important to me. I asked him my essential question. "Daddy, I need to know. Are you my father?"

"Have I not always accepted you as my daughter?" was his reply.

This was not the reply I had hoped for. Even though his name was on my birth certificate under the heading 'Father', I felt he had forgotten all about me in the last three years. All I could see was a lack of support and the fact he had entrusted my care to Stepmother.

He looked at me very sadly. Perhaps there was no other reply he knew how to make. Even though he had been forewarned by my letter, my question must have distressed him, more than ever in these grim surroundings. Surely he must have known I was suffering. All I wanted was for him to put his arms around me in a fatherly hug, to dispel the pain and fear and to mend every hurt. I yearned for it. But he did not touch me.

Just as he was unable to express his feelings to me, I could not force the conversation further. He looked exactly as he had when he had taken me to the Albert Hall recital. He had not changed in any way. He treated me just as he always had and even began to discuss everyday matters.

"How are your studies going then, dear child?" he asked in a friendly way.

"Daddy, I am not studying any more. You remember, there was some financial difficulty concerning my scholarship. I have a job now. It is quite interesting and I think you will be proud of me, even if it isn't music."

"Well done. I always knew you would sort something out. What sort of work is it?"

I told him about the clinic and the children and how much I enjoyed being part of a team. He smiled pleasantly at what I was saying but did not seem to be paying much attention. It was as if the reason for my visit and our previous conversation had never occurred.

He sat down at his desk, limply, sadly, fumbling in a drawer and extracting four tattered pound notes. "You'll be needing some money for your train back to Oxford. This should help. I imagine you must be finding it difficult to manage. I wish I could give you more, but things are not good for me, either."

It was not money I wanted from him. Having no idea of his financial difficulties, because he never expressed his troubles, I did not even know if this would cost him dearly. Perhaps even a couple of pounds was stretching his limited budget. For his generous gift I gave him the briefest of thanks, nodding my head and wanting to hug him but still too uncertain of myself to do so. He gave no indication as to whether he had been upset by my question. He seemed lost in that world to which nobody else would ever belong.

My concern was selfishly for myself and my own confusion, instead of for the isolation of his situation. How much I wished everything could return to normal and that we could both go back to Wahroonga where nothing would hurt us ever again. If only we could have turned the clock back and removed all the pain and suffering. He must have wished for that, even more than I did.

He accompanied me to the door to say goodbye. Even then I felt so sad at seeing how forlorn a figure he had become. I wanted him to hug me but when he didn't, I retreated, tears of anguish soaking into the scarf he had lovingly given me not so long ago. Walking blindly in the cold greyness of that terrible day, I turned back to see if he was still on the doorstep, longing to run back and hear him say that my mother had invented it all, and to hug and comfort me. I was so frightened that he would not do this, that I walked on. This was the last time I ever saw him. I was eighteen.

UNDERSTANDING

Everything I had believed in had been shattered. I had loved my father. How can I explain my understanding of love? With admiration, loyalty, respect, trust, hope, that was how I had loved him. I had been proud to be his daughter. It had been such a wonderful feeling of elation, listening to people speak of him, hearing his concerts, being part of something so much greater than myself, greater than he was too, a world of music.

So when my mother came to see me, after such a long absence, I had not wanted anything to happen between us that was not beautiful. I had wanted to find a way to love my mother. The instinctive love I had had for her had been taken away, strangely enough, by the very nuns to whom my father had entrusted my care. 'Honour thy father and thy mother', they had taught us in the Ten Commandments. No sooner had they explained the meaning of this, than they had decreed that divorce was a sin of mortal importance. My parents were sinners, according to the nuns, and the marriage to Stepmother was yet another sin. The last part I could understand and agree with. But what about my own mother, and my love for her?

I had kept loving my mother, in a distant, hopeful way, convinced there must be something I had done wrong which had made her give me up. Something, I assumed, which had helped her to forget my birthdays and Christmases. The fault had been mine, not hers.

When she had contacted me, it seemed out of the blue, I was ready to discover the wrong I had done so that I could ask forgiveness and then we would love each other 'properly'. Seeing her fragile body, understanding gradually that she had been damaged in every way by life's experiences, that she too had been abandoned, I had given her love and sympathy, and sought to protect her and forgive her and to seek her forgiveness.

The blow she struck by announcing that my father was not my father was like an electric shock, attended by a pain so great that it annihilated my trust. I felt totally betrayed. I wanted no details, and yet I craved them. Ambivalence overwhelmed me.

I had to know that the man I had believed was my father was my father. He had answered me as he always did, not perhaps in the words I sought, but in his own way, for he too must have felt a deep shock and grief at what my mother had said, whether her words were true or not. Had he known? Was there anything for him to know?

It was hard for me to understand all this in any way other than to retrace my life as it had been to date. It was my mother who had abandoned me, and my father who had taken me under his wing, filling my life with music throughout my early childhood, giving it to me as his own special present. It was he who had pressed for me to attend the Conservatorium, to be in the same building where he was director, where I could be even more a part of him than I could have dreamed. He would not have done this if he had not loved me. Of that I was sure.

His way of showing love was different from that of others. I had been satisfied with it, and proud, until my mother's words destroyed the trust. But why should I trust the woman who had abandoned me for twelve important years? How could I know she was even telling the truth?

Was denying that Eugene Goossens was my father my mother's way of protecting me from the scandal? If so it was rather late. I had, on one occasion, phoned about a room-to-let in Oxford, and made an appointment and arrived to see it, and on giving my name as Goossens, suddenly found the room was taken. I had not thought much about it at the time, not knowing of the publicity which had preceded my arrival.

I knew I must discover more about the scandal surrounding my father's departure from Sydney, for my own sake, perhaps to clear my father's name, perhaps to understand my mother's behaviour and her reasons for threatening my emotional security so drastically. I began my quest in Oxford City library. There it was warm, the seats were comfortable, and old newspapers were filed by date, and easy to find. Learning that my father had been front-page news even in England was a big shock to me. Not because it upset me but because I understood how devastating it must have been, not only for him but for his very honoured, famous and successful brother and sisters. The media had done its best to destroy the family name. Father had been involved with a person nicknamed 'The Witch of the Cross'. This is what I found out from a précis of various newspapers. In the past forty years or so, further reports have appeared, a play has been written and produced, and an opera is in preparation. Archives available after the thirty-year secrecy rule have been inspected.

On 9 March 1956, Customs officials detained my father at Mascot airport on his way home from a conducting tour of England and the Continent. Vice Squad detectives at the airport confiscated about 2000 pornographic photographs, films and books as well as three rubber masks found in his luggage.

He had stood down from his positions as chief conductor of

the Sydney Symphony Orchestra and director of the Sydney Conservatorium of Music, giving reasons of health. This giant of Sydney's musical life was shunned by the same people who had once clamoured for his attention.

Just four days afterwards, Father was charged with 'importing prohibited goods'. He pleaded guilty in the Special Federal Court on 22 March. Eager reporters were disappointed that he made no personal appearance, but the poor man was far too ill. His legal representative Jack Shand, QC, read out a doctor's certificate to the court saying that he had examined Sir Eugene Goossens at his Wahroonga home and found him in a state of physical and mental collapse, unfit to attend court. Father was duly fined one hundred pounds, the maximum penalty for the offence.

Just over one month later he secretly slipped out of Sydney by air to Rome, and never returned. To protect his identity, he travelled as Mr E. Gray and was permitted to hide in a small room adjoining the terminal until a few moments before takeoff.

Subsequent reports showed that Rosaleen Norton—known as the Witch of the Cross—played a key role in his dramatic downfall. Daddy had met her in connection with his research for his great oratorio *The Apocalypse,* and became fascinated with the occult. He was a lonely man, seeking not only companionship but distraction and excitement. Alas, a firm friendship had developed, as well as a physical relationship.

In 1954, *The Apocalypse* received its world premiere at Sydney Town Hall. It was my father's sixty-fourth composition. Various reviewers greeted it as a work of great importance. Better still, another performance followed in Britain. Critics there had mixed opinions. That bothered me little, for I was uninterested in the opinion of others, needing no reassurance of my father's excellence, so their approval was secondary.

Much later, in 1982, in honour of Father, the work was performed once more. Fred Blanks of the *Sydney Morning Herald* wrote: "The end of the World came perilously nigh in the Opera House Concert Hall on Saturday afternoon. But then, a violent subject needs violent treatment and it is no wonder that *The Apocalypse* by Eugene Goossens often resembled a sound-track for the Last Judgment. It is the kind of work that invites adjectives such as overwhelming, grandiloquent, flamboyant. Yet beneath its mostly turbulent exterior beats a heart very conscious of sheer musical beauty, for this is an oratorio that elevates the soul as often as it chills the spine. And it obviously emanates from the pen of a composer masterful in the deployment and juxtaposition of orchestral and choral resources.

"It also happens to be so extravagant—double choir, six solo singers (of whom the two females ones have a very lean time) large orchestra, organ, off-stage brass reinforcements—that you could regard Goossens as the last of the big spenders in the oratorio market."

When the performance was recorded for commercial release, happily—according to Blanks—it was a truly splendid reading for which primary credit went to the astute, unflaggingly vivid conducting of Myer Fredman, who made virtuosi of the Sydney Symphony Orchestra, Philharmonia and associated choirs, not to mention the soloists Ronald Dowd and Raymond McDonald. Also outstanding as the Evangelist John (whose revelations started it all) was Grant Dickson.

"In the context of contemporary music the work itself now sounds much less daring and trail-blazing than it did three decades ago," concluded Blanks.

Father had received a knighthood for his contribution to music. After the scandal, questions were asked in the Australian Parliament about whether he could retain this honour. Fortunately, the suggestion was immediately dismissed. Father may have lost his positions in Sydney, but nobody could deprive him of his knighthood.

To me, the disgrace of this man whom I was so proud to call my father was a cruel, unjustified disaster. I was not in Sydney to suffer with him, nor there to hug and comfort him. It was my sister Donie who fended off the press at the doors of his

Wahroonga home. Incorrect reports said I was there, weeping at a window (I was of course in France at the Couvent de l'Epiphanie, unaware of the tragic circumstances). Stepmother, who announced to the newspapers that she would always stand by her husband, never returned to Australia. She did, it appears, meet him in Nice and arrange accommodation for him when he arrived in England.

The most comprehensive biography of my father is *The Goossens: A Musical Century* by Carole Rosen, published by André Deutsch in 1993. Chapters devoted to his life and to his contribution to music throughout the world give a far better overall picture than other books I have read, although there is value in all that is written. I was privileged to know Carole; she was eager to clear my father's name, and urged me to continue seeking evidence to prove that his disgrace was brought about by others who sought to gain from his dismissal. She assumed, as did I at one time, that some conspiracy was involved.

Although it is naturally my wish to clear my father's name, I have been unable to find new material that would prove beyond doubt that the items discovered in his luggage were put there by people who wished him harm. Curiously, it seems that the photographs were burned and never presented at my father's hearing, and he pleaded guilty in order to minimise publicity as much as for reasons of ill health. We shall never really discover either what was in his suitcase or why the importance of its private contents grew out of all proportion to ruin his reputation, his future career, and the rest of his life.

The scandal forced my father to leave a life he truly loved, one in which he was fully engaged, both as a musician and as a teacher, a leader, a mentor and friend to many students who became great musicians and who, today, remember his name with pride and gratitude. In failing health, depressed and deserted by his wife, he found difficulty in obtaining work in England; though scant engagements were available to him in eastern Europe, his real life had ended.

One can easily stand aside and say 'times are different now'. But had my father done wrong? Or had he purchased a bundle of photographs to share among consenting adults in private. There are many possibilities, but speculation is unimportant. What matters is that the great contribution he made to Australian music is often regarded as secondary to the alleged 'thrill' of the scandal.

Even as I read about these events in the newspapers, I realised how necessary it had become for me to eradicate painful memories of unkindness and hurtful remarks. It made me understand more fully the reasons Father had been unable to help me financially at Oxford. Shame filled me at my own selfishness.

How much of my life had I chosen to forget, during the difficult years when I was alienated first from Mother and then from Father? I believe that these memory lapses are as kind as the coma one suffers after a terrible accident, they are one of Nature's ways of keeping us whole. Without blocking out some of the pain, life itself becomes more fragmented than the memories.

It took some time for me to come to terms with Mother's very occasional letters, given the fact we had finally met, and I had had the impression she wanted us to be closer. She mentioned she would be moving but never wrote again with a new address. Without letters I was not to know the parlous state of her health, where she was, or who to contact to find out more about her. It made me realise that she had evaporated, as before, without a means of contact. This made me very sad. Father was absent yet again, conducting. He continued to have occasional concerts, particularly in eastern Europe.

When he returned more permanently to London, he sent me a couple of postcards but didn't invite me to come and visit him again. I hadn't seen him since I had asked him if what my mother said was true. This disturbed me terribly.

I presumed, rightly or wrongly, that his new companion

Pamela Main, who lived in his flat as his 'housekeeper', did not like me, or felt that I intruded on her domain. I did not know why I was not welcome, but I was certain it was not because my father did not want me. I wrote to tell him about finishing my studies and about my job at the clinic, but I was too fragile to go where I was not invited. How sad that during the two years when I could have seen him more often, learned how to understand his suffering and possibly offered him comfort, the invitation never came.

Work absorbed me. I loved my position at the Child Guidance Clinic. I felt part of a team, and regarded Dr Ounsted and Mrs Tow as *in loco parentis,* admiring them and feeling a deep attachment to them both, and to the psychologist Ak Akhurst, whom I was to meet again in a different phase of my life.

As well as working at the clinic I was offered work at the Park Hospital for Children with Neurological Disorders. Dr Ounsted, who was an exceptionally talented neuropsychiatrist, was the superintendent there. The hospital treated children with various areas of difficulty. One area involved autism, another children with epilepsy. The most tragic was that this hospital was deemed a 'place of safety' for children who had suffered physical abuse.

There is some similarity between children who feel they were unloved by a mother and children who have been abused; nevertheless, seeing how these little ones had suffered helped me to feel very strong and privileged.

Teamwork enthralled me, and in an effort to utilise skills I had learned other than secretarial, I was pleasantly surprised by a promotion to research assistant. There I was put in charge of compiling fascinating patient data from records of children both there and in our 'control' group in Gröningen in Holland. It was good to be doing something useful, something that had meaning and was helping others.

It was in this small role that I began to feel a sense of purpose in life independent of the overwhelming pain of my encounter with my mother, and it was in this atmosphere of loving and healing, amongst the team of practitioners, whose whole life was dedicated to others, that I began to feel whole again. I benefited from their care and consideration.

There had not been much time for socialising, and I disliked parties, being afraid of large groups and shy in the company of new people.

But now I was ready to take on the world, or so I thought. However, I was still immature, and made unwise decisions. My greatest wish was to love and be loved, to be part of a family, to have a family of my own. This led me to wrong choices sometimes, with very sad results. I had much to learn.

AN OPPORTUNITY FOR
HAPPINESS

My twenty-first year was the most memorable of my life. I met, fell in love with and married a young scientist from the Atomic Energy Authority at Harwell.

This is how it came about. When Bronwyn left to marry her Thomas, the flat was offered to one of the staff from the salon. It was time for me to move on. A twenty-minute walk down the hill from St Aldate's I found an affordable and spacious bed sitting room to rent.

The first time I met my future husband, by the mailboxes of the building where we were both tenants, I hoped from the glint in his eye that our attraction was mutual. We introduced ourselves. His name was Graham Hopkins. It would have been somewhat forward of me to invite him in for a coffee, but I rather hoped he would say he would like to see me again. This was a silly, unrealistic idea and it was only after several weeks of friendly meetings collecting the mail that I summoned the confidence to approach him beyond the mailbox.

It took considerable courage for me to knock on his door and ask if I might borrow some milk. My head was filled with romantic dreams and I saw us as Mimi and Rodolfo in Puccini's *La Bohème*. I blushed as he answered the door and I made my request. Books and newspapers were scattered around his room, but otherwise it was quite tidy, I thought, for a man living alone. He walked over to the sink, took out a bottle of milk from the cold water it was standing in, and said, "Why not take the whole bottle? I have some more in a jug for my cereal in the morning."

As he said nothing further, I thanked him, accepted the milk and went back to my room with it, annoyed that I had not invited him for coffee. Then I thought, follow your convictions, go back and do so now.

Graham was glad to be asked. I had performed a small miracle of stage management, tidying my room, putting on the gramophone, even being unsubtle enough to put on the love duet from the end of Act I of *La Bohème*. Perhaps it was as well that he was not familiar with it.

"Do you like opera?" I asked, as if it would be the key to my heart.

"I don't know much about music at all, to tell you the truth," he said. He noted my crestfallen expression and added, "But if you have something you'd like to play for me, I'd love to hear it."

Relieved, I told him the story of *La Bohème* and played some excerpts from my secondhand scratched record. Overuse had taken its toll, the diamond needle was older than it should have been and kept sticking and repeating phrases in a most annoying way, but I could not afford a new one.

"I love romantic stories," he said, and I noticed his eyes were very blue. He was handsome, too, with a boyish face and thick, straight, dark blond hair. His clothes were typically English: corduroy trousers, white shirt, dark tie and a saggy brown cardigan which made him look endearingly uncared for. We sat and listened awkwardly to the music, he on the armchair, I on the bed. After a while he said he had better go, I said not just yet, and then he kissed me. It really was like in the storybooks.

Graham was three years older than I. He was five foot ten, (178cm) solid of build and I found him most attractive. He resembled Kirk Douglas and was quite the most handsome man, I thought, as we enjoyed our first movie together. We went to see *Spartacus*, and were very impressed by the scene with the chariot race. It was even more exciting to feel Graham's arm gradually finding its way around my waist on this, our first real date. I liked the fact that he had not rushed at me, but I craved affection and eagerly hoped he would become even more demonstrative.

Then, after we had been out together a few more times, he escorted me back to my room one night. I invited him in. We embraced, removed some of our clothing and began to make love. It was wonderful to be cradled in his arms.

It was comforting as well as exciting, for he was considerate and introduced me to his body gradually, touching me softly all over, kissing me in every single place.

"I am a Catholic," I told him anxiously.

This statement prompted him literally to put his shirt back on, and he strode awkwardly across the room to make us both a cup of tea. It looked as if he was angry with me.

"So you won't use contraception?" he asked.

"Of course I will. I do believe in contraception, because I think it is wrong to have babies unless you are ready for them. If a baby was conceived every time a couple made love, the world would be filled with unwanted children."

"Stop talking, then," he said, not unkindly, "and let me make love to you."

I felt excited, yet scared to be taking the big step with him. The most important thing to me was to be loved, to belong to somebody. Surely making love must be the way. Intimacy would bring us closer together. Breathless from excitement but frightened, I asked, "Do you love me?"

He answered not with the words I needed to hear, but with a passionate kiss.

After a couple of months, he asked me to marry him. This made me very happy. At last, I would belong to someone. Relieved as well as thrilled, I accepted.

"I want to tell my father," I announced, and immediately wrote him a letter. It was such important news, I needed to put it in writing, as it made the whole idea more real. Apart from receiving a couple of postcards from eastern Europe, I had had no news of my father for ages. I did not have a telephone, and on the few occasions I had gone to the public phonebox and dialled Father's number, I was answered by his companion who told me abruptly, "Your father is abroad on the Continent." Her voice never indicated that further conversation would be welcome, and when I enquired when he would be returning, she would say she did not know.

I had never told Graham about my mother's revelation. I still could not bring myself to believe it, although it filled me occasionally with doubt about everything in my previous life. If I accepted what she said as the truth, I would have no sense of belonging at all. That did not seem to matter quite so much now, for I was going to belong to Graham.

On tour in eastern Europe, my father did not receive my letter until his return several weeks later. He wrote me a kind letter, wishing me well and congratulating me. He said he would be going away again soon. He didn't want me to put off our wedding because he could not attend. He said he would like to send us some money towards it, but could not do so just yet. I supposed he would send us a surprise present instead. It never crossed my mind that he could not afford to do so. He gave us his blessing to be married as soon as we wished. Disappointed that he would not be with us, but accepting his absence as I always had in the past, we set the date. A June wedding would be romantic, I thought, believing in the calendar and hoping for summer weather, forgetting that summer was a very movable feast in England. We chose late June and were blessed with sunshine and warmth.

My colleagues from the clinic offered to be our witnesses. We married in the registry office, then all enjoyed afternoon tea together at the Mitre Inn. Mrs Tow and Ak Akhurst represented my side of the family, in the absence of relatives. They were relaxed and happy for me, or so it seemed. Graham's parents came, ill at ease and thus appearing out of place, for this was our first meeting. They lived in Birmingham and did not like to travel. As Birmingham was only some sixty miles away, this seemed bizarre to me. I was upset that they might not like me.

People had told me that the scandal surrounding my father's dismissal in Australia had featured in the English papers. In France there was certainly nothing about it in the Paris papers Stepmother had brought with her on that terrible day when she told me about it.

I had been afraid that Graham's parents might disapprove of me because of something they had read during that time. Graham assured me that they never paid much attention to the newspapers. To add to that concern, I was also terrified of anybody learning of mother's revelation. My fears proved to be totally unwarranted. My new in-laws demonstrated no particular feeling about me at all. They courteously expressed pleasure at meeting me and assured us they were happy to see us getting married. Graham explained that they were not comfortable at social events and unaccustomed to meeting people from what he referred to as 'other classes'. This was not a term people had used in Australia and I was unfamiliar with the notion. I thought of people more in terms of education. Graham told me I was very out of touch with reality and we had our first argument on our wedding night.

To argue about the class system seemed ridiculous, particularly as I did not believe in it. But he explained my family would be regarded as upper class and his as lower working class. The very idea was alien to my experience of life, which I now realised had, in many ways, been of extreme privilege, although also of extreme contrast. He explained that people in his 'class' would never have treated me the way my parents had. This made me defend them all the more, saying that Daddy was far too busy to have looked after me, and had entrusted me to Stepmother. The argument ended with him pointing out how hopeless she had been at it. At least on that point we were able to agree, kiss and cuddle, and fall into a peaceful sleep.

I did not like arguing and avoided conflict, seeking the middle road and general agreement rather than to upset Graham, or indeed most people. My need for approval exceeded my need to defend a strong opinion of my own.

The most important event of my life was the birth of my son on 2 October 1961. Graham and I were still living in lodgings in Oxford, the completion of our married quarters delayed by a builders' strike. The flat we were to move to in Abingdon was so near to being finished that it would have been foolish to move twice. So, due to the endless delays, he was born in Oxford.

The family doctor, a wise and kindly man, decided I was too strong and healthy to require hospitalisation for a 'perfectly natural event', and insisted instead that I merely register at the Radcliffe Infirmary, as was the custom with home deliveries, for blood matching in case of emergency.

The doctor appointed his favourite midwife to be responsible at the birth, intending to be present himself. There was only one possible reason why this might not occur. His own baby was due within days of mine and naturally he wanted to assist at his wife's delivery should both events coincide.

It was a sunlit day, with the glorious warmth of an Indian summer streaming through the windows when my labour started, conveniently at eight in the morning. I phoned the midwife, who scurried around on her bicycle, notifying the Radcliffe that my baby was starting to make its journey into the world. The hospital confirmed that all my details were registered, in the unlikely event that I should require admission.

The midwife was in her early thirties, sturdy and robust of

manner, with a reliable cheerfulness which made her company most agreeable. I knew her from the classes in natural childbirth which Graham and I had studiously attended together. She played a good game of Scrabble, with the generosity to allow me to win a few games, while Graham, who had taken the day off work, made us welcome cups of tea or coffee and sandwiches.

I was not in much discomfort until four in the afternoon, although things were progressing well and normally. Then contractions began in earnest, and I experienced the intense pain of childbirth. The midwife offered me laughing gas, but I had a cold, so my blocked nose did not allow me to inhale it.

My baby was born at half past five, without the use of analgesics until just at the last moment, when I was given a welcome injection of pethidine. He cried lustily. The midwife helped Graham to wash and dress him, and ten minutes later, our doctor arrived.

"Welcome to the world, young man," he told the red bundle of baby. "Sorry I wasn't here to greet you. Been up with my wife all night and all day. She's had a difficult time. We now have a daughter, an hour older than you are."

He was utterly exhausted, and grateful for a cup of coffee once he had checked me, stitched me up a little, examined the baby and declared him perfect. He thanked the midwife and sent her home.

"What are you going to name the little chap?" he asked.

"We're not sure. We were so certain he was going to be a girl, we had only chosen the name Monette, so now we feel rather foolish."

"So do we, we thought the opposite. I think we have six weeks to make up our minds, but you will register his birth, won't you?" he advised Graham. "You just write Baby Hopkins, until a name is chosen, that's quite usual."

It was six weeks before Baby Hopkins became Philip Alexander, and by curious coincidence, the same day my doctor and his wife named their little daughter Philippa.

I don't believe I have ever experienced a happiness so complete as to hold in my arms this adorable child, knowing he was my very own. It made me grateful and all the more loving towards Graham. We were a family, that family which I had desperately missed and had at last found. Never again would I feel lonely or abandoned. Graham worshipped his little son. He cradled him in his arms, sang nursery rhymes to soothe him to sleep, changed his nappies and boasted about him to all his friends.

On sunny days I could put Philip out in his pram in the garden, but when it rained or at night there was no way we could get away from his noise. I felt guilty if I was tired or cross. Graham could escape by going out to work. I was totally engulfed by the constant crying, and anxious as to the best way of coping. None of us had the opportunity for uninterrupted sleep. In the evenings we whispered so as not to wake the baby, reading books rather than listening to the radio. The volume control on the gramophone had stuck at a loud level, and would have been deafening, so we packed it away. We could not afford a television set. It was all a great strain. Friends suggested I was suffering from the 'baby blues'. All we needed, I thought, was more space.

Our move to Abingdon made life much more comfortable. Living in the one large room with shared bathing and toilet facilities down the hall had been terribly difficult with a crying baby.

Abingdon was a bustling market town six miles from Oxford, closer to Graham's work, and with a new housing complex for the employees of the Atomic Energy Establishment Harwell and the County Council. Moving to a newly built two-bedroom flat with its own living room, in immaculate order, was an immense relief.

I became houseproud for the first time in my life, borrowed cookery books from the library and made an effort to budget on one meagre income. Graham was in his first year out of university and paid accordingly. Once the rent was paid, we had eight pounds a week left. The bus to Harwell was free, but food and heating cost six pounds, so we had only two pounds remaining for clothing and savings.

We had only just been managing since I had given up work. How different a life it was for me now. I adored being a full-time housewife and mother, taking pride in polishing floors and in vacuuming and dusting. These tasks had not been part of my upbringing, but I found them most satisfying. I was grateful for the time I had spent in France as an *au pair*, and for the experience and recipes dear Madame had given me.

I could not believe my good fortune as I walked down to the river Thames each day with Philip in his pram, enjoying the ducks and swans, watching the changing colours of autumn. I was so proud of my new baby and delighted when passers-by stopped to admire him.

Graham was home punctually by six each evening, allowing us a routine of regular meals and contented, even romantic evenings together after bathing our baby. I could not have imagined a life more perfect. I still missed Sydney but Graham had said he would consider emigration to Australia, later, if only we could manage to save some money.

As a treat, Graham brought me a kitten. It was a very smart female tabby with a beautiful white chest, white paws and a white tip on her tail. We called her Mimi, remembering our meeting and *La Bohème*. It seemed proper to give cats musical names. I couldn't help thinking about Daddy and wondering why he had always insisted they be called 'George'. It was fun to tell Graham about Pelly and Melly and how much I had loved them. He told me that was why he brought Mimi into the household, because he felt I needed a cat of my own rather than those in my memory.

At first I was anxious about what we would do with my kitten when we emigrated. I met my neighbour on the stairs as I carried her upstairs.

"What a beautiful little kitten," she remarked.

"I'm a bit worried about her, because we may go to Australia in a year or two and I would have to find a home for her," I confided.

"Don't worry! Mr Hadley and I love cats. If you need her

looked after, or if you go away, we'd adore to have her. Funny we never got one ourselves, isn't it?"

The Hadleys were in their late forties and had no children, no pets and never seemed to have any visitors. They were from the north, like Graham's parents. Mr Hadley worked for the council. Mrs Hadley stayed at home. She spent her day cooking, cleaning and keeping the flat spotless. Sometimes I would meet her outside, at the communal washing lines. They always called us Mr and Mrs Hopkins.

One day as we were pegging out the washing, I said, "Please call me Renée, and my husband is Graham."

But Mrs Hadley explained, "Where we come from, unless we're close friends, we always like to stay a bit formal. It doesn't mean we're unfriendly. It's just that we keep ourselves to ourselves. It's the way we were brought up. No offence."

It seemed strange to me, but they were always courteous, and Graham explained "that's the way they do things up north".

"You make it sound like a foreign country," I replied.

"In some ways it is. It's more to do with class than place. Once you've lived here a few years, you'll understand."

He made me feel as if I were foreign and incorrect, and I never understood his insistence on class differences. Musicians had no class. Musicians just were.

I was thrilled and surprised to receive a letter from Mummy announcing that she wanted to come and meet Graham and Philip. I was more than a little amazed, as I had continued to write to her, but had received no replies. Naturally, I had feared she might be dead but knew nobody who could tell me about her. Her letter was written as if she had never lost contact and was in a cheery, friendly style. It said, "I'll stay at a hotel again, darling. I've booked into the same one. I know it will mean taking buses, but it's better than crowding you when you are just getting used to being a family. The last thing you'd want is me sleeping on your sofa."

I was touched by her sensitivity, and grateful, for although

I had told Graham a little about my mother, he remained inflexible on the subject of her having abandoned me when I was so young. He asked me questions about her life with Father. I told him I knew nothing, that when they divorced I was too young to know what questions to ask, and when she had come to see me, she had not been forthcoming about her life at all. I had found it simplest to let her talk rather than to question her.

His parents never came to see us, which I regretted, but Graham said they would be less afraid of being friendly now we had Philip. My new mother-in-law wrote occasionally, and she often mentioned that they hoped to come down by train one day to visit us.

Graham's father worked for a large factory which produced china and bathroom fixtures. For our wedding present they gave us a beautiful dinner service, Autumn Leaves it was called. There was apparently a special concession for employees, at a discounted price. I adored that dinner service, and realised how much it must have cost them, even with the reduction. They had very little money. They were loving and unquestioning parents to Graham in their own quiet way and I hoped I would grow close to them, however different our worlds seemed to be.

My mother's visit was set for late March the following year, when Philip would be six months old. I was so proud of him and longing to show him to her. She wrote regular, lengthy letters concerning the impending visit. She was very keen to tour parts of England with us.

"Darling," she wrote, "Let me pay for you and Graham to hire a car. I cannot drive, but I'm sure with a baby, we will need a car. We always had one when you and Donie were little. Admittedly we had a chauffeur too, finances being rather different. Find out the details and tell me how much it is and I'll pay when I arrive."

All I knew about my mother's work was what she had told me when I was eighteen. She apparently worked as a clerk in a shipping office and was able to get special deals on plane fares because of this, at discount rates, at certain times of the year.

Whether she was finding finances difficult, whether her health was covered by private insurance, or whether she had friends helping her, all this was unknown to me and had never been discussed.

I was going to arrange to hire a car from Hertz, but friends offered us the use of theirs. It was a small black Morris Minor 1000 with a convertible top, the sort one hoped to roll back on a sunny day, but due to years of English weather, the moving parts had rusted stiff from the combination of rain and infrequent use. We were never able to take the top down.

We drove to the airport to meet my mother. She was even thinner this time, pale, and obviously in considerable pain. She was delighted to meet Graham and enchanted by Philip. Graham was courteous and considerate towards her, though disconcerted by her relentless need for whisky. He lacked compassion for her.

"Is there anywhere special you want to see, Mrs Goossens?" Graham asked.

"They tell me that the Cheddar Gorge in Somerset is beautiful. If it isn't too far away, may we go there one day?" she suggested.

We planned a picnic and set off just after breakfast, to make the most of the day. We picked Mummy up at her hotel at half past eight and set off towards Wells, a four-hour drive. It was a perfect late winter's day, clear but cold. Mummy and I wore woollen skirts and jumpers, with jackets in case it turned colder in the afternoon. Philip was bundled snugly into his carrycot in the back seat of the car with Mummy. Graham drove and I navigated.

My mother was thrilled by the deep red cliffs of Cheddar Gorge and the greenness of the Mendip Hills we passed on the way. She said it reminded her a little of the area around Boston where she was born.

We stopped and picnicked on the grass and took photographs of her with Philip. It was a happy family outing. It seemed so perfectly normal, a young couple with a baby and a grandma. I was truly contented.

We listened to an exciting broadcast on the portable radio we had brought with us. It was a repeat of the broadcast of 20 February 1962 when John Glenn had completed three orbits of earth before splashing down in the Atlantic. Hearing his voice in space was so thrilling that we ate our picnic straining our ears, the radio on the rug beside us.

We began our return journey towards Oxford around two o'clock. As we approached Berkshire, twilight set in and heavy clouds gathered. I have little recollection of what happened next, but I remember my scream of terror as I yelled, "Stop!" and a hedge seemed to jump out at us.

Panic-stricken, Graham put his foot on the accelerator instead of the brake. The Morris left the road and flew through the air and over the hedge.

The rest I learned much later from the police. We had been incredibly lucky. The car had jumped the hedge into a farmer's field. We had all been thrown clear. Safety belts were not obligatory then. Mummy and Graham had been knocked unconscious by the impact. The car had rolled three times, then stopped after somehow running me over then crushing me under its weight.

Two hours later, a couple driving by on the other side of the hedge heard a noise, and the wife remarked, "Can't you hear a baby crying?"

The man stopped the car, listened carefully and agreed with her. They followed the sound and searched for the baby. They found Philip, crying from hunger and fear, safe in his carrycot. A few yards away his father and grandmother were just waking from their concussion.

Mummy said, "My daughter . . . where is she?"

The couple hurried towards the car, seeing my bloody arm extending from beneath it.

"Call an ambulance," said the man to his wife.

Within ten minutes, an ambulance was diverted to assess the situation.

"You can take the husband, grandmother and baby to hospital

to be attended to, but this young lady will need a fully staffed ambulance with a doctor and a nurse," said the medical attendant.

I am forever indebted to him for his decision, because the doctor who came later told him that if he had moved the car away from me, by rolling it off as he wanted to at first, he would have punctured my lungs.

The colonel, my rescuer, held my hand until the ambulance arrived.

He told me later, "There was no way you were going to let go of my hand, and when the doctors brought you towards the operating theatre, you clutched my hand as if your life really depended on it. The nurses seemed to understand and allowed me into theatre. I held your hand until the anaesthetic took over."

I was in surgery for nine hours. The injuries were serious. My pelvis was fractured in nine places, crushing the spleen, damaging the liver and several parts of the intestine.

"It was as if a bomb had exploded within the patient's pelvis," wrote the treating surgeon in his notes. After surgery I lapsed into a coma for three and a half weeks.

The coma was a blessing, because it cushioned me from some of the pain. In the moments I drifted in and out of consciousness, I could discover no comfortable position in which to lie. Strung up in a hammock to make a secure binding for the pelvis, I could not squirm as much as I needed to. A massive wound from the chest bone down to the base of my stomach required daily attention. A laparotomy had been performed, my spleen removed, my liver repaired. Due to the wound, the pelvic fracture could not be set in a cast. The fragments of bone which had punctured the organs had to be extricated, and the remaining structure was left to shape itself.

Doctors forget the possible awareness of coma victims. I heard a male voice announce definitively, "This one won't last twenty-four hours."

In reaction to his voice, I found myself trying to yell, "I'll bloody fight and live. You'll see!" I was faintly aware of straining to use the word 'bloody', which was unusual for me, because I was conscious of needing to shock, but I was unable to speak.

My mother suffered fractured ribs but Philip was miraculously unhurt. My darling baby had yelled and saved my life. Graham was concussed, but all three of them were allowed to go home after a few hours of observation.

I remained on the critical list for several weeks. My mother was due to go home to America a week after the accident, and she boarded her flight just as planned, saying to Graham, "There is nothing really that I can do, is there?"

This made him feel even more angry with her, as he considered her to be running out on her responsibilities yet again. I did my best over the months that followed, once I could speak, to defend her. The point I made was that Mummy must have had a difficult, lonely life. Her behaviour didn't mean she did not love me, just that she didn't know how to show it, or to take responsibility. My words partly comforted me and helped me to make sense of her actions. Nevertheless, I felt very let down, and that she had left when I could have done with a mother's hand on mine, with kind words, with consolation. Graham remained unconvinced of her reasons and wrote her off as hopeless.

When I awoke from the coma, everybody told me I had been nattering to them in gibberish, until one day a physiotherapist who spoke French said, "No, she is talking about a man in space, Glenn or something. It isn't nonsense. Perhaps she thinks she is there with him."

I had no memory of speaking in French.

"Where do you think you are?" said a friendly nurse sitting on the side of my bed and checking a transparent glass drip to which my arm was attached.

"I have no idea," I replied.

"I'll go and tell sister you're awake. I've been so worried about you," she told me, looking concerned.

"What I mean is, I don't know what hospital I am in, that's all."

She clutched me by the hand, allowing a couple of tears to trickle down her rosy cheeks. "I've been looking after you for nearly four weeks and I've been worried that with your head injury you might have lost your memory. My name's Sally, by the way," she told me.

Graham's parents came down from Birmingham and stayed with him in the flat for two weeks. When it was clear that I was going to be in hospital for a substantial time, they offered to take Philip back to Birmingham with them, so that my father-in-law could go back to work and Graham could return to Harwell.

They brought Philip in to say goodbye to me. As I was still strung up in intensive care in a hammock, with tubes coming out of me, the nurses suggested it might frighten a baby of eight months. He was wisely protected from so dreadful a sight. Mrs Hopkins cried when she saw me.

Pain was a reliable companion. Every four hours I was given another injection of morphine and a cocktail of analgesics. The deadening effect was marvellous for about half an hour, then the throbbing, ripping, tearing electric shocks in my pelvis brought back memories of childbirth. However, there would be no new baby at the end of this unbearable and unproductive ordeal.

"We don't want you getting addicted to the medication," the medical staff all agreed. The idea of addiction was far from my mind, I had enough problems to deal with as it was.

I felt helpless, totally occupied by fighting the pain. It was so overbearing, so all consuming. It became impossible to think of anything else. Too ill to read, there was nothing to distract me.

I would have liked to have written to my friends but such an effort was out of the question. There were drips in both my arms. One was a slow blood transfusion, the other a low dosage of constant morphine.

Then I realised I needed no pen, no paper, no records. All I needed was to listen to the fantastic tunes in my head. The days were so long. They were also endlessly lonely. Breakfast came at seven, made by the night staff before they went off duty at six. The eggs were solid and congealed in fat. It was a rude awakening. The long day meant I could play several scenes from opera to myself. Some days I would imagine an act of *Madame Butterfly*. Another afternoon I would choose a scene from *Boris Godounov*. There were hundreds of melodies and many dramatic stories to occupy my mind, but the discipline required considerable effort.

My reveries became an inspiration and offered a solution to my concerns about my parents. It all began with the music in my head and one particular scene from *Boris Godounov*. The Tsar goes to his children's quarters to comfort his daughter Xenia and to visit Feodor, his son. An enormous globe is centre stage. The Tsar shows his son the lands he will be responsible for after his own approaching death. The music illustrates the changing emotions of the father as he enjoys the company of his children. His tenderness and concern for them is obvious from his demeanour.

Into my dream walked my own father. He took me on his knee, for I was still quite small. The other characters left the stage. He picked up the globe and set it on the table before us. Sometimes the huge ball obliterated him from my sight and he peeked around from the other side to tell me that he was still there, even if I could not see him. He told me how much he loved me, his youngest, smallest daughter and how he thought about me often. He smiled and said he never thought about anybody all the time. He needed to think about the music he was writing, which was so totally absorbing. He hugged me strongly in his arms. I was aware of stirring in my sleep and turning over. When I awoke, the answer to my question was there. Of that I had no further doubt. I was certainly his beloved daughter.

In the days that followed a peaceful feeling pervaded me but I remained preoccupied with my mother's revelation. She was such an unhappy, lonesome person. I wondered if she might have invented the story about the violinist being my father to make me feel I belonged more fully to her, to take some of her own loneliness away. Again my mind was altered by a musical dream. This time it was *Madame Butterfly*.

A beautiful young woman was on the stage, but in no way did she resemble any Cio-Cio-San I had ever seen. Her clothing was traditional Japanese, a white satin robe around her. She stood with her back to me, looking out to sea. The music of 'One Fine Day' was playing in my head, the words imprinted on my mind. Then, suddenly, the music stopped and the woman turned to face me. It was my mother. She dropped the satin robe to reveal a pretty cotton dress, such as she must have worn when I was very small. She told me that she loved me. Then she stepped away and dressed behind a screen, becoming Cio-Cio-San again, with a sword ready for her suicide. I wanted to rush forward to stop her. A tiny child toddled onto the stage then ran into her arms. They both then ran towards me and hugged me, then moved away as suddenly as they had appeared.

The music continued to play in the background and I saw two people at the back of the stage. One was an elegantly dressed American I knew to be Kate Pinkerton, coming to take her husband's child away. I could not see her very clearly. My mother walked towards me, handing me a pair of binoculars. I thanked her, put them to my eyes and immediately recognised the figure. It was my stepmother.

Aroused from my dream by the noises in the ward, I was much distressed. My mother had given me away in sacrifice, so I could have a better life, as had Cio-Cio-San. This seemed so real to me that its tragedy caused me to take the simile further. Had my mother wanted me to believe I was not my father's daughter so as to protect me from the hurt of the scandal? If this was so, it was difficult to imagine why she had played out that dreadful scene in Oxford.

She must have had reasons of her own, I thought. I could not forget her suffering and that she was dying of cancer. In such a grievous state she must have felt quite desperate. Poor darling. How she must be suffering.

The physical pain was a constant companion. When it was really severe I could float it away on an imaginary balloon. The technique gave me a blessed relief for short periods throughout the day. At night they gave me extra sedation which made me sleep for a while.

Visiting hours were not generous, half an hour each evening and half an hour on Sunday afternoons. Graham came to see me each night, seven till seven-thirty, as was the quota. It was several weeks before I was taken from intensive care to a forty-bed ward, mainly occupied by geriatric patients. I was surrounded by old ladies with broken hips who were completely bedridden.

Conversation was restricted in so public an environment and Graham and I began to drift apart during the eighteen months I was captive.

"What did you have for dinner?" I would ask him.

"Baked beans on toast."

"And tonight?" I would venture.

"The same."

"How about tomorrow?"

"The same. I'm not very good at cooking."

We would hold hands and people would watch 'that nice young couple'. "Shame, isn't it?" they said, returning to their own patter. I grew to feel part of an institution and less of a wife and mother. It was three months since I had seen Philip. It was not possible to converse with the other old ladies, for most of them were hard of hearing, and given the crowded conditions of the ward and the constant background noise, intimate communication was discouraged and we had no privacy.

There was no television, but now each bed had a radio headset so I used to listen to it most of the time, usually the classical music station. I often switched it off in favour of the tunes in my head.

The news seldom interested me. I felt out of touch with the

world and only allowed the words to drone along as background company until the music started again.

However, on 13 June 1962, one item riveted my attention.

"We are sad to announce the death of the conductor and composer, Sir Eugene Goossens."

I could not believe the words. I had not seen my father since our last fateful meeting. That had been almost three years ago. He had been in Europe, on conducting engagements. I had written to him about Philip and an occasional postcard confirmed that he was looking forward to meeting his grandson.

It was heartbreaking to realise that the most important chapter in my life was ending. My father was dead. Every beautiful musical melody which made my life worth living had been introduced to me by him. The appreciation and knowledge of music he had bestowed on me were the most important gifts in my life. And he would never be able to answer the question I needed to ask again.

My institutionalised life as a patient isolated me from reality. There was nobody in the ward who shared my past world, or my love of music.

My inherited fortune consisted of all the music ever composed. Excerpts from my favourite operas played in my head in celebration of my father's life, rather than of his death. To me he would never be dead. His memory would live forever through the gifts he had bestowed on me.

In this way, I would always be able to prevent the chapter called 'My Father' from coming to a close.

CHANGE

My father was buried while I was still in hospital. I did not know where or when. Everything about life and death seemed detached and distant. I felt no part of the world at all. It was a very long time before I learned that his grave was at East Finchley. Perhaps he was buried there because that was close to where his father had lived, and perhaps had also been buried. I never had the heart to go and see it. No longer did it seem part of my reality, and I simply did not want to accept that my father was dead. I preferred him still to live on in his legacy of music to me. If you cannot say goodbye before death, or in a funeral ceremony, it is too late to do anything on a physical level. One must do the process of grieving through the mind and the heart. This may seem like denial and it may be, for of course I knew his body was dead, but his spirit would always live within me and within those whose lives he had touched with his goodness and genius.

Aunt Sidonie came to visit me, to speak about my father and to tell me how sorry she was that I had learned of his death so shockingly on the radio. She also told me that Uncle Léon had been seriously injured in a road accident. He had been catapulted through the windscreen and his poor face was so torn apart that it required over a hundred and fifty stitches to rejoin his mouth. He was world renowned as a great oboist. At last his condition was stable. The doctors said that Uncle Léon would survive, but the surgeons did not think he would ever play the oboe again.

It is testimony to his great courage and tenacity that he did master the oboe again, but was not able to play works such as the Richard Strauss concerto. His embouchure had been badly affected by the stitching and nerve damage. He felt he had been cheated of his greatest gift and was very sad. However, he brought joy through his inspirational teaching, and the fact that he mastered playing again at all was miraculous.

My mother had written to Sidonie from New York to tell her about my accident. Mother's sister Catsie had suffered an immense tragedy of her own in the week of my father's death. Her son and daughter-in-law were killed in a car accident, leaving five orphaned children. The two families were overcome by tragedy.

At last my condition was beginning to improve, but occasionally an enveloping grip of searing, burning pain would shatter my lower back. I experienced a sensation of stabbing in my legs and feet. Gratefully, I realised that this pain indicated I had regained feeling in them.

Months passed, birthdays, Christmas, still I remained in hospital. Daily physiotherapy was beginning to bring tingling sensations to my legs, not just when I was in pain. I was confident that I would walk again.

The daily grind of the ward continued. Five times a day there was a bedpan round. Six, ten in the morning, then two, six and ten at night. Everybody in my end of the ward needed a bedpan. In between times, the poor old ladies would wet the bed. The nurses would go through the process of changing their nighties and their sheets. They did this cheerfully and without a single word of complaint.

The woman in the bed next to mine used to tell them, "Sorry, dears. If you could just answer the bell when I ring it, I wouldn't be such a bother."

"We're sorry too," the nurse would say, "but with forty beds, we just can't answer all the bells in time."

Everybody around me seemed anonymous. We were all lonely in a crowded room. We were imprisoned strangers with nothing in common but pain and disability. Our loneliness was too immense to share. Routine visits from busy or superior doctors filled the mornings. Unspeakably dreadful meals, plonked upon our bed trays by staff clearly resenting the tedium of their task, indicated mealtimes. And finally the ridiculous tinkling of Matron's bell alerted visitors that they must leave. Everything conspired to increase rather than dispel our sense of isolation from the world.

We were given one roll of shiny toilet paper on admission, or to be more exact, it was put in our locker, usually just beyond reach. Visitors used to bring in new rolls for us, soft tissue which was nicer, because the ward was always running out. The noise of the trolley, laden with forty metal bedpans, sounded as if all the percussion instruments of an orchestra had decided to contribute towards the most cacophonous of symphonies.

After about six months in hospital, a junior resident came to my bedside. I had never seen him before, and he did not know me. He drew the green curtains around us, looked at me very solemnly, then announced, "I have studied your X-rays. I am afraid to say, there's absolutely no hope. You will never walk again. You must prepare yourself for life in a wheelchair."

Stunned, I was unable to reply. He walked away without looking back. I needed to talk to somebody. Anybody. The woman in the bed next to mine was asleep. What if the doctor's words were true? I waited for my favourite nurse, Sally, to come on duty that evening.

"Sally, Sally. I need your help. I must talk to you. It's dreadful news. The doctor came and said I will never walk again. I don't believe him. You know he's wrong, don't you?"

Sally took my hand and sat quietly for a while, uncertain of what to say. A bell demanded her attention. "I'm terribly sorry, I have to go now, but I'll see if somebody can take over from me. If not, I promise I'll be back the moment I can. Then I'll stay with you when I'm off duty, if you'd like."

I felt totally alone. Graham did not seem to be a part of me any more. The long period of hospitalisation, the lack of privacy, short visits and truncated conversations had made us lose touch. He was never there during the tough times, through no fault of his own, but because of the archaic visiting hours. He had kept his half-hourly tryst each day, but I had noticed for some time that he came out of habit rather than interest and when he did come, he never discussed anything important to him. So when this tragic diagnosis was made, I felt he would not understand, and to tell him I would not walk again would be to admit failure.

I did not feel he was a person in whom I could place my trust any more. I did not feel he would 'take my side'. He had argued so much against my parents. He had criticised them for their neglect and been particularly judgmental of my mother. He knew I had nobody in the family who would stand by me. Perhaps he would seek total control of Philip if I were disabled.

Philip was miles away. How on earth could I look after him? My precious baby would need my help. Would they bring him back to me? Would Graham's parents insist on keeping him, saying I was not capable? The thoughts raced through my head.

After an endless wait, Sally came back to tell me she could find nobody to help her on the busy ward. She offered to come back later.

"You're a darling, Sally. No. You have to study for your exams next week. Please draw my curtains around me. If I can cry in private, I'll work something out. I need to pretend I'm asleep when Graham comes. He is the last person I want to talk to just yet. Keep him away, will you? I need to think about what I am going to tell him."

Visiting time came and went. The babble of voices around me did not include Graham's, no protest, no discreet glance behind my curtains to see if I was all right.

I lay frozen with fear for the future, occasional episodes of sleep allowing me to escape the bewilderment of how I was going to look after my baby. What if they really said I could never have him back? The important thing was to make myself walk, however difficult. I knew I could do it.

The following day, Sally was on day duty. It was comforting to see her smiling, confident, friendly face. As she walked towards me I could see that there was a bulge under her uniform. She put her fingers to her lips and looked carefully around to make sure Matron was nowhere to be seen.

I could not believe my eyes when Sally gently removed the bulge which had given her an enormous bust. It was a tiny grey kitten. She placed it on my stomach so that I could stroke it.

"I found it in the car park last night as I was going home. Perhaps it has lost its mother. I don't know much about kittens but it certainly looks terribly young and hungry, so I'll take it home and feed it when I go off duty. I know you miss your baby and you said you used to have cats. This can be your own little cat, but I'll look after it for you." Delighted, I named her Musetta.

Three weeks earlier the porters had moved my bed out onto a veranda. It was glassed-in, with a scrubbed wooden floor, but the windows did not fit very well so it was colder than the main ward, but much more interesting. There were things outside to watch, people arriving and leaving, different cars in the car park, dogs being walked, leaves falling. It made me feel part of the world again.

My visitors were few and far between. The dear colonel used to come, because he was on the board of the hospital and an important guest not subject to rules. Matron even smiled when he came to see me. In summer he would bring me strawberries from his garden. He would speak of music and ask me what opera I was up to the day he came. I used to make him guess. His favourite was *La Bohème,* so he used to hope his guess was right. I would save it up for the day I thought him most likely to come. Sally would tell me board meeting days, so I always knew when he was coming. It was a great game.

Mrs Tow came from the clinic, as did Dr Ounsted, but Ak had left and gone to London. They had all come together to see me at the beginning, when I was unconscious in intensive care. Apparently Dr Ounsted had burst into tears the moment he saw me.

The kitten slept on my bed during Sally's eight-hour shift. A wet puddle would be deposited near my feet occasionally, nothing else, fortunately, and we kept the secret for several weeks.

One day Matron, an unfriendly and severe woman who, appropriately, I suppose, regarded it as her duty to keep us clean, neat and tidy at all times, had just completed her round of inspection prior to visiting time.

The kitten was under the blanket and wanted to come out. It meowed loudly and Matron looked everywhere to see what the sound could be. The woman in the bed next to mine began to cough loudly to try to muffle the sounds whilst I stroked Musetta, but it was too late.

Matron's face grew as red as a tomato. She straightened her back, put her hands on her hips, then folded her huge arms aggressively in front of her.

"What is this?" she yelled. "An animal in my ward! How dare you! Who brought it in, this horrid bunch of fur?"

"Matron, please, the kitten walked in all on its own," I said.

"Just like pigs fly in too, I suppose, madam," she replied, grabbing the little cat.

"Don't hurt her, please," I begged.

"I'll ring the RSPCA, I will. They'll put her to sleep."

I began to cry, saying, "You're a cold-hearted, mean-spirited person!" and wanting to say much worse than that, but too scared to do so.

Her tone then quietened, her face softened and she added, "They might even find a home for it. You never know."

But she marched from the veranda imperiously, holding the poor little kitten by the scruff of its neck. I never saw it again.

My mother sent me postcards from New York. 'Hope you are better and can go home soon,' was the usual message. She told me nothing about her life or herself. I felt that I still did not know her at all.

Graham's mother wrote to me faithfully once a week, giving me news of Philip. I treasured her letters because I learned about Philip's progress. 'The little darling can feed himself now', or, 'He is beginning to drink from a proper cup'. Most of all I loved the photograph she sent me, which was on my bedside locker all the time.

Everybody admired the picture and said what a beautiful baby he was and how lucky I was to be able to look forward to going home to him. They handed it around from bed to bed, the nurses proudly carrying 'Mrs Hopkins' little boy Philip'.

The old ladies told me it gave me a reason for getting better. The picture showed Philip in a blue romper suit sitting on a rug outside his grandparent's house. He was grinning contentedly and looked chubby, healthy and happy. He had just celebrated his first birthday and, as I hadn't seen him for five months, I missed him more than ever.

In 1963, after almost eighteen months in hospital, the doctors said I could go home in a wheelchair. Due to intensive physiotherapy, I was able to walk a few steps, take ten paces at most; I crawled confidently, and refused to accept a longer stay and the offer of further rehabilitation.

I would teach myself to walk again, doing the ballet exercises I had done when I was five in New York, until I was told I was going to be too tall for ballet and the lessons stopped. Those early months of learning ballet movements might prove useful for strengthening my muscles now, I thought. The exercises I remembered well, and had used them under the bedcovers in an attempt to strengthen the emaciated muscles of my legs.

Graham had seemed distant for some time, since Philip's first birthday. Certainly, hospital visiting hours had been bleak. How could anybody maintain a close friendship in only thirty minutes each day? True, he had come every day, but at times I sensed his boredom and resentment. I hoped that this was something I was imagining.

Whenever I had asked him if anything was wrong, he always replied that things were fine. Conversations were limited and stilted, very much one way. There was not much of interest I could report about my day, and when I asked him about his work he would say defensively, "You know it is government work," making it sound very mysterious. Certainly he never encouraged me to ask further questions. I supposed my long stay in hospital must have been trying for him as well as for me, although it was very different for us both. Surely once I returned home and cooked him some tasty meals, established a routine and we planned together for the future, things would return to our 'good old days'. I have always remained an optimist!

The eagerly anticipated day finally arrived. Graham collected me by taxi and I waved goodbye to Sally and the nurses, who had become my friends. I knew I would miss them, longing to go home but frightened of the changes and responsibilities to be faced.

The taxi took us to our Abingdon flat. Graham had told me Philip would come down from Birmingham with his grandparents in a few days. He had explained I might be tired at first and that I would need to get used to being home. I was awfully disappointed to think Philip would not be there to welcome me.

To my delight, out under the porch was Philip in his grandma's arms. It was the best surprise in the world. I burst into tears as I got out of the taxi, stumbling awkwardly. Graham helped me by holding my arm as I catapulted myself towards my baby, leaning against the brick wall to stop myself from falling. All smiles and gurgles, he hugged me back, saying, "Ma-ma".

It was the first time I had heard so magical a sound, the words all mothers cherish, a precious moment never to be forgotten.

Graham and his father carried me carefully upstairs, laid me down gently on the sofa and Philip climbed confidently onto my lap. Grandma made us tea. "We're not staying for lunch because our train goes at two, but I've made you a nice casserole and put it in the oven to heat it up. We'll be on our way."

After more than a year of being confined to a hospital bed, I felt strange about being in my own home and exceedingly grateful they would not be staying and sleeping on the sofa. I had been allowed only one visitor at a time and, as none of the other patients could walk or leave their beds, I had grown unaccustomed to the sounds of chatter. The family was all talking at once, asking what I would be doing, how I would manage with Philip.

The Hopkinses left. We waved goodbye and thanked them as they walked towards the bus stop, forlorn and sad after enjoying having our baby for so many months. Grandma was crying but trying to be brave, saying, "A baby should be with his mother. I know how you must have missed him, dear."

Grandma said goodbye to her grandson just as my mother had said goodbye to me. I could imagine how empty she must feel. I thanked her again before she left, not only for caring so marvellously for my darling baby, but also for faithfully sending the letters and photographs which had meant so much to me. She was a sweet woman. Grandpa never had much to say. He supported his family and went to work. That was the way he thought things should be.

The hospital had lent me a wheelchair, which was folded and stored on the landing outside the front door. My plan was to dispense with it as soon as possible. The doctors had given me a large container of barbiturates to take, two each night. The tablets made me feel drowsy all day so I crawled to the bathroom and flushed them all down the toilet. Sally had looked up the side effects for me before I left, making me promise not to tell Matron, because nurses were not allowed to give advice. The prescription had been dispensed as treatment for my head injury and coma. As I suffered no dizziness or headaches, I had no wish to take unnecessary medication. There were painkillers too, for the pelvic pain which remained intense at times, particularly now that I was moving around. I put these safely in a bathroom cupboard and locked it.

We ate our lunch almost in silence, making that silly conversation, mainly about the weather, that people make when they do not quite know what to say. I had expected so much of this moment and now we seemed like strangers.

Philip sat in his high chair, patting at his crushed banana with a spoon. He began to cry as soon as he had finished his unappetising concoction from a Junior Heinz tin.

"Time for your afternoon rest, I suppose," said Graham uncertainly, taking him away, changing his nappy and putting him into his cot. Watching him do this, not particularly confidently, I wondered how I was going to manage, given that I could not stand without support. As usual, I presumed I would work something out quickly. I followed him in slowly, leaning against the walls for support to prevent myself from falling.

The nursery was welcoming, with stuffed toys on the window sill and bright yellow painted walls and pretty curtains with teddies all over them. I had chosen the fabric and stitched them by hand the first week we moved in. Everything looked very clean, which was a relief, because I knew Graham was no good at housework. Like his father, he believed this to be woman's work. I wondered who had been doing the cleaning. A frightening thought crossed my mind, then I dismissed it as ridiculous jealousy. We closed the door of the nursery and went into the kitchen.

I stumbled after Graham awkwardly, my footsteps unsteady, my back aching from the effort, my legs almost crumbling. What I wanted was to have him hold me in his arms. Instead, he pulled out a chair for me and helped me to sit down. He glanced at me in such an uncomfortable manner it was clear that even a cuddle was out of the question.

"I have something to tell you," he began, turning his face away, just as my mother had done not so long ago. "During the time you have been in hospital, I've been seeing another girl."

"Of course you must have seen other people. It's been such a long time."

"Well, more than just seeing," he said, looking even more uncomfortable, clearing the dishes away without looking up at me. "Her name is Rebecca."

"Tell me everything," I said, my heart almost stopping with dread. "Is it someone you have grown very fond of?"

"It is far more serious than that. I love her."

Stupefied by his words, I could feel my world once again coming to an end. My mind rushed ahead with fear. Love. He loved her. That meant he no longer loved me. And his son, Philip. What of his love for us? He must never have loved us, if he found it so easy to turn to another. Maybe he had only had a fling? I looked at him and he began to speak again.

"You see, we work together. One thing led to another. I felt so guilty about you, knowing I was the cause of your accident. I couldn't help it. Really I couldn't. She is a lovely person."

His voice droned on, and the fear came to me again, that same fear that had terrified me when my mother told me about the Swedish violinist. I almost knew what he was going to say, but something inside me hoped I would not have to hear the words.

Graham cleared his throat, looked me straight in the eye and announced, "I know the timing is bad . . . but you will have to know sooner or later . . . Becky is going to have my baby."

He had spoken the very words I dreaded most, the words that were going to change our future forever. Home at last from hospital after eighteen months of yearning for the love of my husband, now it was to evaporate, like everything in the past. All that had been needed to turn our life from that of a happy family was one car accident. Archaic visiting hours. Cruel injuries. A feckless, weak man. A woman he described as 'a lovely person'.

"I never blamed you for the accident," I told him, hoping to redeem something for us both. But I began to feel the cold shiver of defeat. The Italians have a saying, 'I just felt somebody walk across my grave.'

That same chill now froze me.

"Love is not simply a tap one can turn on and off. Of course I still love you," he said in a voice that lacked conviction.

With my own tap having just been firmly turned off, I wondered why he was making an attempt to explain. I had believed that he adored Philip and that he had loved me. Now I knew that the physical love and warmth that I had so longed for would never be mine again. He had said the words. He loved Rebecca. He even referred to her as 'Becky'.

As much as I wanted to plead with him, I did not want him to stay with me out of guilt or pity. What I had to decide, and immediately, was that I had to start life now the way it would be for the future.

"All right," I told him in my bravest voice. "Go to your Becky and enjoy the new baby. Forget guilt and obligation. Make a new life for yourself. I will make my own way, with Philip, and we will manage without you. This is not the way I wanted to bring up *our* baby. But now that I am to bring up *my* baby alone, you may visit him whenever you wish. Go now, please, go tonight. Collect your things later. Go now, though, before I change my mind. I have grown accustomed to being without you. I'll manage with Philip. Just go."

To my further amazement, he went. Just like that. There were mutterings without much conviction to the effect of how would I manage and how sorry he was. He expressed no further guilt, no anxiety for our future nor apology for his betrayal. Released, by my words, apparently, from obligation, he packed a bag, pecked me on the cheek, just as if he were leaving for the laboratory for work on any normal day. He simply walked away from us.

My worst nightmare had been realised. But perhaps it was not the worst. I still had Philip. I was very much afraid of how I was going to manage physically, much more afraid of practical matters than of the emotions that would overcome me later. For the moment, I felt completely numb. I suppose it is like when one hears suddenly of an unexpected death. Death is always unexpected. So is abandonment.

When Philip awoke from his rest, I crawled into his bedroom, stretched up and took him out of his cot. "We are on our own now," I told him.

It was difficult at first, not being able to walk, but I could stumble and crawl. It was imperative for me to overcome this, and quickly. The wheelchair was useful around the house and Mrs Hadley upstairs, who had been looking after the cat, did my shopping. It was good to have Mimi back with her dear little white paws and generous purr of contentment. Even her name brought music back into the house.

My neighbour still called me 'Mrs Hopkins'. She smiled in a friendly manner, was terribly kind and helpful. "You can always count on me to help you out. If you need any shopping, or somebody to help you to get down the stairs safely. Or to mind the lad. My husband could mend a fuse for you or change a light globe, that sort of thing. Just knock on my door."

It was comforting to know they were there, and I did call on their help, but only when it was essential.

Music played constantly on my gramophone and it put rhythm and vitality into my exercises. Fortunately my memory firmly held every movement from that one year of ballet work at the age of five. It had intrigued me, and I had found the movements awkward then, but realised how strong it had made my legs, how much faster I had been able to run as a result. I knew there must have been a good reason why I had done them then, and was enormously grateful to put them to important use now. As I was strengthening my muscles, Philip adored mimicking me. It is very funny to watch a little boy not quite two years old trying to perform a pirouette! He would also watch amazed as I tried to do straight leg raising, lying on the floor beside me, imitating me, then clambering all over me and hugging me. We would crawl around indoors, and take our meals sitting together on the floor. It was fun, and it was not difficult. When a beloved child giggles and makes you laugh, it is not possible to be unhappy for more than a moment.

It was obvious that the pram would make a marvellous walking frame, so I used it to increase my distances outside, and gradually I walked a little further each day until I could do my own shopping. By increasing the distance by a hundred yards each day, I knew I would achieve that, as the shops were close by and I would have no weight to carry, as I could put everything in the pram. My plan was to take the wheelchair back to the hospital by bus within six weeks and to visit the nurses with my baby.

Household tasks were made amusing by Philip's desire to assist. Hanging out the washing was difficult, as I still could not stand without holding on to something, but by dragging a chair out from the ground floor laundry I could lean on it and peg clothes to the line. Philip would hand me the pegs and the clothes, one by one. It took an incredibly long time, but all we had to do was play and make up for lost time. It was wonderful to have so much free time to enjoy my favourite little companion. He was a million times better than all those cats I had adopted around the world, giving them love and hoping for some in return. Now I had all that love. But I no longer had the love of a husband. I missed Graham immensely, longing for his once-loving arms to hold me, but I was determined that such a loss must be privately endured.

Philip was a smiling, cheerful baby, and I was proud to take him to meet Sally back at the hospital. Mrs Tow from the clinic had driven over to help us. She insisted it was impossible for me to get a wheelchair, a pushchair and a two-year-old onto a bus, however determined I might be. It was particularly grand to see her then, on one of the many visits when she had 'just popped in to see how we were managing'. It was pleasing to hear Sally praising me for walking in such a short time. She declared Philip to be the most beautiful child she had ever seen.

Now that the wheelchair was officially disposed of there were other goals to attain. Money was needed. Graham promised to give us the rent money and something towards our food, but I would obviously have to get a job. I wanted to become a teacher, so that my hours would fit in with being a mother. Money must be saved, too, for our return to Australia. This priority offered me a positive goal and a concentration of purpose to overcome all obstacles. It was my driving force.

Pen and paper in hand, I calculated the money we would need. My sums showed that I could manage on ten pounds a week. The rent was two pounds ten, paraffin oil for the heating the same, food the same, leaving the remainder for clothing and extras.

Graham was not sure he could manage ten pounds but said he would try. I pointed out that a court of law could compel him to pay for our maintenance. He was very angry at my words. The notion of doing overtime or taking extra work tutoring, for instance, never crossed his mind. There was no question of state aid; it was not available in those days and in our case, there was no need for it. We would manage. I had never been afraid of work.

I wrote to various teacher training colleges in the hope of securing a place.

THE PURSUIT OF
KNOWLEDGE

Westminster College, halfway between Oxford and Abingdon, offered me a place. To my surprise, my former boss Dr Ounsted had filled in an application form on my behalf. He sent it to me for signature when he knew I was well enough to embark on a career. He had always wanted me to train as a teacher, telling me in the past that I could gain much more satisfaction from working directly with children than being a medical secretary and researcher.

When the papers arrived they included a questionnaire and some test material which I completed. To my delight the offer of a place was followed by the allocation of a grant. It was relatively easy, at last, to access an education. I would have loved my father to be alive so I could show him that things were going to work out for me and that everything would be all right. I knew he would be happy for me.

Westminster College was only about seven miles from my flat at Abingdon, but while I could still only walk a few hundred yards it remained inaccessible for me by public transport. The principal of the college insisted I purchase a motor car. With a kindness and foresight which was to enrich my three years at college, he and his wife volunteered to be guarantors for my small hire purchase agreement.

The principal was a tall man, his deportment stately, his language eloquent. His wife looked as if she had been chosen for the role by Central Casting. Her pretty, short, curly grey hair framed the perfect features of her oval face. The clothing she selected was traditional English, as displayed on covers of *Country Life*, pearls and twinsets, practical woollen skirts, never trousers. She was both surrogate mother and perfect lady.

In their home they welcomed many students who visited frequently and often stayed to tea. Their hospitality was generous, the reception unconditional and they never offered advice on personal matters unless pressed to do so. They were the very image of perfect married bliss which most of us hoped to attain. As a single parent, I was grateful for their example. In common with many mothers who manage alone, I felt guilty that my son had no man to rely on, or on whom to base his ideals.

My grant was for ten pounds a week which, despite my optimistic calculations, barely covered essential provisions. To stretch these funds to their limit, they also had to include the purchase and running of a car: Renée's red Renault.

It was a cute little car, dented from previous adventures, sufficiently scratched to avoid the compulsion to wash and polish it, for clean or dirty, no difference was apparent. It represented freedom, the four wheels which would take us to see our friends and enable me to obtain my qualification.

To earn extra money, in term breaks I returned once again to the Children's Hospital as a medical research assistant. Dr Ounsted was still medical director of the hospital and the clinic where I had worked earlier. Philip was welcome to come along with me and play, in the care of the nurses, while I worked. Arrangements were flexible and the knowledge I acquired while assisting with projects gave me new insight into areas of special education, invaluable to my future college assignments, as well as providing guidelines for my future career.

These spells of additional work provided for unexpected expenses such as car repairs, excessive electricity bills or the purchase of clothing for us both. We joined the category to which people refer as 'poor but happy'. The cliché did not sit well, because there were moments when I did feel immensely rich spiritually, but at other times I was very unhappy. The summer vacations were best for increasing my income and enabled me to save as much as I could for our return to Australia.

People were dismissive and unkind about Graham. I had no wish for Philip to remember him unfavourably and had long overcome the anger I once harboured towards him. In many ways, our life was now much more complete and focused than ever before. My energy was reserved for the future, not for the past. Graham continued to express remorse over the accident, often bringing it into the conversation during his weekly visit.

"How are things going at home?" I asked one day, eager to hear that he was making positive plans for his new family's future at least. The mastery of my feelings in public was becoming more than satisfactory, and I was proud of that. Privately I remained devastated by the accident and its consequences.

"Well, thanks for asking. Not so well. My time with Philip is making things difficult at home. Becky is always on at me about it."

I nodded. "So, what do you suggest?" I said, beginning to follow his drift.

"I think I should make it alternate Saturdays," he announced.

Disappointed to see him depriving his son of a father, I decided nonetheless to agree and see how things developed. My conviction was that Philip needed regular visits from his father, but I would not dream of demanding anything that was not offered willingly.

Music continued to be the foundation of my life. It was something of which I could be certain. When he had first returned to England after his miserable scandal in Sydney and before Philip was born, Daddy had occasionally put an extra ten shilling note in his occasional letters to me 'to buy something I needed' and I had always used that money for second-hand records. Often he would remember my birthday or Christmas and again send me a pound which I converted immediately into records too. How I treasured them, and how much more so when I learnt how dearly those small financial offerings had cost my father. Also, I bought myself a couple of second-hand records whenever I could find a bargain at a church fete. There were now twenty altogether, and my record collection, scratched and used as it was, offered a variety of symphonies, *concerti* and opera ensembles to which we listened constantly in the background.

Philip particularly enjoyed the Saint Saens Piano Concertos Two and Four, describing them as 'the horsy music, Mummy'. He used to jump up and down when he heard them and hum along as he listened to melodies, pretending he was a singer and pulling extraordinary faces.

Unpredictably, pain occasionally returned in huge waves and my pelvis felt as if it was cracking. Walking would become so painful I could hardly bear it. At college I would press on, but at home I could lie down. Philip would bring me a book and we would lie on the sofa together and enjoy looking at books or reading stories.

I was afraid of pain, frightened not because it hurt so much, but because it might prevent me from continuing with my studies, or caring for Philip adequately. There was no treatment. The local medical practice was inevitably impersonal, with five doctors seeing patients on a roster basis. You never knew who you would get to see. They gave me pain killers and told me to rest. My back pain never caused me to miss a lecture and fortunately I always managed to make it into work at the children's hospital when the opportunity arose. Then suddenly an unpredictable event changed our lives dramatically.

One warm Sunday in late spring I took Philip to Abingdon, where a new paddling pool had been built by the river. It was an attractive area within a small park where many children gathered to play, the toddlers sitting in the water, pouring it over each other's heads with buckets and spooning it into their mouths with spades. The sound of happy laughter rippled merrily.

That evening, Philip began to vomit. He was very sick indeed. Then his stomach started losing its contents into his nappy. I knocked on my neighbour's door and asked her to come in to mind him while I went out to the phone box to call the doctor.

The doctor came, examined Philip and told me to give him a pint of water with a teaspoon of salt and a teaspoon of sugar, as much as he could take. He promised to come and see us the following morning.

All night poor Philip continued being sick, distressed and exhausted, his eyes dark in their tiny sunken sockets. I was grateful to hear the doctor's knock at seven in the morning.

"Mrs Hopkins, how's the wee lad?"

I told him. He looked at Philip again.

"We'll need to send some faecal specimens to the laboratory."

He gave me a container and told me the district nurse would visit in a couple of hours.

Philip's condition continued to deteriorate. By the time the nurse arrived, I was frantic with worry. Everything else I should have done had been forgotten, meetings, exams, lectures. I slipped a note under my neighbour's door asking her to ring my college to say I would not be at college for a while.

When the nurse came, she took Philip's temperature. The thermometer gave a reading of one hundred and three. She helped me take the specimens for examination.

"I don't want to worry you, Mrs Hopkins, but there are nine children in the area with similarly serious symptoms. They are all extremely ill. Either it is food poisoning, or an outbreak of salmonella."

"How bad is that?" I asked her.

"The laboratory will test these specimens right away. I'll drive them into Oxford myself. It should take about twenty-four hours to check for the disease. Meanwhile, please do not touch or come into physical contact with anybody else. If we cannot contain whatever it is, there will be an epidemic."

"But I live alone with my child. How am I to shop, make phone calls, hang out the washing?"

"I'll have a word with your neighbour. She seems a pleasant lady, and when she met me on the landing she asked if there was anything she could do to help. I'll be back this afternoon. Doctor will call tonight at tea time. If you know we are definitely coming, and I promise you we will, you won't need to go out to telephone us. Obviously, get word via your neighbour if anything changes for the worse."

With my baby not quite three years old and unable to retain nourishment, I could not see how anything *could* be worse. I cradled him in my arms between his bursts of sickness, over-whelmed to see him weakening and in such distress.

The nurse visited as promised, helped me to clean Philip up yet again, took his temperature, which was now even higher, and reassured me I was managing everything very well. Then the doctor arrived.

"I'm afraid the news is not good. The initial diagnosis is *salmonella typhi*. It is not as serious as typhoid, but it is never-theless a notifiable disease that is important and requires very careful monitoring. Fluids for your baby, plenty of rest for you, although you'll laugh at me for saying that, and absolute quaran-tine. There is no other treatment at this stage. Nurse will tell you how to manage the quarantine."

I was devastated. Typhoid. When as a child I had travelled

through the Suez Canal, a man on board had died of typhoid and the entire ship was quarantined. I was well aware of the seriousness of the disease. Nurse assured me once more that *salmonella typhi* was not as serious as typhoid, but all I could think of was that my precious baby could die if I failed to manage his illness perfectly. Surely he would be better cared for in hospital, however much I would hate to be separated from him again.

"Don't be afraid," said the nurse. "We are isolating all nine babies in their own homes. It is much safer to contain the disease this way than to risk spreading infection throughout a hospital. I have been allocated to all nine of you and I will visit twice a day. Your doctor will attend to each child personally. This way, we minimise cross-infection. We will be popping in and out several times a day."

It was comforting to have our own special nurse and doctor. They looked after us with great kindness and care.

"How on earth did Philip pick up this illness?" I asked the doctor.

"From the information you gave us, we are checking out the two factors which seem common to you all. One possibility as a source is a type of canned corned beef which comes from Argentina, which some of you used in sandwiches this week. The other, and the very idea of it renders me speechless with fury, could be the paddling pool itself."

"But I can't bear canned beef, and Philip certainly doesn't eat that sort of thing," I told him. "Somebody must have made a mistake."

"As soon as we've done further tests, I promise to let you know the cause. We've closed the paddling pool as a precaution."

Philip began to respond to the fluids. His temperature vacillated alarmingly. His cheeks would burn flame-red for a few hours, then he would shiver at times and his tiny body would feel so cold I had to wrap him in several layers of blankets. The nurse advised me on every aspect of his care, dressed him, humoured him, and even made me cups of tea. She took shopping lists to my neighbour, instructing her to leave the purchases at my door and not to come inside. The quarantine was the key to containment.

Mrs Hadley did as instructed, and would ring the doorbell cheerily three times just to say 'hello' as she did so. When I hung out my washing, she was not to come out to see me either, and I was to wipe the washing line after using it and bringing in my laundry as an added precaution against spreading the disease. So I rang on her bell three times, using a rubber glove, to give my 'hello, I'm going downstairs' signal. All the other neighbours were at work during the day, so it was only the two of us who risked contact.

The drama continued for three weeks, then Philip's blood tests came back showing he was clear of infection. It was a wonderful moment. I was so grateful to the doctor and the nurse. As soon as I was given the all clear I went out and bought them each a thank-you card, and a small box of chocolates for my devoted neighbour.

There had apparently been some administrative confusion over the purification for the paddling pool; in consequence, the lives of nine babies had been placed in mortal danger. It was a credit to the local medical and administrative services that no life had been lost and that the situation had been contained without press reports that could have led to widespread panic. I was exceedingly grateful that Philip had been fully restored to health.

I had missed three weeks of college lectures, but all my tutors, as soon as they were told of the emergency, had kept notes for me. I would be able to make up the lost assignments in craft and French before the end of term. The principal and his wife congratulated me on Philip's resilience and recovery.

Philip and I were beginning to have a wonderful time. My college schedule was not taxing and fitted in perfectly with his nursery school, which he attended only in the mornings. At three years old he was such a sturdy and interesting little chap that I hated leaving him at all.

When I first arrived in Oxford, it had not occurred to me to try to discover if any of our Australian musician friends were there, or in London. My life had been concerned mainly with survival, establishing myself, getting through exams and finding work. Then one day, happily, I caught sight of a poster announcing a production of *Carmen* at the Oxford Playhouse. Among the names on the playbill I saw those of Jenifer Eddy and Geoffrey Chard. These were friends I had known since I was a child back in Sydney. I saved up for a ticket, and went backstage afterwards to see them both. It was so exciting and comforting to see them and to hug them. Through our discussion I realised that many other old friends from the Con were singing in London. Neil Easton was there, too, with his wife Doreen, who immediately insisted on inviting me to come up to London, giving me their phone number and address. They had three children and invited me to bring Philip to meet them for a weekend whenever we were free.

They lived in Harrow and the journey should have not been difficult, but I was always hopeless with directions, and things never changed! Driving around London with which I was scarcely familiar, seemed a nightmare of spaghetti junctions and no through roads. To anybody else, it was not a difficult journey, as they had said in their first letter of invitation, just straight up the A40 from Oxford and turn off after High Wycombe towards Harrow. But it was hopeless. I became lost time and time again, going around in circles, and on one particular occasion when I finally thought I had got it right, there was a Detour sign ahead. I pulled the car over. Philip was asleep in the back. I put my head down on the steering wheel and stupidly began to cry.

A massive lorry pulled up beside my car, obstructing the flow of traffic. Out stepped a man who looked like Eliza Doolittle's father. He was smiling broadly, the whites of his eyes in stark contrast to his coal-stained face.

"What's the matter, me duck?" he asked with much concern.

"I'm lost, that's all!" I told him as cheerfully as I could. "It's nothing really. So sorry if I worried you."

"That's all right, me lovely, just wait while I park me truck," he said. "Won't be a tic." He moved his truck, parking it on the pavement, returning with a wink.

"Nobody minds if it's a coal delivery," he assured me. "Now, where are you going?"

I pulled out my tattered map and showed him the street I was looking for.

"Goodness, gracious, no, luv! You're quite out of yer depth. You're miles away from yer friends."

My crestfallen look inspired him.

"Now you listen to me," he began, tweaking Philip's cheek and leaving a sooty patch on it, "you and the little lad shouldn't be a-wandering around London all alone now it's getting dark. How about I show you the way? I'll lead in me truck. If you're in trouble and can't follow me, give four toots and I'll wait for ye."

Off we set, a curious pair, in convoy. He drew his truck up in front of my friends' house, waited for me to park safely, then was about to be on his way.

"No. Don't go, please. You've been so kind," I said to him as my friends came out to meet me.

"Who's your escort?" they asked kissing me on both cheeks and taking Philip's tiny hand as he wriggled sleepily out of the car.

"This is the kind man who showed me the way," I introduced the coal man.

"Well, you'd better come in and have some tea," they said, inviting him to sit down with us at the kitchen table.

"We don't even know your name," I said.

"T'is no matter. Glad to be of service, me lovely." He downed a cup of tea, munched two biscuits, putting one in his pocket 'for later'. Then he stood, thanked my friends, tweaked Philip's cheek again, and bowed to me saying, "Now I'll be off."

Neil Easton was a baritone singing at Sadler's Wells and his wife Doreen had made their home an agreeable and welcoming centre in London for homesick Australians. They had three children about Philip's age.

There would congregate various Australian singers: baritones, basses, tenors and sopranos; we even had a mezzo. In summer the men would play cricket on the village green or in winter find a football match to attend. Doreen and I stayed with the children, doing the cooking and enjoying a chat. It was like having an extended family, and I adored seeing them.

We used to talk about Sydney all the time and our dreams were centred on when and how we would return. We all loathed the cold, wet English climate. But because we all shared in this feeling, it became far less awful as we joked about sunburn, surf and mosquitoes, pretending to swat them away, particularly on freezing wintry days.

Occasionally, when we stayed overnight, Doreen would mind Philip so that I could go and hear her husband Neil sing. Among his roles was that of Rigoletto. I couldn't afford to pay for opera tickets and treasured the gift of 'complimentaries', so whenever there was one to spare, Doreen would invite me to use it.

Australian singers were very successful in London in the 1960s. Joan Sutherland, whom I remembered from her debut in Daddy's opera *Judith*, was now one of the most important sopranos in the world. Elizabeth Fretwell, Ronald Dowd, John Shaw, Jenifer Eddy, Geoffrey Chard, Marie Collier, Margreta Elkins and Gregory Dempsey were performing regularly at Sadler's Wells or at the Royal Opera House at Covent Garden. It was said, at that time, that if the Australians were to go home, London would have no opera at all.

Doreen suggested, "Why don't you go back to Australia and see if you can persuade conductors to have operas performed in their original languages? You could do the French coaching."

We all laughed, but firmly believed that we would all eventually return, either to sing or to retire, and I would go on to teach French. We all wanted our children to grow up in the fresh air, with warmth and sunshine.

The best things of my childhood had been music, opera, friends and sunshine. All these were gradually returning to my life again, even if the sun shone less ardently. I intended to ensure that Philip had as happy a time as I had before I left Australia. We could not afford a piano, so recordings would have to do for the meantime. Maybe later I would be able to afford an instrument and lessons for him. At least he deserved the opportunity, if he wanted to learn.

THE FLYING HEIFER

My college course was in French and craft, selected to afford maximum time with Philip, and using skills that could be formalised without too great or studious an effort. Although I had considered doing music, not having a piano, and having had no practice for so long, I lacked the confidence to expose my abilities, or lack of them.

At Abingdon we were always pleased to see visitors, particularly if it meant having foreign exchange students to stay. A French girl from Lille came to live with us for a week, sleeping on the sofa bed. She attended lectures with me at college, and was particularly eager to see the countryside. She spoke little English, had no desire to change this state of affairs, and taught me idioms the nuns would never have known, useful for cursing motorists whose behaviour irritated us. I found her company most amusing. She declared Philip to be the most adorable child she had ever met.

Our most memorable excursion was to see the ancient white

horse on the hill at Uffington in Berkshire, about five miles west of Wantage. According to legend, this was the place where St George killed the dragon. Of course Philip was fascinated by the idea and wanted to see a dragon this very minute. The white horse was best viewed at a distance, which meant that it must have involved considerable feats of planning at the time of its construction. The French girl said that she had never seen anything quite like it.

We also drove through the Cotswolds, admiring the picture-postcard villages, detouring to places that had names which amused her, such as Stow-on-the-Wold and Shipton-under-Wychwood. It was worth taking her there simply to hear her extremely weird pronunciation of the names. She bought us a drink in the beautiful cobbled high street of Burford, stopping to buy souvenir spoons for her parents' collection.

We travelled mainly on secondary roads and country lanes. My French friend was a reasonable navigator, but she was a city girl like me, and had little idea of the countryside. I had always been hopeless at directions, and country ways, so we were both astonished when our progress was suddenly halted by a herd of cows being moved at milking time.

A farmer, ruddy of face and cheery of manner, alighted from his mud-splattered Land Rover and approached us. "Never mind, me luvs. Sorry to hold thee up. Me cows be powerful slow this afternoon. I'll lead them to the left side, mind how you go, overtake on the right and no harm will come to thee."

Cautiously, I negotiated a path around the herd as the heavily plodding, uncomfortable cows with their full udders thumped along placidly beside me. To my right was a grassy bank, sloping quite steeply towards the road. At the top of the ridge was a young heifer, sprightly and rapid of movement. All of a sudden she crashed onto the bonnet of my car, her weight crushing the metal and sinking into the front of my little red Renault. With the engine at the back, there was little resistance. Frightened, she extricated herself the moment I stopped, bashing the left headlight with a violent explosion of glass which caused the timid older cows to stampede around my car.

"Cows everywhere looking in," said Philip delightedly, waving to them.

The farmer approached the window. "Sorry, me love. I be not knowing what to do 'bout this. Me farm be over the hill, if thee needs me. Bit of damage she done, the rascal." He laughed contentedly, surveying the damage and shaking his head, then touched his cap respectfully with his hand by way of farewell.

I wrote down the number of his Land Rover, we shook hands and he said, "Phone me wife if thee have bother with insurers. Never ye worry, suppose the farm be covered for this sort of thing."

Reassured, I drove home, the caved-in bonnet a curious twist of metal, but as it grew dark, the absence of a left headlight was bothersome. We passed no telephone boxes, so the best thing to do was to press on regardless. It was six in the evening, and businesses would be closed. In the morning, I'd go to the phone box and look up the name of a solicitor. I was in the Automobile Association. They would be sure to help me, I thought. Unconcerned, I set about making supper.

Philip was busy on the floor of the living room, my French guest finding paper and paints for him as he enthusiastically completed a picture. It was a vivid yellow, blue, black and red creation. The red Renault took the central position and in his blue sky was a black circle. He pointed to it explaining, "I can't draw cows, Mummy," and then showed me the green he was going to introduce to represent the grassy bank.

"Cow jumped over the car, Mummy," he announced, immensely pleased by his own wit as he also included a large smiling moon.

The solicitor was not as confident about my rights as I had been. When he consulted his law books, he discovered that under a law passed around the turn of the century, a farmer was only liable for thirty-two shillings of damage per head of cattle. He therefore telephoned the farmer.

"That be the law, then. I'll give the poor lass a cheque for forty shillings. That'll be fair," my generous farmer told him.

The local mechanic proclaimed the vehicle unsafe. The bodywork and a new light would cost me forty pounds, four whole weeks of my full grant. My farmer's forty shillings would not be of much help. The mechanic offered to carry out the work, saying I could pay him when I had the money. That meant my next holiday secretarial pay was spoken for, but what luck to find such an understanding mechanic, not only trusting but also willing to wait for his money.

During that first year, Graham had visited Philip once a fortnight, but unreliably, for four months. When he next came to see us, he wanted to change our agreement again. His new baby daughter was now three months old.

"Could we make it once a month?" he declared without displaying emotion of any particular kind.

"How do you really feel about such an arrangement, Graham?" I asked.

"It seems a good idea," he replied.

The request came as no surprise. He had frequently missed visits of late, although I appreciated that he had always fore-warned me. My son was never going to wait expectantly for an unreliable parent. Graham was becoming a very shady figure in our lives. It was hard to believe how much we had once shared.

With the aim of shocking him into some sense, I thought carefully about my next statement. "If Philip means so little to you that you only want to see him once a month, I suggest you forget all about him."

Graham agreed. It seemed unbelievable to me. I was appalled, but not particularly surprised. It was as if for him the past had never existed.

"All right, then. I won't be coming at all." His remark was neither spiteful nor petulant. He just did not seem to care.

I consoled myself that this meant he probably would raise no objections when I arranged to take my son to Australia.

PLANNING TO LEAVE

In 1966, at the end of the second year of my three year course at Westminster College, I could not believe my eyes when I read an advertisement in the *Sunday Times*. In Australia, the New South Wales government was conducting a massive campaign to recruit teachers.

I rushed to see my principal, waving the advertisement at him, laughing with happiness.

"I suppose you want me to do something about this for you?" he asked good-naturedly. He made a phone call to Australia House, as the paper instructed. "I believe quite a few students due to graduate next year will be keen for an interview," he told them.

The response was sufficient to justify a visit from a departmental inspector. He was offered accommodation in the college guest apartment, and one hundred students applied for an interview. Twenty-five applicants were successful. To my great joy, I was one of them.

My future employment was assured, dependent upon my gaining my diploma, of course. Now it was up to me to get the very best marks possible for all my final exams. The only further hindrance would be a medical examination, to be held in London. Perhaps my body was less fit than my mind, and I really dreaded the possibility of being failed on medical grounds. I wanted nothing to stand in the way of my plans.

Because I had moved around so much, I had lost the Versailles address of dear Madame de la Chapelle for whom I had worked as an *au pair*. I would have loved to have written to her about college, Philip, my plans to return to Sydney. She really would have cared and been interested. I had been bad at keeping in touch and had lost contact with many friends and relatives.

My sister Donie wrote regularly. It was good to know she was well and that things were working out for her. Sadly, her personal life had not always been happy. We did not seem to have much luck in our family. When children grow up without experiencing the happiness of their parents' togetherness, through good times and bad, it is hard to find a role model for one's own marriage. Certainly neither my sister Donie nor I had been fortunate and as in later years I got to know some of my cousins, I learned of their difficulties as well.

Aunt Sidonie had been the mainstay of the family, but a very busy one, working full time in the BBC Symphony Orchestra until she was in her eighties and then teaching at the Guildhall for a further ten years. Aunt Marie's daughter Jean had been in touch with me, and I had been able to see her family a little during my late teens, but we had also lost touch. Usually when I left a place, and I had moved many times, I would write enthusiastically to members of the family whom I knew and to friends, but if they did not reply, I assumed they had written me off. This was foolish of me, but it is perhaps explained by my lack of self-esteem and genuine belief that there was no particular reason they would be interested in maintaining contact.

Aunt Sidonie had visited me in hospital at Oxford when she

learned about our accident, but due to her busy schedule she came only once. She did her best to maintain a correspondence with me, however many times I moved, and I believed in her love and interest and hoped she would be glad to see me and Philip. We drove down to Surrey to see her before leaving for Australia and I have a photo of Philip enjoying himself riding their large industrial lawnmower alongside their beautiful German pointer Fritz. Uncle Norman was still alive then, and it was good to visit them both and feel part of the family. But I was not then in touch with anyone else in the family other than my sister Donie in Australia. She was the only family member still there and I longed to join her.

It was a disappointment that Mummy wrote only at Christmas and that she did not put an address on the back of the cards. The letters I had sent her were returned marked 'addressee unknown', so I had no way of staying in touch with her.

When anybody wrote to me, they always received a reply, but if people stopped writing, I assumed they were no longer interested. Betsy Brown had remained steadfast. Her letters were much more than a pleasure to receive, they were my most reliable point of reference. Arriving faithfully once a fortnight, they were as dependable as the rising and the setting of the sun. They were my lifeline.

I wrote to her enthusiastically now, in greater detail, telling her of my plans, asking for advice on where we might live, and whether she was in touch with any of my old friends. She wrote of everything, from economic conditions, kookaburras singing, the end of the Australian winter, to the antics of her spaniel dogs. With each letter, and the marking of the calendar on the wall, the possibility of our return became a certainty.

In August 1967 I had written to Donie asking her to sponsor our return home. She had not replied. This concerned me, as she had always seemed enthusiastic about my return and usually replied promptly to my letters. Perhaps she was not well. I must contact her as soon as I arrived, I thought. As I required a sponsor, someone who would be responsible for me during my first week in Sydney, I wrote to Miss Brown asking her if she would be that sponsor. She cabled an immediate reply, 'I have registered as your official sponsor and will be at the airport to meet you'.

On the morning of my French examination my car broke down. It was the oral, and I hoped to get my best marks for it, so I was particularly anxious for the rescue service to come and fix my car quickly. I decided to put my misfortune to good use. There weren't many examiners around, or so I had heard, who spoke idiomatic French. Even if they did, they might not know much about the inner workings of the motor car. In my briefcase was a large Collins dictionary with a diagram of a car at the back, with arrows to identify the various motor parts. I was unaware of these terms in English, let alone French, but while I waited an hour for the repair man, I learnt how to say that the gear box was jammed so that my car would operate only in reverse. I identified a few further dazzling terms, just for good measure.

When the repairman arrived, he took less than ten minutes to fix whatever it was, something quite simple which defied translation. Then I was on my way.

The examiner was a grey-haired man who told me he was a retired Army colonel. I wanted to ask him if he knew the colonel who had rescued me from the accident, but this did not seem the right time. He greeted me in English, which was not a very impressive beginning, and ushered me into the tutor's room.

I introduced myself, changing the language to French, then launched into my verbose explanation concerning the reasons for my tardiness, elaborating every minute detail of the bothersome vehicle. Fortunately he was as dazzled as I had intended him to be, even asking if I had taken a mechanic's course.

The oral exam continued over coffee, and the examiner confessed that his knowledge of colloquial French was limited.

He assured me, rather pompously, that he did possess an exceptional ear for fluency and linguistic skill and indicated that he
appreciated my efforts.

My chief interest at college had been preparation for teaching
children with special learning difficulties. There had been no particular course to follow, which had been a disappointment. It was
arranged that some of the work I had done at the Child Guidance
Clinic and subsequently at the Park Hospital for Children during
the vacations would be used as assignments for this. So, as a substitute for some of the education topics, I wrote about autistic and
emotionally disturbed children and their learning difficulties, some
of which were attributable to medication which caused them to be
drowsy or inattentive. My clinic colleagues had been generous with
their time in helping me write these essays. I hoped to teach special
education when I finished college.

The craft exam was going to prove much trickier. Craft should
never have been an option for me. After reading the syllabus I had
hoped to learn skills that would be useful in home making. My
ideas of becoming a brilliant toy maker were soon dashed as I
settled for the simpler skills of knitting and making felt stuffed
toys. The construction of furniture for the home was another
dream to remain unrealised.

I had had rather a chequered career with the craft master, who
was a perfectionist. Before becoming a lecturer he had been a
craftsman in industry. He was a true professional who expected
dedicated work and the highest standards.

Eschewing modern glues, he made us boil up a thoroughly
vile, evil-smelling concoction that took ten times as long to work
as anything used in the home. He was a stickler for accurate
measuring, to a millimetre, whereas I possessed no constructional
skills and had no idea of measurement, let alone technology.

Six months before the final examinations we were allowed to
nominate our main subject and to relinquish the subsidiary. Our
final woodwork test had been to make tongue and grooved wood
panels, followed by a perfect dovetail joint intended for a

completed coffee table. I measured the pieces with unprecedented diligence but found that instead of joining as they should, at right angles, the pieces only fitted together in one straight line.

This was the only time my craft master lost control. He almost made himself ill, he was so angry. His face as purple as an aubergine, he stood in the middle of the room and shouted, "You damned fool of a girl, why on earth must you ruin my days by attending classes?"

"Quite right too," said the smug smarty-pants who had done everything right, including making a dining table and eight chairs, three beautifully turned table lamps and a wooden rocking horse.

The last time I went to see the craft master was undoubtedly one of the happiest days of his life. Having glared at me for two years, he now looked up from his gluepot, scarcely interrupting the movements of the large wooden stick with which he sluiced the glue continuously.

"Yes?" he muttered crossly. "What is the cause of this interruption?"

"I've come to tell you, sir, that I am going to spend my last six months on French only. I have completed my assignments, so I'm giving up craft."

He took his right hand off his stick, grasped my hand in his as if we were the greatest of friends.

"May the Lord be praised! That is the most wonderful news I have had all year," he said, and for the first time in two years I detected the faintest glimmer of a smile.

For the examination it was agreed that I could submit the practical work I had completed to date. This consisted of some masterpieces of children's toys, bedside lamps—made on the lathe, no less—and a sculpture of a dachshund which nobody recognised but assumed to be abstract. "Deeply meaningful," muttered the craft master with a look of unprecedented tolerance.

It is a matter of pride that Miss Brown kept this abomination on her mantelpiece until her death in 2002. Visitors often enquired about the nature of the specimen.

Fortunately I passed—on the grounds, I suppose, that I had managed to complete my assignments on time.

The next essential was to do exceptionally well at teaching practice. I was concerned that for this I would have to be out all day for two whole weeks, which would be difficult for Philip, so I sought the advice of the principal's wife.

She greeted me with an invitation to Devonshire tea. She brought in a tray of freshly baked scones, served with lashings of cream and plenty of homemade strawberry jam. I wondered if I would ever be as capable as she was. "Are you concerned about teaching practice?" she enquired immediately.

I explained to her that it was not the teaching practice that worried me, for I was truly looking forward to that. My worry was about practical arrangements for Philip. I reminded her that he was only five and a half years old and that his day would be too long without me. Usually we were only parted for four hours a day whilst he attended nursery school. Although the teachers had kindly said they would keep him until four p.m., and I knew they'd be kind to him and look after him properly, I felt uneasy. I feared something might make me late, the car might break down or the children in my care might require me to stay back for some reason. It was so good to be able to share my worries with her unreservedly. I felt rather like a mother lion.

She reassured me and reminded me of her promise that she would always help me if something like this happened. Immediately she set out a practical plan, which was to drive down to Abingdon at lunch time each day and to pick up Philip from school. He would come back to her home at college and have his usual afternoon sleep, and when he woke up he would be able to play with the other children in her care.

I probably still sounded anxious as I rushed out words of uncertainty and gratitude all mixed up. "Are you sure you can manage it? Isn't it going to be an awful bother? Would you like me to pay for the petrol?"

"Don't you worry about things like that, my dear. You just go off and do the very best teaching practice you can. You'll be a credit to my husband if you do well. This is the first year we've had mothers with children. It's terribly important for him, too, that you have every chance of becoming an excellent or even exceptional teacher. No need to worry about a thing. Give it your very best effort."

Her kindness thrilled me. Just to be sure that Philip would be happy with her, we went up together the next day and spent an afternoon with her, sorting out cupboards. She said it was good to do something normal when a child was being minded, specially in an unfamiliar environment. That way they could find their own way of playing and settle in. Philip enjoyed the afternoon and I could see that he would be happy.

The morning the teaching practice posts were announced, we all rushed to the notice board to see where we were to be sent. I had hoped for a secondary school French post, but to my dismay found myself allocated to a village primary school on the other side of Oxford. It would mean a forty-minute drive. Alarmed, I went to see my Education tutor.

He was a solemn, bearded man and his lectures had often been ponderous and lacking in humour. In contrast, tutorials with him were a delight. He explained problems deftly, his essay correction was helpful and informative, and he even granted us the occasional benevolent smile.

"How am I going to manage at a primary school?" I asked accusingly. "You know my subjects are French and craft. I don't know anything about developing ideas for primary age. I don't even know how to teach reading correctly."

"Well, it's time you learned," he replied. "The idea of training college is to prepare you for the profession. These days, that can mean a job anywhere in teaching. It is the teaching and the child which matter, not the subject. The skill you use to impart knowledge is what matter. You must adapt to any situation in which you find yourself."

I blinked, unable to believe he would say this to me six

months before the end of my course, having previously failed to intimate any such ideas and expectations.

"Well, I've got some urgent learning to do. Can you help me, please?"

"Ring the headmistress of the village school and ask her what she expects you to do in the fortnight," he said, not unreasonably. "When you know what's required, I'll give you an hour before lectures each day this week."

"It's kind of you to suggest it, but the times won't work out, because I can't leave my little boy at nursery school until half-past eight. My lectures start at half-past nine and it takes me half an hour to drive here."

I realised I was making it all sound too hard, and feared he would withdraw his much-needed offer of assistance.

He shrugged his shoulders, looking most inconvenienced by my outburst. "I always wondered how one could expect mothers with young children to study and do their teaching practice."

"Dare I ask if we could make it half an hour each day? Even that time would be terribly precious for me," I wheedled.

He sat at his desk, took out his diary, put his head down and gave the impression he had finished with me. Then, to my surprise, he closed the diary, stood, and walked towards me. "Of course I'll help you. Forgive me if I sounded unkind. I simply don't see how mothers can juggle home life and study without something or someone suffering."

"Sometimes we have no choice," I said, then, not wanting to sound ungracious or self-pitying, added, "and I am very grateful to be given the opportunity of a career which will allow me to bring up my son. He's just a bit little yet, that's all. I have to put his needs first. That was the basis on which I accepted my place here."

"You're quite right. Students with children need all the help they can get. Count on me."

When I rang the headmistress, my heart sank at what she expected me to do. I was to take a class of twenty-five children ranging in age from six to ten. In the mornings we were to do maths, reading and social studies and in the afternoon singing, writing and gym. It all sounded absolutely impossible. I wished I had stuck with music, even the violin. A sense of panic overcame me.

My tutor was not reassuring, either, when I relayed the information.

"How's your maths?" he asked, thinking this might be one area in which I showed some degree of competence.

"You'll be shocked to know that I got only four marks for my A level maths," I told him, mortified.

"How ever did you manage that?" he asked, his voice filled with uncharacteristic admiration.

"I didn't do well, that's how!"

"No, I mean how on earth did they choose to give you four marks?"

I admitted, "I got two marks for getting my name right and another two for remembering my serial number."

To my relief he burst out laughing, then put his arm around my shoulders. Due to my experiences as an *au pair* girl, I flinched, fearing this might be the beginning of a sexual advance.

"Don't worry, there will be nothing like that in this college," he said perceptively. And nor there was.

He made me a list of possible subject plans and drew up an emergency lesson chart. It was the best thing I learned during my three years at college.

When I arrived at the village school I was greeted by the head-mistress, who explained she was sole teacher. Her name was Miss Braithwaite. A spindly, straight-backed spinster of around fifty years old, she reminded me of my first piano teacher, in looks if not in manner.

"Now, dear," she instructed me, "you're to arrive at school half an hour early each morning, because you are to fill the coal scuttle and start the fire so the classroom warms up a little."

I told her about Philip and explained why I couldn't leave him at nursery school early.

"This is the real world now, young lady. You will have to make special arrangements for this fortnight. I have my cats to feed before I come to school, followed by an hour's drive. I will not see myself put out over your boy."

Crushed and belittled by the idea that she considered Philip to be less important than her cats, I took an instant dislike to her, probably because she scared me. And we were only just beginning.

"And you'll teach music during part of the lunch break. I saw on your application form that your maiden name was Goossens, so that means you must be musical. Anything will do. Play to them, sing to them, it doesn't matter. They must have music. Every child must have music to thrive. It would be like failing to give a cat its catnip, or a plant its fertiliser. Bring your own records, if you like."

"Where did you learn about music and how important it was?" I asked, then feared my question must have sounded impertinent.

Her immediate reply reassured me. "Music just is. You must know that. Oh, yes, I've seen your father conducting. I was just a young girl at the time and it was at the Royal Albert Hall. It made a great impression. From that moment on, music became part of my life. Music simply is. Every child must be given music so that it becomes a part of them."

Hearing her ideas brought me immense pleasure. Suddenly there was vitality and a joy in her voice. Her knowledge from many years of experience, combined with her attitude, would prove to be an inspiration.

The children were bustling around by the end of the afternoon, requiring help with the important matters of putting coats on, tying shoelaces, finding hats and attaching gloves to strings through sleeves. There was too much of a commotion to allow for further discourse. The first day had been exciting, and yet my sole contribution had been as an observer. Miss Braithwaite looked as fresh as a daisy, ready to start all over again. There was so much for me to absorb. Then, tomorrow, it would be my turn to face the class.

Next morning I arrived at just before eight, brought in the coal, stoked the fire and put on the kettle so that I would have a cup of coffee ready for Miss Braithwaite.

Before the children arrived, I played the overture to *The Mastersingers*. As it had been my own favourite, I knew I could bring it to life for the children.

"Heavens, how simply marvellous, child," said Miss Braithwaite brightly. "And what arrangements did you make for your little nipper?"

I explained that my neighbour had kindly offered to walk Philip to his nursery school and how I had promised to bring in her washing and do her ironing in exchange. Miss Braithwaite seemed embarrassed by the details of such domestic trivia.

"There you are then, as you have discovered, everything can be arranged. It's important for you to learn to be flexible. Never neglect your child, but make sure your employers are happy with you. Make them feel they come first, even if in your heart they do not. You need your job, don't you?"

I had been concerned that she might take advantage of my need. But as the first week slipped by, I learned so much from her example that I realised I had discovered an impressive, kindly ally.

"Tell me about your cats," I asked her one lunch time, during a relaxed moment as we served up the children's lunch. The food was not as unappetising as it looked. The meat had a greyish hue and the hot vegetables looked as if a blue dye bag had been dropped in with the water: blue peas were one thing, blue potatoes positively forbidding. At the mention of cats, her face shone with delight.

"Oh yes, my darling cats! My life would be ruined were it not for cats. I loved a young man once, but he was killed in the war. My mother suffered a long and painful illness and I spent my days caring for her and never got around to meeting anybody else. My cats keep me company. Do you have a cat?" she asked, her voice warm and enthusiastic.

I told her about my cats, past and present. "I'm lucky, though, because I have Philip too," I told her.

"And your husband?" she asked.

"We have been divorced for a year. He's married again. He has a new baby now. We don't see him anymore."

She put her arm around me and gave me a friendly squeeze.

"What we need to do, in that case, is to make you the very best teacher in the world," she said hopefully. Then, with a shrug which suggested a compromise might be a more realistic option, she added, "A very good one, anyway." She smiled again.

Whenever I had sought a role model in matters of teaching, I had always remembered my beloved Miss Brown in Sydney. I had watched her carefully, as children will when they admire a person. She moved briskly, but with an economy of movement. She spoke quickly, but wasted no words. She seldom raised her voice, except to great effect at moments when we were being less than reasonable. Her lessons were a perfect example of the dispensing and acquisition of information.

Once I had started at Westminster College, I realised that not even the lecturers quite possessed her ability for communication. I appreciated that hers must have been a rare gift. Miss Brown punctuated her sentences with facts; her timing was almost theatrical in its impact. Each subject was rounded up and polished towards the end of a lesson, much as a skilled writer uses the end of each chapter to make a reader long for more. Geography was connected with history, with music, with literature. Separate disciplines were taught with rigour but their interrelationship was never in question.

Faced with a class of boys and girls at such different stages of learning, I recognised that what my tutor had told me was correct. The subject matter meant little without expert presentation by a skilled teacher.

"Instead of your usual lessons, Mrs Hopkins is going to tell you about life in different countries. You may never have this opportunity again. Listen carefully. This week, she's going to tell you about Australia. Next week, she's going to tell you what it was like to go to school in France," Miss Braithwaite informed the children.

"I will write you out some notes for tomorrow," she promised me.

To my amazement, I found she had written all my lesson plans, but at the bottom she had written, 'or develop, as the situation arises'. Her aim was for me to capture the children's interest by demonstrating a change from her own style. She hoped my freshness of approach would captivate them. How could I possibly live up to her expectations?

Miss Braithwaite placed great importance on reading, and showed me by example the best way to help children to attain the basic skills. She asked me to write out the story of *The Mastersingers* on the blackboard and spontaneously produced an impromptu scene. A tall shy boy became Walter, a blonde awkward girl was Eva. Whirling around her with excitement, the others were divided into two groups. The smaller children were designated apprentices, the remainder masters of guilds. She gave a whirlwind explanation of apprenticeships, guilds, and their importance. We were all caught up in her enthusiasm.

Singing along to the recording, boisterously and not at all as Wagner had intended, the class joined to give an unprecedented rendition of the rather difficult 'Prize Song'. Improvised banners were deftly made from coloured sheets of cardboard. A procession assembled readily and marched along the corridor, around the building, then back into the classroom. When the music started for the Dance of the Apprentices, a gay and animated dance began, the older guild members clapping rhythmically at first but then joining in with the young apprentices, considering dancing more agreeable.

"People set far too much store by visual aids and having the technical equipment for a lesson. A good teacher is able to use almost anything to create a vital and exciting learning experience," Miss Braithwaite emphasised.

"I wish you could come and be a lecturer at college," I told her.

"Some of us are much better at doing what we do than at talking about it. Different skills are required. I would not make a good lecturer. I love the immediacy of teaching, or I would not have stayed. There is never a single day that I fail to be grateful for my choice of profession," she said.

I could see by her face that she had discovered contentment.

At the end of my second week I was having such a splendid time that I finally understood how wonderfully fulfilling teaching could be. At first I had regarded it, I am ashamed to say, merely as a means of providing for Philip and sharing his vacation periods. Teaching would obviously demand far more dedication than that. If I were to achieve excellent results not just for myself but for the children entrusted to me, I could do no better than to follow the example of Miss Braithwaite and Miss Brown.

"Your school positions will not always work like this," she said, "but let us make your first memories happy ones. That is what I try to do with the children."

I looked around me. The twenty-five children in her care were well behaved, attentive, obedient, contented and fun to teach. Her approach certainly achieved her aims.

"This is the secret of teaching," she told me proudly. "Make them enjoy learning."

During the last few days I followed Miss Braithwaite's plan by telling the children about France, interspersed with answering their requests for words in French. I wrote key words on the blackboard, we practised pronunciation, then learnt two songs, 'Frère Jacques' and 'Sur le Pont d'Avignon'.

The class particularly liked the second one, because they could do both words and actions. After singing the line, 'L'on y danse tout en rond,' a small boy called Bevan asked, "Who is Lonny?"

I explained the meaning of the text. "They dance in a circle."

He looked at me with a quizzical expression and once more said, "I still can't see where Lonny comes into it."

"Never mind, Bevan," said a pigtailed girl who had appointed herself his minder, "just accept that it's 'in foreign'." This apparently appeased his need to discover the whereabouts of Lonny.

I had been concerned about an item on my timetable referred to as 'gym'. There didn't seem to be a plan for that.

"I can't do gym either," Miss Braithwaite admitted, "so we do running on the spot when the children are cold, and hands up and down when they are restless." She laughed. "Nobody is good at everything!"

On my last day she brought a homemade cake with lemon icing. "Wrap up a large piece and put it in your bag for the wee lad, won't you? And do bring him to see us all one day before term's over. Promise?"

I promised.

My kind neighbour Mrs Hadley would not let me do her ironing, although I had offered it in exchange, but she did allow me to bring in her washing for two weeks because I absolutely insisted. I also noticed she invited Mimi in to be cuddled during the day, particularly when it was wet. The cat would be curled up in front of their gas fire if she was not out on the landing to greet me on my return.

I bought the principal's wife a large cyclamen plant to thank her for looking after Philip. She said it had been a pleasure and that she looked forward to hearing my results.

At the end of June 1967 I learned that I had won the French prize, passed craft, astonishingly, and obtained a distinction for my teaching practice and a credit for maths and reading. Now my diploma in teaching was secured, I photocopied it and sent it to Australia House, as this was the penultimate step towards my proposed immigration.

A letter of acknowledgement came by return post, requesting a payment of ten pounds by money order for registration as a migrant. Attached were several documents for me to complete, one inquiring whether I required transit by air or by sea, another a notification that medical examinations could be held any time before the end of the year. A teaching position would be offered to me on arrival in Australia for the beginning of the school year of 1968.

This meant I would have to choose between starting a teaching job after the summer holidays, knowing that I would disturb the children's routine by my sudden departure, or taking a temporary position as a secretary. I went to see Dr Ounsted at the Children's Hospital, where he now spent most of his time.

"You may rely on a position here for as long as you need it. I'll pay you the same as you'd get as a first-year teacher. On second thoughts, as we did before, I'll pay you ten per cent more. That way, we'll have the benefit of you and you'll do somewhat better than you would without us. Can you start next week?"

I was glad I would have time to keep my promise to Miss Braithwaite to visit the school and show them Philip. It is difficult to describe the pride I felt in him, and the joy in the older teacher's face as she held his small hands in hers and told him he had a very special mother.

I was extremely grateful for Dr Ounsted's offer. The experience of working with his team had inspired me, and the knowledge I had acquired from working in the college vacations was probably responsible for my doing well with my essays. It felt like going home, working at the hospital again.

Unfortunately, Mrs Tow did not work for the hospital, only the clinic, so I didn't see much of her, except when I went to visit her at her lovely old village cottage, twenty minutes drive from my home. Being Australian, she travelled to and from Sydney frequently, and I was dying to tell her about my plans. Ak had left long ago, to lecture at London University. Our happy, united team had broken up.

The new work involved me with two clinical psychologists, the husband-and-wife team of John and Corinne Hutt. John was good company, and emphasised the importance of 'being seriously silly' to counteract the pressure of work. He suggested at the outset that we called each other after characters in *Winnie the Pooh*, particularly on written memoranda.

Dr Ounsted, whose first name was Christopher, became Christopher Robin. John was Pooh, I was Kanga because of my impending voyage. Corinne was Piglet, a name about which she naturally had her reservations. Nevertheless, all our correspondence was initialled accordingly, so that when I left, much scribbling out was needed.

The man who looked after the electro-encephalograph department, was known as Eeyore because of his predominantly solemn outlook on life. If someone said it looked like a nice day, he unfailingly replied, "But the clouds are gathering. It will be raining before the end of the afternoon." If a report read, "This child appears to be showing some signs of improvement," Eeyore would reply, "Yes, but then of course they often do, before deteriorating."

Our clinical work was fascinating and varied. The money was generous and the hours flexible. If Philip had a day off school, I could take him to the playroom and the nurses would look after him while he played with the hospitalised children.

We adapted amusing devices such as our Winnie the Pooh names to defend ourselves against the desperately sad parts of our work. One of my first duties was to classify photographic slides of children who had been battered by their parents. Dr Ounsted worked beside me, passing slides for the screen projector, instructing me what to write: 'head abrasion, sexual abuse, genital deformation,' and so on. Tears were running down my cheeks. I was extremely distressed at what I saw.

"You must pull yourself together. You must never show your emotions when you meet the parents, or when you feel strongly about the children and their injuries," he said. "Don't you imagine I have the same feelings when I see a father who has criminally assaulted his child? As professionals, we all have to hide what we feel."

After our gruesome task was completed, he smiled and put his hand on my shoulder. "Thanks for doing this with me. I hadn't wanted to face it alone," he said.

It was nearly Philip's sixth birthday and he was going to start at the local infants' school, as his nursery only took children until they were six years old. As we hoped to leave for Australia before the end of the year, I felt sorry for him having to change schools for so brief a time. However, the school was within easy walking distance for us and Philip already knew some of the children moving there with him.

His teacher was a disagreeable woman with furious red crimped hair, who wore blindingly bright clothes and spoke in a raucous voice. I could think of nobody less suitable for a class of five- and six-year-olds. She seemed to regard parents with distaste, as if we were a race to be endured, and did not encourage conversation. When clusters of mothers exchanged pleasantries with each other at the school gates she appeared to see this as a sign of potential gross sedition, and on more than one occasion actually shooed us away. This had the effect of making us linger even more and adopt a united stand, as it were, against 'the enemy'. Imagine my surprise when she sent Philip home with a note requesting me to see her.

When I answered the summons, with some trepidation, before school the following morning, she invited me into the staff room.

"Mrs Hopkins, your little boy stood up in the front of his class yesterday and said it would be his birthday on Friday. He invited all thirty-six children to come to tea. I thought you might like to come in and make other arrangements."

I was both mortified and amused. The idea of thirty-six children in our tiny lounge room was terribly funny. Winter had replaced autumn more than a little suddenly, and the driving, chilly rain precluded outdoor activity.

I was thankful that I had some teacher training now that I had to face a class and, without wishing to embarrass Philip, un-invite them all.

The teacher suggested, "Why not call Philip out first and have a quiet word with him?"

I felt foolish at not having thought of the idea myself. She hurried in to fetch him.

"Sorry, darling," I told him. "You can't have everyone to your party. Why don't you choose your six best friends?"

"I can't remember their names," he said.

Poor little chap. I knew just how he felt, for this was exactly what had happened to me at his age. Already he had encountered several changes, with nursery school, then being with the children at the Hospital school room, how could he possibly recall everybody's names so quickly?

"After school, then, bring the children you like over to me when I come to meet you. I'll ask their names, talk to their mothers, and we'll arrange a party for you on Friday, okay?"

He seemed very pleased by my suggestion.

I entered the classroom, feeling idiotic and embarrassed. I cleared my throat. "Children, I am very sorry to tell you that we really cannot fit you all in at a party on Friday. Philip wanted to invite you all, because he likes you all so much, but we really don't have room. I hope you won't be disappointed."

To my surprise, Red Hair handed me a box of Smarties to distribute as if they were a gift from me, so I passed them around, each child delighted to receive one. I decided Red Hair wasn't so bad after all.

Friday afternoon's party was going to be a great success, or at least so I planned. I made a donkey onto which tails could be pinned, bought balloons to blow up, made complicated layers of parcels for pass-the-parcel, baked fairy cakes, made hundreds and thousand sandwiches and a birthday cake shaped like a teddy bear (well, almost), and savoury sausage rolls.

Before I took him to school that morning, Philip asked, "What will you be wearing, Mummy?"

The pride of my wardrobe was a dark purple woollen trouser suit with a Nehru collar and elegantly tapered trousers. It was, I was convinced from endless borrowed magazines, the height of fashion.

"I'm going to wear my lovely new purple suit," I told him.

"Oh, Mummy!" he implored in a voice of vehement disapproval. "Proper mummies only ever wear skirts."

It was his birthday, after all, so I wore a comfortable corduroy skirt.

He smiled, hugged me and said, "You really are a proper mummy now!"

THE ULTIMATE PRIZE

With the morning post came a letter with OHMS on the envelope, setting up an appointment for the dreaded medical examination. I was terrified that the doctors might refuse to pass me on the grounds of my back injury. There was a form to fill in, declaring any previous illnesses or surgery. It took me an hour to complete the details. I carried my reply to the post office, registered it as requested, and entered the appointment in my diary.

November the first was four weeks away. I made a particular effort to do no lifting, or anything else that would make my back sore or line my face with pain.

Although I dreaded the medical, I optimistically imagined myself back in Sydney quite shortly. No more months of cold grey fog ahead. If we flew away soon, we would enjoy the warmth of summer.

Betsy Brown's most recent letter had mentioned early bushfires, temperatures in the nineties, and her spaniels were so hot they had taken to sitting in their water bowls when she was late home from the Con.

I arrived at Australia House ten minutes before the appointment and talked nervously to another woman in the waiting room. A stiffly starched uniform crackled in to greet us, the voice behind it coming from a small, thin nursing sister obviously overcome by her enormously ill-fitting clothing.

"Come along in, Mrs Hopkins," she said, discreetly handing me a glass vial, popping a thermometer into my mouth, asking me to step onto some scales and then measuring my height.

"Fantastic, on all counts," she said, checking the colour of a paper slide against the contents of the vial. "Now go on in to see the doctor."

I must have looked nervous for she added, "He's really rather a sweetie."

A tall man with white hair and a snowy tuft of beard greeted me.

"I'm the locum," he announced. He sat down at a large desk, indicating an armchair in front of him. All the paperwork I had recently completed was in a file he was inspecting.

"So you've had a bit of an accident?" he enquired wryly, shaking his head.

I winced as he read aloud a comprehensive list of my injuries, fearing it might cause him to pronounce me unfit for duty.

"Well now, so you are going to Australia with your young son. Been there before, have you?"

"Oh yes, doctor. I was brought up in Sydney. I adored it there and all I have ever wanted was to obtain my qualifications so I can go back there to teach and to bring up my son in the sunshine."

He smiled. "You do sound keen. Let me take a look at what sister has written down. Weight eight stone ten pounds, height five foot four inches. Urine, normal."

Conversationally, he continued, "We'll just take your blood pressure." He expertly placed the blood pressure cuff around my arm, checked the readings of the mercury.

"One hundred over seventy. Couldn't be much better than that. We'll have you teaching for us forever!"

He seemed pleased with what he had discovered so far. Looking carefully at the file on his desk, he nodded his head agreeably. "I see from your college record that there have been no days of absence due to your back injury. Just the normal things, flu, colds, and not too many of those, either."

By now I was so nervous that my breathing was becoming unsteady. I was terrified something would still go wrong. What if he was worried about Philip's salmonella? But then, I realised rapidly, he wasn't employing Philip, and there was no medical inspection for him.

"Stand up. Let's take a look at you." He walked around me and I feared the moment when he would ask me to remove my clothing, witness all the scars of surgery and have second thoughts, or measure my legs and discover the discrepancy between them due to the missing area of shattered pelvis.

There was a pause and he looked at me very carefully. Then he asked *me* to walk up and down the room.

"You do very well. How do you manage without limping?" he enquired in a voice of esteem rather than criticism.

"To be honest, I do limp sometimes, especially when I am tired. I make a real effort to walk normally. Vanity, I suppose!"

He laughed and carefully closed my file. "I think that about wraps things up," he said.

"You don't need me to take my clothes off?" I asked.

"No need for that at all. I can see how well you are. Anyway, there's no heater in here and it's a terribly chilly morning," he replied, extending his hand to shake mine. "I hope you enjoy Australia," he said, and he escorted me out of his room. I could have hugged him.

Relief and happiness combined and I burst into tears as I went down the stairs. I couldn't wait to get home to tell Philip.

The train journey back to Oxford provided a pleasant relaxation after the tension of the interview. I was in such an ecstatic mood I scarcely noticed the time, thinking ahead of all there was to do.

I rushed in to tell Philip the news.

"Philip, I've done it. Your mummy's actually done it! All this time I've planned to take you to Australia. You'll be going there when you are six, just like your mummy was. Isn't that wonderful?"

Philip climbed into my lap, put his arms around my neck and kissed me. "I'm pleased you're so happy, Mummy."

The next day I went up to the hospital as usual, but was so full of excitement I could hardly concentrate on my duties.

"So you're finally leaving us," said Dr Ounsted, coming out of a meeting.

"I'll miss you and my research here. I'm so grateful for the help and encouragement you've given me, specially since the accident," I told him. I really wanted to hug him, but he wasn't a demonstrative sort of man and I supposed he would not like it.

"The place won't be the same without you," he said, "but I know you're going where you want to be. It will be a great start for Philip too, in the sunshine. I hope you'll be very successful and happy. You will write and let us know how you get on, won't you?"

I promised I would.

Just as I began to walk from the room, he rushed over to me, cleared his throat, put his arms around me and gave me the biggest hug imaginable.

"I'll really miss you, too," he said. There were tears in his eyes.

It made me very glad to think he would miss me. It was lovely to be missed, just as important, but not as painful, as missing someone.

As I still had no definite departure date, we agreed I would work up till the last moment. I rounded up my summaries on the research project, and a secretary was interviewed to take on my work. I was proud to show her what we were trying to achieve.

Philip couldn't understand why we should have to leave some of his toys behind, but we took the important things, his electric

train set, his teddies and his books. We gave some kitchen imple-
ments and a few pot plants to my neighbours, as well as last-
minute pantry supplies of tins and food. They were looking
forward to adopting Mimi.

I took the little cat across the landing, hugging her. "Oh Mrs
Hadley, you really will love her, won't you? I'm going to miss her
so much. You will cuddle her, please, won't you?"

My neighbour took the tabby with its coat dampened from
my tears. She held her closely. "We're great friends already, aren't
we, Mimi?" She patted the cat's head and I could hear a
contented purr.

"Don't you worry now, I know she'll be happy here. We'll
probably spoil her to death. Goodbye. Good luck. Just let us have
a postcard of this famous Harbour Bridge of yours."

We were permitted a very small baggage allowance. Forty
pounds each, it said on the air tickets. Eighty pounds of belongings did not seem much for setting up home again.

We had pared things down to a few clothes, records, toys and
favourite reference books. No linen, bedding, no electrical goods.
It would mean starting afresh and buying as I earned. I would
need to find us a furnished flat.

On 15 November I received official notification of our
departure. We were to leave on 27 November, less than two weeks
away.

I was worried that Donie had still not responded to my letter,
but I knew Miss Brown would be there to greet us, and I was
certain it wouldn't be long before we met up with childhood
friends again. My hopes for a new and happier life exceeded any
doubts or insecurities.

It did not seem much, but I had saved one hundred pounds. That
was all we had to begin our new life in Australia. It gave me a
great feeling of adventure, of freedom and pride that we had
achieved this much.

Saying goodbye to Oxford was fraught with mixed feelings. I was nervous about the new adventure, however much I had anticipated it. Yet I was so excited I could scarcely sleep. There was so much to consider. I wished so much my father had been alive. I remembered the time he had greeted us from the deck of the Customs' Department tug when we first arrived in Sydney by ship from America and he had clambered aboard to hug us.

At the airport we checked in our baggage, taking a few items under our arms for the journey so Philip would have something to occupy him on the plane.

It was a noisy, exciting, bustling place full to bursting with travellers. The weather was foggy. At one stage an announcement was made over the loudspeakers: 'Flights today may be delayed and in some cases cancelled, due to poor visibility'.

My heart sank, but within moments came a further announcement: 'Would passengers for Flight QF1 proceed to Gate Number 15. Boarding will commence in approximately forty minutes.'

"Is this it, Mummy?" asked Philip, looking at the waiting area and finding it not at all what he expected. "It's a bit like when we go to see the doctor, only no magazines." His voice betrayed his disappointment.

"No darling, this isn't the plane yet, it's just where we have to wait again."

"Why do we have to keep on waiting? We're ready now." The poor little chap was beginning to feel tired.

A further announcement told us to follow the attendant and we were led down a flight of stairs to a waiting bus.

"I thought we were going by plane, Mummy," said Philip, his voice deflated by this further betrayal.

The man in the queue behind us burst out laughing and Philip began to cry. Then his little eyes lit up brightly as we approached a huge airliner.

"This is it, my little one," I told him. "We're on our way."

Once on board, I drifted in and out of sleep. The journey,

long in distance, was a short and uncomfortable means to a new life. Then came the announcement I had longed for: 'In ten minutes we shall be making our descent to Kingsford Smith airport at Sydney. We hope you have all enjoyed your flight.'

Enjoyed it? It had been the most significant flight of my life.

I woke Philip and we gazed through the window, waiting for our first magic sight of my beloved city. When we saw the Harbour Bridge, a lump came into my throat and the tears flowed freely. "Look darling," I said to Philip. "We're home."

FINALE

When you have wanted something very badly for a long time, as I had, returning to Australia was my dream come true. Dreams, as we all know, require fulfilment. So much that I had hoped for did come true, but there were inevitable disappointments.

Hoping to be reunited with my sister Donie, I had been extremely sad that she had not responded to my request for her to sponsor me, and when we did meet, it was brief. I was not welcome to visit her in Canberra, particularly once I began to work at the Conservatorium. One can only surmise that, after the scandal, the pain of my being again involved directly with Sydney musicians might have been too great for her. Perhaps she regarded me as a traitor. I do not know this for a fact, but the idea was put to me by many of her former friends, whom she also no longer wished to see. She had left Sydney, given up music and sold her harp; possibly she would not have considered me 'correct' in returning to take up work within my father's former home ground. Despite many attempts to mend the 'rift' with my sister with whom I had grown up and whom I admired and loved so dearly, regrettably we lost touch. Her reasons may go beyond anything I comprehend, so in the end, one must respect silence and the wish for separation.

I had hoped my mother would come to Sydney, possibly even that she could have lived with us. But this was not to be. Five months after my arrival, I received a telegram notifying me that she had died in New York. The telegram came from her sister Catsie, who gave no address to which I could write for further information. It was devastating that Mother had not been able to share my joyous return, or even knowledge of it, for she had written so infrequently that I was unaware of the advanced state of her illness.

My mentor, sponsor and now 'adopted' mother, Betsy Brown, took over her role as Philip's grandmother, being there for all birthdays, Christmas and his graduation, giving him total and unconditional love and acceptance.

In 2001, the year I returned to Sydney definitively after eight years in Europe, she was in her mid eighties and in failing health. I was glad to be able to spend considerable time with her, reminiscing, reassuring her and just simply being there with her. When she passed away her memorial service was attended by her ex-students from all over the world. If they could not come in person, they sent loving letters, all of which were read in her honour. Alas, when I made my speech in which I credited her as the best mother anybody could have hoped for, I broke down and cried. She had been that to me, and I was proud to say so. Betsy was a uniquely wonderful woman who, unmarried herself, had mothered literally hundreds of musicians, whom, as they travelled the world, she constantly supported by her frequent correspondence. Some of us had followed a musical profession as expected, and others fulfilled our destinies in other ways.

My greatest delight was in the development of my son Philip, who has been my reason for being since the fortuitous day of his birth. His schooldays were over all too quickly. And although

I saw little of him during term time, as do most working mothers, every shared moment was important. We savoured and held sacred holiday times together and made the most of Sydney's beaches, visiting them most weekends. I was overjoyed when he graduated with honours from Sydney University. His writing skills were displayed early in the performance of two of his plays at Sydney theatres during his university days. His subsequent career, also successful, was, unsurprisingly, in publishing, the media and technology.

Just as I had hoped, I was able to find work in the field I loved most and for which I was best qualified, teaching. Beginning in special education with the NSW Education Department, I worked with autistic and emotionally disturbed children, and those with physical and developmental disabilities.

Later, to my great happiness, I applied for and was granted a position as lecturer in French at the Sydney Conservatorium of Music, and for ten years taught diploma students and future opera singers as much of the French operatic repertoire as time would allow. Participating in rehearsals and performances, watching the growth and development of my students as they made their way first to the Opera House and then, if lucky, to impressive careers overseas, brought me great joy.

In addition to this, I was French coach to the Australian Opera, working with famous singers and musicians both Australian and from overseas. Many were old friends and acquaintances. It was thrilling to work with Joan Sutherland and Richard Bonynge on their first major return to Australia, and to become part of a company of which, to this day, Australia can be truly proud.

To be part of a team at the Opera House that was the physical fulfilment of my father's dream was particularly exciting. I felt as if the circle of my life had been completed. I knew too that he would be happy for me to be part of his world, and perhaps even pleased with my accomplishments.

The launching of a television station devoted to multicultural broadcasting, SBS, offered me another career change, and I worked as an editor and subtitler there for twelve years, enjoying especially the challenge of subtitling operas for the international market. Surrounded by colleagues from over forty nations, I felt not at all isolated from the rest of the world. With international news and current affairs beamed in daily, as well as films, dramas and documentaries, it was a revitalising way of keeping up my vernacular language skills.

I have been most fortunate to work in fields I loved, and which challenged and refreshed my mind and soul and gave my life a sense of purpose.

We never heard from Graham, but the Oxford phone book shows that he still lives in the area. I presume he has now retired from his position at the Atomic Energy Establishment at Harwell, but as Philip had wished for no further news of him, I never contacted him.

Before I went to Europe for my recent longer stay, my Aunt Sidonie continued to correspond with me, and I planned to go and visit her, which I was able to do in 1985 and again in 1992. The first visit was brief but the second marked the beginning of my enforced retirement.

The back injury caused by my car accident in 1962 worsened, and after a lifting incident at work I required complex spinal surgery to be able to walk again. It was not long before I became partially confined to a wheelchair. While visiting my aunt and a former colleague in France I sought medical advice and received treatment and further surgical intervention, but none of this enabled me to return to work in Sydney.

I remained in Europe for several years, enjoying a satisfying and mature relationship which helped me to grow in confidence and strength and which also fostered my writing skills. Travelling in a wheelchair is a challenging activity, and I wanted to write about the positive gains and to set down practical advice for others who found themselves housebound. Therefore I journeyed, often lying flat on my back on a special mattress, throughout

France and England and to Italy, keeping a record of events. I followed this up with some twenty articles published in the UK.

It was wonderful during those eight years to be able to get to know Aunt Sidonie better, and to meet my cousins. Jennie Goossens, Léon's older daughter, visited her at home regularly and I would, on occasion, see her there. I also enjoyed a couple of meetings with Benedicta, Léon's daughter by his first wife. Sadly, she had been in New York too when we were children, and although she was fourteen years older than I, it would have been lovely to have known her then. Corinne, Léon's youngest daughter, my age, whom I had not seen since our brief teenage encounter, came to meet me and we found we had much in common. It is pleasing to have filled in the gaps of our lives, and to have caught up as real cousins. Regular phone calls and letters continue to keep this friendship alive.

My life has been filled with enriching relationships. Some have endured, others have not. I realise now that when we meet a potential lover, it is not uncommon to 'fall in love' with qualities they do not possess, and to hope to find in them all that is missing in ourselves. It is therefore impossible for any one person to meet those needs, and also totally unrealistic to expect it. It is the same for the partner who takes us, seeking to find their missing selves within us.

People whose parents enjoy apparently ideal and blissful relationships do not always make lasting or happy marriages, but perhaps those of us who have had unusual role models find it even harder. Marriage requires much love and understanding, so we can only learn from mistakes and try the best we can with the abilities we have. If, despite all efforts, it is impossible to make a relationship work, one has to move on, rather than to drag down the partner in despair and disappointment.

While I was away in Europe at this time, my homesickness for Sydney became more overwhelming with each year. The dark and long winters of Europe depressed me, and feeling the cold more than ever, I needed to be back where I knew I belonged. Philip had been working in Amsterdam for a couple of years and I had been able to travel to see him, by taxis and planes, within a day, but he then was transferred to Hong Kong. I visited him there a couple of times, and found conditions there for disabled people particularly grim. When he came to England to see me our meetings were always far too short and I missed him terribly, despite phone calls and emails.

In 2001 we both returned to Sydney to live permanently, he in his house, I in mine. With only ten minutes by road between us, life became much more on an even keel and we are able to keep our small family intact. It is wonderful to be home again and to be able to attend concerts and operas in two of the buildings which I still regard as my father's domain: the Sydney Opera House and the NSW Conservatorium of Music.

The years progressed slowly in the rehabilitation of my father. A bust, a carefully worked likeness by sculptor Peter Latona, was commissioned and is the only one which stands in the foyer of the Concert Hall of the Opera House. It was put in place in 1982 to coincide with the second of two performances of my father's choral work *The Apocalypse*, which formed part of the fiftieth anniversary celebrations of the ABC.

The ABC finally moved from their higgledy piggledy buildings scattered all over Sydney to one main centre at Ultimo. The Recital Hall there, where the Sydney Symphony Orchestra rehearses and where many concerts and broadcasts are produced, has been named after Father. So, in her quietly slow manner, Sydney has finally done her best to rehabilitate my father's memory. Concerts of his compositions heralded the opening of the beautifully refurbished Conservatorium of Music and I was happy to be on the guest list and to continue to attend the most interesting musical events held there. Unlike the Opera House, the new building is fully accessible for wheelchair patrons.

Aunt Sidonie is the only surviving member of the wonderfully talented family of five children of Eugene Goossens II, and at 103 still speaks happily with me on the phone when I call her each fortnight in Sussex. She is increasingly frail, but her quick wit and humour remain vital. Her lifelong friends enjoy her company and lighten her life, as she does all who come in contact with her.

In 2003 I am writing more, involving myself in committee work, trying to make Sydney more disabled-friendly, and keeping a particularly firm eye on the Opera House renovations, as this must be one of the most difficult and challenging buildings for the frail elderly, those in wheelchairs, and even parents with small children in pushchairs.

My current project is a book for parents, on how to cope when their children suffer pain. This is an underrepresented field in publishing, and although there are many medical articles available, I want to write a work in layman's language that will help parents understand how to manage procedural, acute and chronic pain in children. Fortunately, I am being assisted by an internationally respected physician in this field, and a clinical psychologist.

When I look back on all that has happened to me and to my son, I am grateful we have been able to share such a rich life together, and one we enjoy still. My hopes for him include all the hopes I had for myself and more, as any parent wishes. Life teaches us lessons all the time, and it is up to us to retrieve the best, the most useful and the most glorious moments, to build richly on them, to learn from our mistakes and to do our best to help others develop their own talents and hopes. The ability to teach is within us all, and to teach we must continue to learn, to strive and to hope.

Also from ABC BOOKS . . .

UNDUE NOISE
Andrew Ford

On a stretch of highway I travel is a sign that reads UNDUE NOISE IS AN OFFENCE. There is no obvious reason for its existence and it irritates me – perhaps because it questions the very basis of what I do. I am a composer of Western Art Music and by definition most of this has been undue noise for around 200 years.

In this selection of articles, reviews, lectures and essays, some new, others originally published in a variety of newspapers and magazines, Andrew Ford shares his thoughts on music of all kinds – from Bach to Cole Porter to John Lennon, from Peter Sculthorpe to Joni Mitchell to Eminem.

'One can't imagine very many Australian composers who could sustain the volume or quality of Ford's critical commentaries and radio broadcasts ...' Martin Buzacott, *24 Hours*